Between Growth and Stability

Between Growth and Stability

The Demise and Reform of the European Union's Stability and Growth Pact

Edited by

Leila Simona Talani

Director of Studies, MRes, MACEP, MAIP, Department of European Studies, University of Bath, and Research Associate, London School of Economics, European Institute, London, UK

Bernard Casey

Faculty of Finance, Cass Business School, London, UK

Edward Elgar

Cheltenham, UK • Northampton, MA, USA

Published by
Edward Elgar Publishing Limited
Glensanda House
Montpellier Parade
Cheltenham
Glos GL50 1UA
UK

Edward Elgar Publishing, Inc.
William Pratt House
9 Dewey Court
Northampton
Massachusetts 01060
USA

A catalogue record for this book
is available from the British Library

ISBN 978 1 84720 206 2

Printed and bound in Great Britain by MPG Books Ltd, Bodmin, Cornwall

Contents

Figures

Tables

Boxes

Contributors

Professor Michael J. Artis, Director, Manchester Regional Economics Centre, Institute for Political and Economic Governance, University of Manchester, UK

Professor Alan Cafruny, Henry Bristol Professor of International Affairs, Department of Government, Hamilton College, Clinton, NY, USA

Professor Bernard H. Casey, Faculty of Finance, Cass Business School, London, UK

Dr Giorgio Fazio, Lecturer in Economics at the DSEAF, University of Palermo, Italy

Dr Benedicta Marzinotto, Lecturer in Political Economy at the University of Udine, Italy

Luca Onorante, Economist at the European Central Bank, Germany

Professor Magnus Ryner, Professor of International Relations at Oxford Brookes University, UK

Dr Leila Simona Talani, Director of Studies, MRes, MACEP, MAIP, University of Bath, Bath, UK and Research Associate, London School of Economics, European Institute, London, UK

Professor Robert Woods, Head of Global Economics at HM Treasury. Formerly the Head of Fiscal and Macroecnomic Policy at HM Treasury, UK

Abbreviations

AUD	*Allocation Unique Dégressive*
BDI	Confederation of German Industry
CEECs	Central and East European countries
CFSP	Common Foreign and Security Policy
CMO	collateralized mortgage obligation
CMU	*Couverture Maladie Universelle*
DGB	Deutscher Gewerkschaftsbund
DSS	dynamic stochastic simulation
ECB	European Central Bank
ECOFIN	Economic and Financial Affairs Council
EDP	excessive deficit procedure
EMP	exchange rate market pressure
EMS	European Monetary System
EMU	Economic and Monetary Union
ERM	Exchange Rate Mechanism
EU	European Union
FSAP	Financial Services Action Plan
GDP	gross domestic product
IPE	international political economy
IR	international relations
MPC	Monetary Policy Committee
MTO	Medium-Term Objective
OCA	optimal currency area
ORF	other relevant factors
PPP	purchasing power parity
RIR	real interest rate
RMI	*Revenu Minimum d'Insertion*
SEM	Single European Market
SGP	Stability and Growth Pact
TEU	Treaty on European Union
UIP	uncovered interest parity
ULC	unit labor costs
VARs	vector autoregression models

Introduction[1]

Leila Simona Talani

When it was adopted by the European Council in Amsterdam in 1997 the Stability and Growth Pact (SGP)[2] was celebrated as the guardian of the strength and credibility of the forthcoming Economic and Monetary Union (EMU), and as an additional support for German fiscal conservatism against the inflationary, free-riding proclivities of the 'club-Med'. Yet, ironically, when in 2003 the SGP died at the hands of its mother and father, Germany and France,[3] the Euro appeared to be stronger than ever. There was, moreover, little evidence that the markets questioned the credibility of a post-SGP EMU.

The Maastricht Treaty protocols on EMU resolved the long-lasting controversy between the 'monetarist' and the 'economist' approaches to monetary union. The distinction between 'monetarists' and 'economists' emerged in the course of the discussions over the Werner Plan (1969) and referred to the strategy to be adopted during the transitional period leading up to monetary union. The 'monetarists' stressed the importance of achieving exchange rate stability through European institutional arrangements, while the 'economists' pointed out the necessity of policy coordination and, ultimately, convergence before agreeing on the adoption of a European fixed exchange rate regime or a currency union.[4] The Treaty established a rigid institutional framework with a clear-cut economic objective (that of pursuing price stability) and a three-stage timetable to achieve EMU (cf. Gros and Thygesen, 1998). At the same time, it devised a set of convergence requirements to which applicant member states had to conform before entering. These requirements included permanence in the 'new' Exchange Rate Mechanism (ERM) (within 15 per cent bands) for at least two years; inflation rates no more than 1.5 per cent higher than the average of the three most virtuous member states (that is, the member states with the lowest levels of inflation); interest rates no more than 2 per cent higher than the average of the three most virtuous member states; a debt-to-GDP ratio not exceeding 60 per cent, subject to conditions; and, most importantly, a deficit-to-GDP ratio not exceeding 3 per cent (TEU art. 104(c) and art. 109 (j)).

Whilst the Maastricht Treaty set out strict anti-inflationary requirements, the emphasis on price stability was buttressed by the adoption of the

Stability and Growth Pact in 1997 (Eichengreen and Wyplosz, 1998: 71). The pact confirmed the objective of a deficit-to-GDP ratio not exceeding 3 per cent and commited EMU member states to a medium-term budgetary stance close to balance or in surplus. It also defined the terms and sanctions of the excessive deficit procedure (EDP). Exemption from respecting this fiscal criterion within EMU was allowed only in the case of a decline in GDP of 2 per cent or more and of a temporary and small excess deficit. With a GDP declining by between 0.75 and 2 per cent, the decision on exemption from sanctions was left to the Council of Ministers. With lower decreases in GDP, the excessive deficit procedure was to be implemented in any case, and countries obliged to keep up to 0.5 per cent of their GDP in non-interest-bearing mandatory deposits with the ECB until the excess deficit was re-absorbed. If this did not happen within two years, deposits were transformed into outright transfers (Gros and Thygesen, 1998: 341).

The book examines the demise of the original version of the SGP and the consequences of its subsequent reform. It recognises that debates concerning whether there actually was any demise of the SGP and what were the implications of the reform remain open. Nevertheless it demonstrates that the events of November 2003 and the changes to the SGP adopted in March 2005 configure a different political and economic instrument from the one which had been originally approved.[5] This is why the authors often refer to the crisis of the SGP as its demise or death despite the fact that we still have a (reformed) SGP. The book questions the rationale of similar events from both the political and the economic standpoints. Political scientists have adopted different interpretations and theoretical perspectives in order to understand the complex issues surrounding the SGP. Among economists, there is a great deal of controversy concerning the scope for, and direction of, fiscal coordination in the EMU.

Accordingly, the contributors to this volume examine the demise and reform of the SGP from different and yet complementary perspectives. They seek to find a solution to the dilemmas posed by fiscal policy coordination in the context of a single currency area and to compare and contrast the utility of alternative heuristic frameworks and theoretical perspectives on the EMU and SGP. Special attention is devoted to the question of credibility. Chapter 1 addresses the definition of credibility of international economic agreements in theory from the political scientist and from the economic perspective. Chapters 2–4 focus on the performance of the Stability and Growth Pact in terms of credibility from three different perspectives. Chapters 5 and 6 put forward proposals to ensure the future credibility of the European fiscal rule.

The analysis of fiscal and monetary policy in EMU in general – and of the role of the SGP in particular – has been dominated by economists who, responding to domestic and/or to international developments, have offered policy recommendations for the EU as a whole or for specific member states.[6] In contrast, most political scientists have drawn from a number of disparate theoretical traditions. Scholars working within the framework of intergovernmentalism have sought to describe and explain the development of the SGP with reference to domestic politics and conflict among member states. They have studied decisions taken by the heads of individual member states, while emphasizing the central role played by the nation-state and national interests in the evolution of European integration.[7] For example, Moravcsik has adopted a domestic politics approach to explain why the position of Germany in the negotiations over EMU did not reflect the strong anti-inflationary position of the Bundesbank but rather a compromise between the Bundesbank's strict anti-inflationary stance and the preferences of the business sector for a devalued exchange rate, low interest rate and macroeconomic flexibility (Moravcsik, 1993a: 387, 1998: 401).

Another important application of a domestic politics perspective is that of Frieden *et al.* (1998). These scholars sought to develop an analysis of European monetary policy by using a two-level game framework that examined national monetary policy objectives with reference to domestic sectoral interests. The model identifies economic sectors' preferences vis-à-vis the two interrelated dimensions of exchange rate regimes (fixed or flexible) and levels (appreciated or depreciated).

Neo-constructivist perspectives on the establishment of EMU can be divided into two basic groups: 'identity oriented constructivists' and 'economic ideas oriented constructivists'. The first and, perhaps, more radical group includes scholars such as Minkkinen and Potomaki (1997) and Risse (1998). These scholars argue that the process of monetary integration, and in particular the establishment of EMU, can be explained within the context of identity politics. Their effort is therefore mainly oriented to asserting the 'symbolic' nature of the 'Euro' in relation to the national collective identity and symbols. Importantly, these authors discard as contradictory economic motivations for EMU and attribute explanatory value only to non-economic political constructions.

In the second group are scholars such as McNamara (1998) and Dyson (2000). This group acknowledges the importance of economic factors in the development of EMU, but also stresses the role of economic ideas as opposed to economic interests. According to these scholars EMU became a necessity in the context of the establishment of a new economic consensus, the neo-liberal 'consensus of competitive liberalism' amongst the political elites of all EU member states.

Some political scientists have developed more eclectic approaches that combine elements of neo-constructivism and intergovernmentalism (Dyson and Featherstone, 1996; Martin, 1994; Sandholtz, 1993; Young, 1999). Verdun, for example, has adopted a neo-constructivist framework to analyse the establishment of the SGP while applying a more eclectic approach to its demise (Verdun and Christensen, 2000; Heipertz and Verdun, 2004, 2005). She argues that the signing of the SGP was made possible by a convergence in basic ideas about the relationship between monetary and fiscal policies held by experts in ministries of finance, central banks and the Commission and by academics and relevant international organizations. However, ideational convergence only provided the basis for a political compromise. The decision to adopt that compromise was possible thanks to the prominent position of Germany in the intergovernmental talks that led to the approval of the pact and to the creation of a convergence of German and French interests of a sort that is typical of international power-politics (Heipertz and Verdun, 2004: 1–2).

The domestic actor perspective is exemplified by the work of McKay (1999, 2002), who addresses the issue of the fiscal coordination. While some political scientists have considered this in terms of a legitimization crisis (Verdun and Christensen, 2000; Weale, 1996), McKay is interested in how individual countries would react to the requirements of coordination. He argues that reactions will be different in different countries and that, in times of recession, member states might seek to breach fiscal rules such as those included in the SGP. This prediction is in line with those of many economists who had forecast that the SGP was unlikely to be sustainable (Eijffinger and De Haan, 2000).

Crouch also has examined the EMU and SGP from the perspective of domestic politics. He has focused on the impact of EMU and the budgetary constraints of the SGP on labour markets and trade unions (2002), seeking to understand how national governments will react to the lack of competitiveness of their labour markets without the option of competitive devaluations. Along similar lines, Martin Rhodes (1997, 2002) had argued that the reform of labour markets and of the welfare state would not happen in an unregulated fashion, but through a neo-corporatist strategy or, as he calls it, through 'competitive corporatism'. Paradoxically, rather than decrease, the EMU would increase their role (although not necessarily their power) in the welfare and wage bargaining processes.

This book will provide a deeper analysis of the subject of the Stability and Growth Pact from the perspectives outlined above, focusing in particular on:

- What happened to the credibility of the EMU with the collapse and reform of the SGP?
- Which is the role of the nation states and their domestic constituencies in the crisis of the fiscal rule?

- How did financial markets react at the news of the collapse of the SGP and why?
- What was the impact of the strength of the Euro on the SGP?
- Does the crisis of the SGP signal a crisis of the European integration process?
- Is the reformed pact a guarantee of growth and stability?
- What kind of technical solutions have been devised to solve the shortcomings of the previous versions of the pact?
- Where does this leave the EU and its economic future?

The book is aimed at political scientists and political economists with an interest in European policy making.

CHAPTER OVERVIEWS

In Chapter 1 Leila Simona Talani and Giorgio Fazio apply a political economic approach to the problem of exchange rate credibility, which is treated as an example of international economic agreements. Whilst political scientists focus primarily on a socio-political analysis aimed at tracing back the 'interests' underlying exchange rate commitments, economists tend to focus exclusively on financial and economic variables as connected to the 'expectations' of the markets. Only recently have political scientists sought to devote more attention to the issue from an integrated political economy perspective, which mainly focuses on the role of partisanship and governments' stability in influencing speculative behaviour (Leblang, 2002; Leblang and Bernard, 2000).

Despite these important contributions to the development of this branch of international political economy (IPE), there is still some scope for speculation concerning the relation between socio-political and economic accounts of financial phenomena. There is, in a few words, the possibility of finding a 'synthesis' of the two cognitive and interpretative models and this is, ultimately, the aim of Talani and Fazio's contribution. Accordingly, they argue that each of these perspectives taken separately can account only for a partial representation of reality and does not prove exhaustive of the many implications arising from the issue of exchange rate credibility. Therefore, the study of exchange rate credibility requires an integrated political economy model like the one which is defined and tested in the chapter. The theoretical aim of this chapter is that of confronting economists' and political scientists' approaches to exchange rate commitments and trying to reconcile them in an integrated political economy model, where 'interests' and 'expectations' appear as the two sides of the same coin.

In particular, this contribution seeks to explain why a country commits itself to fixing its exchange rate, and why, at a certain point, the credibility of this commitment may fade, triggering the rational expectations of the financial markets to re-orient towards a realignment of the exchange rate, eventually producing speculative attacks.

In Chapter 2 Alan Cafruny and Magnus Ryner adopt a structural approach to account for the crisis of the SGP. They argue that the fate of EMU – and by implication the SGP – is closely tied to transatlantic relations and Europe's subordination to what they term US 'minimal hegemony'. Cafruny and Ryner argue that the design of EMU is inconsistent with the goal of European autonomy and growth (although this is not to say that policies do not serve the interests of particular – and powerful – European class fractions and regions). Finally, they address the socially disintegrative implications of EMU. Focusing on France and Germany – EMU's core states – they account for a crisis of representation resulting from a politics of welfare state retrenchment that is counterproductive in its objective to revive growth in the European economy or indeed to underwrite the long-term stability of pacts such as the SGP. The EU's aspiration to build a monetary union to promote competitiveness, sustained growth, regional autonomy and social cohesion is self-limiting because the Maastricht design of the EMU is inherently connected to a neo-liberal transnational financial order that displaces socio-economic contradictions from the US to other parts of the world, including Europe. Europe's subordinate participation within this order pre-empts the possibility of resolving structural problems of post-industrial or, better, post-Fordist society in a manner consistent with Europe's social and Christian-Democratic social accords. Economic stagnation, uneven development, and the widening gap between new forms of economic governance and social citizenship amplify legitimation problems and political conflicts, with adverse effects on the EU's political ability to mobilize as a counterweight to the US.

In Chapter 3 Leila Simona Talani assesses the credibility of the fiscal rule with reference to the performance of the Euro after the collapse of the SGP. With the crisis of the SGP a fundamental paradox arises: how can a currency remain as strong as ever in the midst of a serious crisis of the fiscal rule? This paradox seems to point towards a political economy interpretation of the making and enforcement of fiscal coordination in the Euro area.

The explanation for the paradox is sought within the framework of a revised, 'embedded' version of intergovernmentalism based on Moravcsik's liberal intergovernmentalism (1993a), which adds to the traditional intergovernmentalist framework an explicit theory of national preferences formation. As it is applied to the working of the SGP, intergovernmentalists would predict that the interests of the most powerful member states will prevail over those of smaller states in the ECOFIN decision-making process. Based upon previous research (Talani, 2004), embedded intergovernmentalism would trace back the interests of the most powerful Euro-zone member states to the position of their leading socio-economic sectors. Therefore, the shift of emphasis from strict fiscal policy to more relaxed fiscal policy enshrined in the new outlook of the SGP does not detract from the credibility of the member states' commitment to EMU. This is why, after the decision by the ECOFIN not to impose sanctions on France and Germany, financial markets did not reduce the value of the Euro, which indeed continued to increase in relation to the Dollar. This chapter employs a definition of credibility rooted in the consensus to EMU of the most powerful socio-economic actors. Here, credibility derives primarily from structural considerations relating to the institutionalization of a set of favourable macroeconomic policies following from this particular form of monetary union.

In Chapter 4, Benedicta Marzinotto provides an analysis of the credibility of the ECB from a German perspective. She adopts a domestic politics perspective to explain the collapse of the SGP in a country that has a long history of fiscal discipline, mostly pursued with the tacit support of the principal social actors. Different hypotheses have been put forward in the literature to account for Germany's undisciplined behaviour. Some observers still insist on the revolutionary impact of the 1991 re-unification on public finances. Deviation from the 3 per cent deficit target would thus be indicative of the difficulty in funding welfare programmes, especially in eastern Germany, at a time when unemployment in this part of the country remains comparatively high. For others, instead, the presence of fiscal rule imposed from above is in itself responsible for fiscal misbehaviour in periods of slow growth. The argument is that the SGP has forced fiscal authorities into a pro-cyclical action, thus depriving economic policy of any stabilization function. A relatively stringent fiscal policy in recession is believed to further compromise growth, leading to even greater fiscal imbalances in the following years. Against these explanations, Marzinotto argues that the timing of fiscal deterioration is not well explained by the re-unification shock. Fiscal discipline relaxed quite remarkably after 1999, and the same happened in most Euro-zone countries. This suggests that the establishment of EMU has probably softened the incentive structure in favour of fiscal discipline. In addition, Marzinotto addresses the issue of pro-cyclicality and argues that it is inappropriate to state that the SGP has twisted fiscal authorities' arms into pro-cyclical action. Empirical evidence shows that German fiscal policy has been fairly pro-cyclical since the early 1990s and earlier. In this respect, it can hardly be said that the SGP, whether strictly applied or not, is a self-defeating device. Why, then, is fiscal 'misbehaviour' more evident under EMU than in the preceding period? The argument developed here is that German social actors have resorted to fiscal authorities more than in the past to obtain compensations in exchange for wage moderation. Strong domestic pressures would thus be at the root of fiscal misbehaviour.

In Chapter 5 Robert Woods evaluates the SGP with reference to the analysis of effective macroeconomic policy frameworks. He considers the impact of recent reforms of the SGP and the challenges that are likely to arise in the immediate future. Effective macroeconomic policy frameworks help to achieve high and stable levels of economic growth and employment. Accordingly, Woods offers a set of general principles for effective policy frameworks characterised in terms of credibility, flexibility and legitimacy. Experience has led countries to adopt frameworks with 'constrained discretion', including clear long-term goals, a pre-commitment to sound institutional arrangements, and maximum transparency.

Evaluating the performance of the SGP with respect to the three criteria of credibility, flexibility and legitimacy, Woods argues that the recent reforms can improve the operation of the SGP. He concludes by discussing future challenges in implementing the pact, including: the development of complementary national fiscal frameworks and increasing ownership; taking structural reforms into account; the challenge of EU enlargement; discretionary fiscal stabilization in the context of a monetary union; and data surveillance and transparency.

Finally, in Chapter 6 Michael J. Artis and Luca Onorante propose an economic reading of the reformed SGP that challenges the widespread assumption that the demise and reform of the SGP have rendered it useless. They treat the SGP as an example of regime-based international policy coordination. Drawing on a comparison of the SGP and the Bretton Woods System, they point out that both regimes were founded on rule-based coordination, multilateral surveillance, a central inspection body, and sanctions that were ultimately unenforceable. These arrangements do work, but are always subject to contestation and the need for revision. What did we learn from the recent reform of the SGP? The answer, according to the authors, is almost nothing. This means that the formal sanctions procedure of the SGP is still unreliable and the system is likely to come under stress in periods of slow growth/recession. Nevertheless, surveillance 'works' and the '3 per cent' has acquired credibility. The reforms capitalize on this credibility despite the limited capacity for real sanctions.

The reforms retain the emphasis on the deficit constraint of 3 per cent, but they admit some relevance for debt considerations and they relax the conditions under which an excessive deficit procedure would be inaugurated and extend the adjustment period, whilst substantially adjusting the role of the medium-term target.

As far as cyclical adjustment is concerned, the SGP started with a declaration of a medium-term aim of reaching balance or slight surplus. Subsequently – and now – this takes the form of a cyclically adjusted target which in the reformed version (a) is designed to ensure that the actual deficit will not exceed 3 per cent and (b) can be modified to ensure a transition to a stable debt ratio. The reform is based on two arms: a preventive arm and a corrective one. The preventive arm rests on Medium-Term Objectives (MTOs). These are differentiated among member states. They may diverge from a close-to-balance or in-surplus position depending on their current debt ratio and potential growth, will provide a safety margin with respect to the 3 per cent deficit limit and will ensure rapid progress towards sustainability. Country-specific MTOs would be, in cyclically adjusted terms and net of one-off and temporary measures, between −1 per cent of GDP and in balance or surplus.

With respect to the corrective arm, there are different scenarios:

- free fiscal policy (no pact)
- SGP: below 3 per cent after two years, −0.75 per cent threshold, immediate correction
- (severe) economic downturn: 0 per cent threshold
- one more year to go back to 3 per cent
- progressive structural consolidation(−0.5 per cent structural yearly)
- the three above (interaction effect?).

The evaluation criteria are the variability of the cycle and the average deficit.

It is of course very difficult to define which scenarios are more likely and draw elaborate conclusions. However, the authors demonstrate in the chapter that the new range of MTOs appears reasonable overall.

The current and modified rules of the SGP are unlikely to bite and, therefore, they will make little difference to stabilization.

NOTES

1. This is to express my gratitude to Professor Alan Cafruny, who read and edited this Introduction and the Conclusions.
2. When European finance ministers agreed at the Dublin Summit in 1996 on the need for a fiscal framework to reinforce the powers of the future European Central Bank, they called it the Stability Pact. The words 'and Growth' were added later, at the Amsterdam European Council of 1997. The Amsterdam resolution establishing the Stability and

Growth Pact may be found at the following web-site: http://www.ena.lu/mce.cfm, accessed on 6 September 2005. The EU legislation relating to the Stability and Growth Pact may be found at the following web-site: http://europa.eu.int/comm/economy_finance/about/activities/sgp/sgp_en.htmb, accessed on 6 September 2005.
3. For a thorough account of the role of France and Germany in the making of the SGP see Heipertz and Verdun (2005).
4. For more details see Tsoukalis (1997).
5. For other references to the death of the SGP see *Financial Times*, 22 March 2005, 'Death of a Pact'; and *Economist*, 29 November 2003, 'The Death of the Stability Pact: Europe and the Euro'.
6. For the most recent literature see Allsopp and Artis (2003); Annett, Decressin and Deppler (2005); Artis (2002); Artis and Buti (2000); Balassone and Franco (2000); Balassone *et al.* (2004); Begg and Schelkle (2004); Buti and Franco (2005); Eijffinger (2005); and Wyplosz (2002, 2005).
7. For a complete analysis of the neo-functionalist and institutionalist approaches to EMU see Talani (2004), Ch. 1.

BIBLIOGRAPHY

Allsopp, C. and M. Artis (2003), 'The Assessment: EMU Four Years On', *Oxford Review of Economic Policy*, **19**(1): 1–29.
Annett, A., J. Decressin and M. Deppler (2005), 'Reforming the Stability and Growth Pact', *IMF Policy Discussion Paper*, PDP/05/2.
Artis, M.J. (2002), 'The Stability and Growth Pact: Fiscal Policy in the EMU', in F. Breuss, G. Fink and S. Griller (eds), *Institutional, Legal and Economic Aspects of the EMU*, Springer: New York.
Artis, M.J. and M. Buti (2000), 'Close to Balance or in Surplus – a Policy Maker's Guide to the Implementation of the Stability and Growth Pact', *Journal of Common Market Studies*, **38**(4): 563–92. Edited version in Buti and Franco (2005).
Balassone, F. and D. Franco (2000), 'Public Investment, the Stability Pact and the Golden Rule', *Fiscal Studies*, **21**(2): 207–29. Edited version in Buti and Franco (2005).
Balassone, F., D. Franco and R. Giordano (2004), 'Market Induced Fiscal Discipline: Is There a Fallback Solution for Rule-Failure?', mimeo, Banca d'Italia: 389–426, www.ceistorvergata.it/conferenzedsconvegni/mondragone/XVI-papers/Paper-balassone-franco-giordano(06.04).pdf, accessed 19 November 2007.
Begg, I. and W. Schelkle (2004), 'The Pact Is Dead: Long Live the Pact', *National Institute Review*, **189**: 86–98.
Boyer, R. (2000), 'The Unanticipated Fall Out of the European Monetary Union: The Political and Institutional Deficit of the Euro', in C. Crouch (ed.), *After the Euro: Shaping Institutions for Governance in the Wake of European Monetary Union*, London: Oxford University Press.
Buti, M. and D. Franco (2005), *Fiscal Policy in EMU: Theory, Evidence and Institutions*, Edward Elgar: Cheltenham, UK and Northampton, MA, USA.
Crouch, C. (1994), 'Incomes Policies, Institutions and Markets: An Overview of Recent Developments', in R. Dore, R. Boyer and Z. Mars (eds), *The Return to Incomes Policies*, London: Pinter.
Crouch, C. (2002), 'The Euro, and Labour Markets and Wage Policies', in K. Dyson (ed.), *European States and the Euro*, London: Oxford University Press.

Dyson, K. (2000), *The Politics of the Euro-zone*, Oxford: Oxford University Press, Scholarship Online.

Dyson, K. (2002), 'Germany and the Euro: Redefining EMU, Handling Paradox and Managing Uncertainty and Contingency', in K. Dyson (ed.), *European States and the Euro*, London: Oxford University Press.

Dyson, K.H.F. and K. Featherstone (1996), 'Italy and EMU as Vincolo Esterno', *Journal of South European Society and Politics*, **2**(3): 272–99.

Eichengreen, B. and C. Wyplosz (1998), 'The Stability Pact: More than a Minor Nuisance?', *Economic Policy*, **26**, April.

Eijffinger, S.C.W. (2005), 'On a Reformed Stability and Growth Pact', *Intereconomics*, **40**(3): 141–7.

Eijffinger, S. and J. De Haan (2000), *European Monetary and Fiscal Policy*, Oxford: Oxford University Press.

Engelmann, D., H.J. Knopf, K. Roscher and T. Risse (1997), 'Identity Politics in the European Union: The Case of Economic and Monetary Union', in P. Minkkinen and H. Potomaki (eds), *The Politics of Economic and Monetary Union*, Dordrecht: Kluwer Academic Publishers.

Frieden, J. (1991), 'Invested Interests: The Politics of National Economic Policies in a World of Global Finance', *International Organization*, **45**.

Frieden, J. (1994), 'The Impact of Goods and Capital Market Integration on European Monetary Politics', Preliminary version, August.

Frieden, J., D. Gros and E. Jones (1998), *The New Political Economy of EMU*, Oxford: Rowman & Littlefield.

Gill, S. (1997), 'An EMU or an Ostrich: EMU and Neo-liberal Economic Integration – Limits and Alternatives', in P. Minkkinen and H. Potomaki (eds), *The Politics of Economic and Monetary Union*, London: Kluwer.

Gros, D. and N. Thygesen (1998), *European Monetary Integration*, London: Longman.

Heipertz, M. and A. Verdun (2004), 'The Dog that Would Never Bite? What We Can Learn from the Origins of the Stability Pact', *Journal of European Public Policy*, **11**(5), October: 765–80.

Heipertz, M. and A. Verdun (2005), 'The Stability and Growth Pact: Theorising a Case in European Integration', Paper prepared for delivery at the Ninth Biennial International European Union Studies Association Conference, Austin, TX, 31 March – 2 April.

Hemerijck, A. (2002), 'The Self Transformation of the European Social Model(s)', *International Politics and Society*, **4**.

Howarth, D. (2002), 'The French State in the Euro-zone: Modernization and Legitimising Dirigisme', in K. Dyson (ed.), *European States and the Euro*, London: Oxford University Press.

Leblang, D.A. (2002), 'The Political Economy of Speculative Attacks in the Developing World', *International Studies Quarterly*, **46**(1), March: 69–93.

Leblang, D. and W. Bernard (2000), 'The Politics of Speculative Attacks in Industrial Democracies', *International Organisation*, **54**(2), Spring: 291–324.

McKay, D. (1999), 'The Political Sustainability of European Monetary Union', *British Journal of Political Science*, **29**: 481.

McKay, D. (2002), 'The Political Economy of Fiscal Policy under Monetary Union', in K. Dyson (ed.), *European States and the Euro*, London: Oxford University Press.

McNamara, K.R. (1998), 'Economic and Monetary Union: Do Domestic Politics Really Matter?', Paper Presented at the American Political Science Association Annual Meeting.

Marsden, D. (1992), 'Incomes Policy for Europe? Or Will Pay Bargaining Destroy the Single European Market?', *British Journal of Industrial Relations*, **30**: 587–604.

Martin, L.L. (1994), 'International and Domestic Institutions in the EMU Process', in B.J. Eichengreen and J.A. Frieden (eds), *The Political Economy of European Monetary Unification*, Boulder, CO: Westview Press, pp. 87–106.

Minkkinen, P. and H. Potomaki (1997), *The Politics of Economic and Monetary Union*, Dordrecht: Kluwer Academic Publishers.

Moravcsik, A. (1993a), 'Preferences and Power in the EC: A Liberal Intergovernmentalist Approach', *Journal of Common Market Studies*, **31**(4): 474.

Moravcsik, A. (1993b), 'Integrating International and Domestic Theories of International Bargaining', in P.B. Evans, H.K. Jacobson and R.D. Putnam (eds), *Double-Edged Diplomacy: International Bargaining and Domestic Policy*, Berkeley: University of California Press.

Moravcsik, A. (1998), *The Choice for Europe: Social Purpose and State Power from Messina to Maastricht*, Ithaca, NY: Cornell University Press.

Pochet, P. (1998), 'The Social Consequences of EMU: An Overview of National Debates', in P. Pochet and B. Vanhercke (eds), *Social Challenges of Economic and Monetary Union*, Brussels: European Interuniversity Press.

Rhodes, M. (1997), 'Globalisation, Labour Markets and Welfare States: A Future of "Competitive Corporatism"?', *EUI Working Papers*, 97/36.

Rhodes, M. (2002), 'Why EMU Is, or May Be, Good for European Welfare States', in K. Dyson (ed.), *European States and the Euro*, London: Oxford University Press.

Risse, T. (1998), 'To Euro or not to Euro? The EMU and Identity Politics in the European Union', *Arena Working Papers*, WP 98/1.

Sandholtz, W. (1993), 'Choosing Union: Monetary Politics and Maastricht', *International Organization*, **47**(1): 1–39.

Streeck, W. (1994), 'Pay Restraints without Incomes Policies', in R. Dore, R. Boyer and Z. Mars (eds), *The Return to Incomes Policies*, London: Pinter.

Talani, L.S. (2000a), *Betting for and against EMU: Who Wins and Who Loses in Italy and in the UK from the Process of European Monetary Integration*, London: Ashgate.

Talani, L.S. (2000b), 'Who Wins and Who Loses in the City of London from the Establishment of EMU', in C. Crouch (ed.), *After the Euro: Shaping Institutions for Governance in the Wake of European Monetary Union*, London: Oxford University Press.

Talani, L.S. (2003), 'Interests and Expectations: A Critical Political Economy Approach to the Credibility of the Exchange Rates. The Cases of Italy and the UK in the EMS and EMU', in A. Cafruny and M. Ryner (eds), *A Ruined Fortress? Neoliberal Hegemony and Transformation in Europe*, New York: Rowman & Littlefield, pp. 123–47.

Talani, L.S. (2004), *European Political Economy: Political Science Perspectives*, London: Ashgate.

Talani, L.S. (2005), 'The European Central Bank: Between Growth and Stability', *Comparative European Politics*, **3**: 204–31.

Talani, L.S. and G. Fazio (mimeo), 'Interests or Expectations: A Political Economy Model of Exchange Rate Commitments'.

Tsoukalis, L. (1997), *The New European Economy Revisited*, Oxford: Oxford University Press.

Verdun, A. and T. Christensen (2000), 'Policies, Institutions and the Euro: Dilemmas of Legitimacy', in C. Crouch (ed.), *After the Euro: Shaping Institutions for Governance in the Wake of European Monetary Union*, London: Oxford University Press.

Weale, A. (1996), 'Democratic Legitimacy and the Constitution of Europe', in R. Bellamy, V. Bufacchi and D. Castiglione (eds), *Democracy and Constitutional Culture in the Union of Europe*, London: Lothian Press.

Wyplosz, C. (2002), 'Fiscal Policy: Rules or Institutions?', Paper prepared for the Group of Economic Analysis of the European Commission, April.

Wyplosz, C. (2005), 'Fiscal Policy: Institutions versus Rules', *National Institute Economic Review*, **191**: 64–78.

Young, R. (1999), 'The Politics of the Single Currency: Learning the Lessons of Maastricht', *Journal of Common Market Studies*, **37**(2): 295–316.

1. Interests or expectations? A political economy model of the credibility of exchange rate agreements

Leila Simona Talani and Giorgio Fazio

The notion of the credibility of international economic agreements has acquired in recent times a very important role in trying to understand why some economic regimes fail and others are successful. The notion of credibility itself is very vague and can only be applied through further specification of its main components and its realm of application. In this chapter the authors will identify the sources of credibility of exchange rate commitments by elaborating a political economy model synthesizing the political scientists' approaches to the credibility of international economic agreements and economists' approaches to the credibility of exchange rates. In turn, the theoretical considerations stemming from this analysis represent the basis for understanding why the EMU project is credible despite the substantial reform of the European fiscal rule and why the crisis of the Stability and Growth Pact (SGP) did not eventually trigger a crisis for the Euro.

Indeed, the authors of this chapter believe that the issue of the credibility of the Euro cannot be separated from considerations relating to the existence of a structural, political economy consensus to the Economic and Monetary Union by the most relevant domestic socio-economic actors in the most powerful Euro-zone member states. Therefore the monetary policy of the ECB, the Euro and the whole EMU project did not lose credibility with the breach of the SGP by Germany and France because this did not signal to the markets any lack of consensus to the macroeconomic policies enshrined in EMU. However, this is further elaborated in Chapter 3. This chapter is concerned only with the assumption that the credibility of the exchange rate is related to the consensus of the leading socio-economic sectors.

Economic and political science analyses of exchange rate credibility tend to differ consistently. While political scientists focus primarily on a socio-political analysis aimed at tracing back the 'interests' underlying exchange rate commitments, economists tend to give importance to purely financial and economic variables as connected to the 'expectations' of the markets.

Only recently have political scientists devoted more attention to the issue from an integrated political economy perspective. This mainly focuses on the role of partisanship and governments' stability in influencing speculative behaviour (Leblang, 2002; Leblang and Bernard, 2000).

Despite these important contributions to the development of this branch of international political economy (IPE), it seems to the authors that there is still some scope for speculation on the relation between socio-political and economic accounts of financial phenomena. There is, in other words, the possibility of finding a 'synthesis' of the two cognitive and interpretative models and this is, ultimately, the aim of this chapter. In this chapter it is argued that both perspectives, if taken separately, can account only for a partial representation of reality and do not prove exhaustive of the many implications arising from the issue of exchange rate credibility. It thus becomes important to underline that the study of such an issue needs an integrated political economy approach in order to bring together in the discussion the two poles of the question.

The theoretical aim of this research is therefore that of confronting the economists' and political scientists' approaches to exchange rate commitments and trying to reconcile them in an integrated political economy approach, where 'interests' and 'expectations' appear as the two sides of the same coin.

In particular, this contribution seeks to explain why a country commits itself to fixing its exchange rate, and why, at a certain point, the credibility of this commitment may fade, triggering the rational expectations of the financial markets to re-orient towards a realignment of the exchange rate, eventually producing speculative attacks.

Thus, the following research questions will be addressed: Why does a government decide to commit itself to fixed exchange rates? On what is the credibility of this commitment based? Why and when do the markets decide to bet on the lack of credibility of a similar commitment?

In this work it is argued that the markets, in deciding whether to attack a currency peg or not, evaluate a wide range of factors, including socio-political and structural ones. In particular, the credibility of an exchange rate agreement and, therefore, markets' expectations about devaluation depend crucially on the behaviour and interests of socio-economic actors and interest groups. The main hypothesis to be tested is that an exchange rate peg credibility and resilience to a speculative attack increases when it receives support from socio-economic groups. Secondly, this effect is greater when the support comes from the most powerful interest groups. Where power is defined in terms of their contribution to the economy as a percentage of GDP or, for trade unions, by the number of members.

In particular, this research investigates the exchange rate stability of the Italian Lira and the UK Pound during their adherence to the Exchange Rate Mechanism (ERM) of the European Monetary System (EMS) and up to the entering into operation of EMU. The analysis is carried out following the literature on speculative attacks (Eichengreen *et al.*, 1995). Two types of crisis episodes are identified. The first refers more closely to events where a large depreciation or devaluation has taken place. The second relates to the occurrence of speculative attacks, defined as episodes of 'excessive speculative pressure'. The speculative pressure index is calculated as a weighted average of exchange rate changes plus interest rate changes minus reserve changes. Once the crisis episodes have been identified, it is possible to apply simple qualitative response models and estimate the probability of a speculative attack, as a function of both a set of fundamental control variables drawn from the economics literature and commonly used to predict currency crises, and a set of variables which are designed to capture the role of interest groups. Different measures of consensus originally constructed by Talani (2000) are used. A coefficient significantly different from zero and negatively signed is expected in order to validate the hypothesis that consensus decreases the probability of a speculative attack.

The chapter is structured as follows. The first section reviews theories of international political economy and economic theories concerned with the credibility of exchange rate agreements. The purpose is to identify a common basis on which to ground a synthesis between the two disciplines. This is discussed in the second section of the chapter, where the political economy analytical approach to the issue is presented and the research hypotheses proposed. In the third section, empirical evidence is presented on the validity of these hypotheses. Finally the conclusions summarise the objectives and the outcomes of this contribution.

1   SETTING THE THEORETICAL CONTEXT: POLITICAL SCIENCE AND ECONOMIC APPROACHES TO THE CREDIBILITY OF EXCHANGE RATE COMMITMENTS

1.1   'Interests' Political Science Approaches to the Credibility of Exchange Rates

The social science background in which to insert the issue of exchange rate commitment is represented by those international relations (IR)/international political economy (IPE) approaches concerned with the sources of a government's commitment to international economic agreements.

In this context the first relevant stream of theories is represented by the literature on European economic integration and on EMU.

The theoretical debate over the issue of economic and monetary integration is traditionally characterized by the dichotomy between neo-functionalism and intergovernmentalism (Sandholtz, 1993).

Ernst Haas and other neo-functionalists (Haas, 1968; Lindberg and Scheingold, 1970) sought to explain integration through the concept of 'spill-over'. Integration in one issue area will generate functional linkages to other issue areas; as a result, the desire to obtain the full benefits of integration in the first area will produce pressures for integration in a second linked area. Neo-functionalists identify two types of spill-over, each of which deepens and widens integration by working through interest group pressure, public opinion, elite socialization or other domestic actors and processes. The first is a *functional* economic spill-over, which occurs when incomplete integration undermines the ability to achieve all the benefits of the existing policies both in the areas that are already integrated and in related sectors of the economy, thus automatically creating the need for further cooperation among the EC countries. The second is a political spill-over linked to the fundamental role of existing EC institutions in giving impetus to a self-reinforcing process of institution building.

When applied to the issue of Economic and Monetary Union, the concept of spill-over, in its milder political form, implies that the 1992 single-market process increased the level of support among public opinion and EC governments for all those EC initiatives that could enhance the gains coming from the single-market programme. In terms of economic spill-over, the Treaty on European Union (TEU) was portrayed by the EC Commission, and by Jaques Delors in particular (Commission of European Communities, 1990), as functionally linked to the internal market process and necessary for its success. The Commission's case rested on the argument that the completion of capital liberalization in July 1990, coupled with exchange rate stability, as provided for by the European Monetary System (EMS), is incompatible with divergent national monetary policies.[1] In an environment of capital liberalization there is a sort of trade-off between stable exchange rates and independent national monetary policies, the so-called *trilemma* of monetary policy. As Tomasso Padoa-Schioppa argues (Padoa-Schioppa, 1988), since the first brings about gains in efficiency and transaction costs savings, considered particularly important for a single market to work properly, the only viable solution is the pooling of national monetary policies in a monetary union, thus establishing a common monetary policy governed by a European Central

Bank (ECB). In the neo-functionalist interpretation of the role and functions of the ECB there is no doubt that the ECB would, by definition, meet the interests of the entire Euro-zone, which will coincide, by definition, with the interests of all the member states. This happens because, from the neo-functionalist perspective, the establishment of the ECB is an economic necessity and the implementation of a common monetary policy is a Pareto optimal outcome of the integration process.

However, the deterministic nature of the economic argument for the functional linkage between the internal market and the process of monetary union cannot be considered as exhaustive, as demonstrated by the fact that some governments were willing to reap the full benefits of the single market without entering EMU. The UK, for example, successfully remained in the single market after the establishment of the EMU, thus preferring monetary independence to the transaction gains provided by the adoption of a single currency.[2] Moreover, the whole debate about whether the Euro-zone is an optimal currency area (OCA) and the related possibility of asymmetric shocks[3] fundamentally challenge the neo-functionalist view that the implementation of a common monetary policy by a European Central Bank necessarily enhances the welfare of all the EMU member states. In other words, the interests of the member states can still diverge and therefore the implementation of a one-size-fits-all monetary policy will not necessarily result in a positive sum game.

This brings to the forefront realist and intergovernmentalist interpretations of European monetary integration. Both realists and intergovernmentalists, indeed, postulate that nation states dominate EC politics and that outcomes directly reflect the interests and relative power of the member states. Thus both of these related schools of thought analyse the EC as the result of strategies pursued by rational governments acting on the basis of their preferences and power. However, whereas realist scholars tend to identify the interests of the state in geopolitical terms,[4] intergovernmentalists assert the primacy of political economy considerations.

David Andrews offers an exemplary mixed realist/intergovernmentalist account of the negotiations over the EMU.[5] Andrews's central argument is that the Maastricht Treaty resulted from the confluence of interests of the French and German governments. On the one hand, Germany was particularly keen to secure European acquiescence to re-unification. On the other hand, France acted on the basis of a mixture of political-economic and geopolitical considerations, aiming both at restoring some control over its monetary policy making dominated by Germany within the EMS and, at the same time, at firmly securing a re-united Germany within the European sphere. Importantly, according to the author, the issue of German re-unification cannot be separated from geopolitical changes in the international system such as the collapse of the Soviet Union. This event opened, in the words of Andrews, 'a window of opportunity' for France and Germany to come to an agreement on the substance of the EMU. However, since the window of opportunity created by the diplomatic imperative for France of binding Germany to the community following German unification closed after 1992, the actual implementation of the EMU project was doomed to face increasing difficulties, as indeed was the case.

Thus in contrast to neo-functionalists, Andrews emphasizes the national interests of the leading European powers in monetary union: French and German elites recognized a changing set of interests resulting from extra-ordinary developments in the global geopolitical order and political economy, and they reacted accordingly.

Whilst French and German foreign policy goals may have become con-gruent with monetary union, these goals do not by themselves explain the origins of the process, which pre-dated both the collapse of the Soviet Union and the fall of the Berlin Wall. Moreover, this approach cannot account for the interest in EMU shown by smaller countries such as Belgium and Italy in 1988 and early 1989. Nor is it clear that the fear of German unification, in the absence of other motives, was sufficient to inspire the other EC states to overcome the difficulties involved in design-ing supranational institutions and transferring monetary sovereignty to them. Furthermore, this explanation does not account for the role played by political economy interests, namely interest group pressures in promot-ing the goal of Economic and Monetary Union. A more comprehensive and complete explanation requires an analysis of domestic interests.

The need for such an analysis was indeed noted by Moravcsik himself. Building on his earlier intergovernmentalism, he proposed a novel 'liberal intergovernmentalism', which refines the theory of inter-state bargaining and institutional compliance and adds an explicit theory of national preference formation grounded in liberal theories of international interdependence.[6]

In particular, as Moravcsik points out,[7] this domestic politics approach would explain why the position of Germany in the negotiations over EMU did not reflect the strong anti-inflationary position of the Bundesbank but rather a compromise between the Bundesbank's strict anti-inflationary stance and the preferences of the business sector for a devalued exchange rate, low interest rate and macroeconomic flexibility.[8] These two conflicting positions did indeed dominate the whole German domestic debate in the run-up to the Maastricht negotiations and agreement. As a result, in the intergovernmental conference in Maastricht, Germany supported an EMU that fulfilled almost all the 'economist'[9] conditions posed by the Bundesbank but which also paved the way for a softer Euro,[10] a welcomed outcome for German exporters.[11] However, the stress on macroeconomic flexibility by the business community required, at least at the onset, a fiscal straitjacket, like the one devised with the Growth and Stability Pact. Indeed, in the lack of a common fiscal policy or even tax harmonization, the Maastricht way to EMU, complemented by the fiscal constraints of the SGP, points at labour market flexibility as the only feasible tool to react to asymmetric shocks and to tackle unemployment. The connection between EMU and labour market flexibility is reflected in the rhetoric and practice of the EU Commission's interventions within the framework of the European Employment Strategy.[12] Therefore, when Lafontaine sought to give a new priority to growth and employment objectives through Keynesian-style demand management, and to accompany monetary union with exchange-rate stabilization and tax harmonization, he was in overt opposition not only with the interests of the Bundesbank but also of the German business community. The necessary outcome of this situation was his sudden resignation in March 1999 and his replacement by Hans Eichel, who represented the agenda of supply-side reforms and restructuring of the welfare state and of labour markets.[13]

On the French side, it is indisputable that the country's interest since 1984 was to increase the symmetry of European monetary arrangements, which, after the implementation of the ERM of the EMS, had clearly been dominated by Germany as the 'hegemon' of the system.[14] However, according to Moravcsik what it is important to verify is the reasons underlying this particular policy preference. Geopolitical factors, especially those related to the need to keep Germany firmly within Europe after its unification, are discounted on the grounds that the French policy preference did not change with the collapse of the Berlin Wall or with the unification of Germany, but rather remained steadily consistent from 1984 until the Maastricht negotiations. Indeed, political economy motivations ultimately explain French policies and actions. In fact the EMU was seen as perfectly consistent with long-standing French international monetary goals. France had long been committed to an anti-inflationary policy and had supported a strong Franc (the so-called Franc fort policy) and capital liberalization since Mitterrand's macroeconomic policy shift in 1984. However, the European monetary arrangements established with the ERM of the EMS gave a structural advantage in terms of monetary policy making to Germany. Therefore France had a clear interest in seeking to retain the same policy preference within a more symmetrical system like the one devised at Maastricht for the establishment of the ECB. In this regard, a more symmetrical monetary policy offered more advantages than the asymmetrical EMS, including, as listed by Moravcsik, lower risk premia and exchange rate volatility, greater political legitimation and more symmetrical obligations vis-à-vis Germany which would translate into looser constraints on macroeconomic policy and therefore in a slightly more competitive European currency. All these factors explain the very strong support given to EMU by the French business community.[15]

Finally, the case of British opposition to EMU is particularly revealing in terms of showing the extent to which national preferences were formed on domestic political economy considerations and not on geopolitical strategic or neo-constructivist ones. Whilst there is little evidence that Britain's rejection of EMU was based on 'antipathy' towards Germany, there is a great deal of evidence in favour of a political economy approach. Political economy theory, according to Moravcsik, correctly predicted that the British would accept only minor monetary or exchange rate commitments, mainly favoured by the British business elites, for on the one side they were concerned by 'the slide in competitiveness that might result from any firm commitment to stable exchange rates' (Moravcsik, 1998: 417) and, on the other side, they 'would seek to avoid any permanent exclusion from monetary arrangements, for exclusion was perceived as undermining the global position of British industry and, above all, finance' (Moravcsik, 1998: 417). Talani (2000), however, demonstrates that the interests of particularly the financial community lay outside the EMU, and the fear of being sidelined in the European integration process by remaining outside the EMU led the British government to try to destroy, or at least delay, the process of European monetary integration.

Thus, as Moravcsik acknowledges, the question facing international relations theorists is no longer whether to combine domestic and international explanations, but how best to do it.

One solution to the problem is Robert Putnam's two-level games theory (Moravcsik, 1993: 9). Putnam first defines the conceptual framework applicable to all kinds of issues, including foreign economic policy ones. Then he tries to answer the questions of when and how domestic politics and international relations become entangled. Putnam's approach rests on the metaphor of the two-level game for domestic–international relations: at the national level, domestic groups pursue their interests by pressuring governments to adopt favourable policies, and politicians seek power by constructing coalitions among these groups; at the international level, national governments seek to maximize their own ability to satisfy domestic pressures, while minimizing the adverse consequences of foreign developments. Since each national political leader appears at both game boards, international relations scholars can ignore neither of the two games (Evans *et al.*, 1993).

With reference to European monetary integration, different scholars have focused their attention on different aspects of the integrated international–domestic politics approach, often reproducing the institutionalist/ intergovernmentalist dichotomy at one or both levels of analysis. Some applications of the two-level game approach focus on the institutional implications of bargaining links, arguing that it is important to view the debate over EMU as embedded in an institutional pattern of inter-state cooperation in many dimensions (Martin, 1993). Others adopt an institutionalist approach at the national level and an intergovernmentalist one at the international level (Andrews, 1993; Garret, 1993; Sandholtz, 1993; and Wooley, 1993).

Finally, some scholars use an intergovernmentalist application of the integrated international–domestic politics approach to the process of European monetary integration (Wooley, 1993).

Wayne Sandholtz (1993) has provided a synthetic account of the process of European integration by simply juxtaposing the three main theoretical approaches to the process of European monetary integration – namely the intergovernmental approach, the institutional approach and the domestic politics one – and claiming that each of them explains a different aspect of the overall phenomenon. Sandholtz also grounds the discussion of the Maastricht Treaty in the conversion to neo-liberal monetary discipline in several European countries during the 1980s. The convergence to low inflation rates that occurred in the EMS during this period, in fact, was not due to any EMS change that rendered it more effective. Rather the success of the EMS derived from the new inclination of a number of EC countries, particularly the weakest ones, to commit to low-inflation policies. This line of thought is also the basis of neo-constructivist or liberal constructivist reconstructions of monetary integration.

Neo-constructivist explanations of the establishment of EMU can be divided into two basic groups: 1) identity-oriented constructivists; 2) economic ideas-oriented constructivists.

The first group of scholars (Engelmann *et al.*, 1997; Risse, 1998) is, to a certain extent, more radical in the adoption of neo-constructivist assumptions in that they believe that the process of monetary integration and, in particular, the establishment of EMU can be explained within the context of identity politics. Their effort is therefore mainly oriented to verifying the 'symbolic' nature of the 'Euro' in relation to the national collective identity and symbols. Importantly, these authors discard as contradictory economic motivations for EMU and attribute explanatory value only to non-economic political constructions.

For example, according to Thomas Risse, because French and German political elites of all political orientations have incorporated European identity into the national identity, the debate in these two countries was not about whether to join EMU but when and why. In Britain, on the other hand, Europe remains outside and, to some extent, contrary to the collective definition of British identity. Hence political elites continue to resist joining EMU.

Insofar as this strand of constructivism highlights the cultural terrain on which debates on European Union are generally framed, it has a certain appeal. However, the approach is problematic because it is based on a tautology: every single step in the process of European integration, including EMU, can be referred to a particular aspect of the collective perception of national vis-à-vis European identity. Thus constructivist approaches to EMU face the same problem as all idealist explanations in the social sciences: the analysis takes the existence of ideas as given rather than seeking to explain how and why ideas originated and changed as a result of political and economic factors. Moreover, the definition itself of national/European identity is not as straightforward as Risse seems to believe and might be the object of even more controversies than the author claims is the case in relation to the definition of the economic interests involved in EMU. Indeed, the author seems to discard too easily and in too simplistic a way the economic case for the single currency.

The second group of authors, particularly Kathleen McNamara (1998) and Kenneth Dyson (2000), on the contrary, still attribute importance to economic factors to explain EMU, but stress the role of economic ideas as opposed to economic interests. In their view, EMU became a necessity in the context of the establishment of a new economic consensus, the neo-liberal 'consensus of competitive liberalism', amongst the political elites of all EC member states (Dyson, 2000). According to Dyson, 'the success of the economic paradigm of sound money in becoming dominant in the design of the Euro-Zone was the result of the failure of the Keynesian paradigm of the managed economy to tackle the insidious combination of inflationary and unemployment problems in the 1970s and 1980s' (Dyson, 2000: 30). This change in the ideological paradigm allowed the ECB to acquire a central role in the EMU, what Dyson calls an 'ECB centric Euro-zone' (Dyson, 2000: 11).

Clearly, the change in the prevailing ideological paradigm from the mid-1970s onwards is one side of the spread of the new credo in macro-economic policy, a credo emphasizing strict monetary and fiscal policy in the context of exchange rate stability. However, what is lacking from this interpretation of monetary integration is the reasons why this shift happened at that particular historical moment. The solution to this dilemma is to be found in a more comprehensive analysis of the economic interests underpinning this ideological shift and of the related socio-economic groups taking advantage of it in the context of the change in the power relations taking place in the socio-economic arena within a particular historical conjuncture. So, the question to answer is: Who is interested in what in European monetary policy making?

The one author who has contributed substantially to the development of a political scientists' approach to monetary policy making from within a two-level game theoretical framework is Jeffrey Frieden (1994). Indeed, Frieden has proposed a 'two-step' model of national monetary policy making based on domestic sectoral interests. The model identifies economic sectors' preferences vis-à-vis the two interrelated dimensions of exchange rate regimes (fixed or flexible) and levels (appreciated or depreciated). With respect to the second dimension of the model, namely groups' preferences vis-à-vis the level of the exchange rates, Frieden notes that export-oriented traditional manufacturers and primary producers of non-agricultural products have a vested interest in supporting the devaluation of the currency. Indeed, from a differential distributional point of view, the lower, that is, more depreciated, the exchange rate, the higher is the price of tradable goods relative to non-tradable ones.[16] This, in turn, tends to favour the producers of tradable goods, whose output prices rise more than the prices of the non-tradable inputs they use, and to hurt producers of non-tradable goods. Producers in the tradable sector, therefore, gain from depreciation, which makes their products more competitive in home and foreign markets, while producers in the non-tradable sector generally benefit from currency appreciation, which raises the domestic relative price of their products and lowers the domestic relative price of tradable goods. Moreover, international traders and investors, who are interested in purchasing assets abroad, favour a strong currency. On this basis, it is plausible to presume that countries more heavily relying on the exports of manufacturing goods outside the EU would gain most from the devaluation of the Euro. In other words, these countries are the ones benefiting most from the adoption of a policy of 'benign neglect' of the depreciation of the single currency by the ECB.

However, the application of Frieden's model does not explain the credibility of a country's commitment to a fixed exchange rate regime. It is only helpful in defining the economic interests pursued by socio-economic interests groups in relation to a particular dimension of monetary policy: the level of the exchange rates (Talani, 2000).

A structural definition of credibility of exchange rate and monetary commitments is not based on pure economic expectations, but rather on a much more complex set of political economy considerations. In particular, it is possible to hypothesize that the more foreign economic commitments in general, and exchange rate policies in particular, are rooted in the interests of a given hegemonic bloc, the more these commitments are credible. That is, in the case of fixed exchange rates or target zone commitments, the more they can count on the 'consensus' of the most powerful sections of society, the more credible they are.

This interpretation of credibility is rooted in an analytical framework based on three different levels of analysis, which correspond to three different levels of explanation. The first level of analysis, which might be called the 'political economy analysis', is represented by an organic analysis of the domestic structure of capital and of power relations between the various socio-economic actors as historically developed. It represents the limits within which further developments must necessarily take place. This first level of analysis, then, allows for the identification of the power relations among the social forces under consideration within a given mode of production and historical conjuncture. It also provides a basis for comparison with different sets of power relations in different countries.

However, these kinds of structural considerations cannot account for the whole history of the process of European monetary integration. Nor can they provide the basis for reliable predictions of future behaviour. Therefore, it is necessary to connect this first level of analysis with the more conjunctural analysis of the second and the third levels, in order to obtain a dynamic picture of the phenomenon under consideration. The second level of analysis, 'purely economic analysis', focuses on the identification of the concrete interest groups' preferences in a short-term time scale. It focuses on the concrete struggle for economic power, and particularly on the competition amongst interest groups to obtain favourable economic policies. It is at this level that classifications of socio-economic preferences towards exchange rate levels and regimes may be tested empirically. Finally, the third level, 'purely political analysis', focuses on the day-to-day political struggles or the specific means by which economic interests become policies after having been processed through the political and institutional system. It is here that the political bargaining process, the role of political parties and leaders, and the incentive/disincentive mechanism are taken into consideration.

Before turning to the empirical evidence, however, it is worth analysing how economists cope with the problem of credibility.

1.2 How Do Economists Cope with the Problem of Credibility?

In the economics literature, the credibility of an exchange rate system is related to the sustainability of the domestic authorities' commitment in a world with free capital mobility. Whereas credible policy makers will benefit from the possibility of violating, if only temporarily, the 'rules of the game', non-credible ones will be punished even more severely by the international capital markets. Hence, the credibility of an exchange rate agreement can be measured through the calculation of 'realignment expectations',[17] which are higher when the credibility of the commitment is lower.

The seminal work on the behaviour of the exchange rate in a target zone is that of Krugman (1991). In his model, the credibility of the system determines the behaviour of the exchange rate. Indeed, if the market believes that the Central Bank will abide by the 'rules of the game' and is fully committed to 'marginal intervention', the exchange rate will follow an S-shaped relationship with 'fundamentals', i.e. it will adjust less than proportionally to a shock to its fundamentals. This is a direct and free benefit from credibility, due to a 'honeymoon' between the authorities and speculators. Speculators believe that, had the exchange rate depreciated (appreciated) and hit the upper (lower) band of the zone, a positive (negative) shock to, for example, money supply would have been offset by a Central Bank reduction (increase) in money supply. Indeed, since once the 'S' has reached the upper (lower) band it can only decrease (rise) because of a negative (positive) shock to velocity, on average expectations will be of an appreciation (depreciation).

The easiest way to measure realignment expectations is through raw interest differentials. The target zone theory predicts a negative correlation between the exchange rate and the interest rate within the bands. However, most of the empirical evidence is in disagreement with the theory, and a positive relationship is more often identified (Rose and Svensson, 1994; Svensson, 1991). The main explanation for this result lies in the intrinsic lack of credibility of target zones.[18] If the regime is less than fully credible, speculators who observe a shock to money supply and do not know whether it is due to a temporary random disturbance or a change in policy may interpret a rise in the exchange rate as a negative signal and buy foreign currency instead of selling it. An initial rise in the exchange rate can be considered by speculators as a signal that the authorities are not following the 'rules of the game' and lead them to buy foreign currency instead of selling it. Speculation will consequently be destabilizing. Svensson's 'simplest test' of target zone credibility (Svensson, 1990), for example, is built on the consideration that if a fluctuation band is imposed on the exchange rate there is also an implicit band on the rate of return of foreign investment. This is due to the relation linking the rate of return on foreign investment to the actual and the future spot exchange rate.[19] Thus, given free capital mobility, in a credible target zone domestic interest rates must move within this 'rate of return band'; otherwise there would be completely safe arbitrage. Therefore, if indeed the domestic interest rate is outside this 'rate of return band', the no-arbitrage assumption implies that the target zone is not credible and that the expected future spot exchange lies outside the exchange rate bands.[20]

Other economists have adjusted interest rate differentials for the expected drift in the exchange rate,[21] which can be particularly important in a system like the ERM, where some flexibility of exchange rates around central parities is allowed.[22]

When applied to the case of the Pound and Lira's experience within the ERM before their departure in September 1992, these measures of credibility give contrasting results. Indeed, the application of these methods led to the conclusion that, while the British government's commitment to the ERM was fairly credible up to the very last minute before the currency crisis, the Italian one was not sustainable throughout the whole of 1992.

This result is puzzling because both currencies were indeed involved in a major wave of speculation in September 1992, and both governments were forced not only to devalue their currency but also to leave the system altogether. There must be an explanation for the similarities between the countries' experience in the ERM, and it must be possible to trace back 'the common nature of ERM credibility' (Rose and Svensson, 1994).

Fratianni and Artis (1996) have found a solution to this problem by broadening the definition of credibility of the exchange rate commitment to include its sustainability in terms of fundamentals. Thus, even if financial indicators, such as interest rate differentials or forward exchange rates, did not enshrine the lack of credibility of the British government's commitment to the ERM, a closer look at the fundamentals might signal the unsustainability of the currency peg.

Indeed, according to Fratianni and Artis, the markets form their exchange rate expectations not only on financial variables but also on their understanding of the 'average' response of the authorities to the performance of business cycle factors, in particular inflation and output rates.[23] The argument then runs as follows: the British commitment to the ERM became not credible because the markets knew that the UK authorities would respond to the performance of the inflation and output rates in a way which was inconsistent with the maintenance of the Pound in the system.

However, in Britain the recession started long before that in the other ERM countries. Therefore, if the markets based their assessment of exchange rate credibility only on monetary authorities' response to the performance of the leading business cycle indicators, they should have attacked the Pound within the ERM well before they attacked the Lira and the Franc.

On the contrary, Sterling's performance within the ERM was by no means disastrous. Although it had been given the possibility of fluctuating against other ERM currencies within a 6 per cent margin, for most of its experience in the ERM it had moved safely within the 2.25 per cent band accorded to the core EMS countries, without interest rates being forced up. Instead, UK nominal interest rates showed a clear downward trend in the period Sterling remained in the ERM, while the inflation rate fell drastically from 9.5 per cent in 1990 to 5.9 per cent in 1991 and 3.7 per cent in 1992 (OECD, 1991). Moreover, British authorities had justified British entry in the ERM mainly on business cycle considerations, namely the necessity to reduce inflation rates and to keep interest rates in line with the needs of an economy in recession.[24] This was actually what happened in the course of British adherence to the Exchange Rate Mechanism. This conclusion would be consistent with the idea that the markets considered the British government's commitment to the ERM credible up to the very last minute before the British decision to leave the ERM.[25]

The chronic instability of the international monetary system, especially during the last three decades, provides strong evidence that speculation has been in most cases destabilizing. The presence of bands does not necessarily provide the desired monetary policy flexibility, as is evident from the historical authorities' propensity to early intervention. Ultimately, target zones are exposed to speculative attacks.

A large economic literature has discussed the causes of currency crises and speculative attacks on exchange rate pegs. Research in the area can be tracked back to the seminal work of Krugman (1979) and Flood and Garber (1984). It is now customary to separate the literature into so-called first and second generations of models. A fiscal imbalance ending in monetization lies at the heart of the first generation type of crises. The inconsistency of persistent deficits makes the currency peg a perfect target for speculators, and the crisis outcome is the most obvious and almost deterministic result. While these models provide a reasonable characterization of crises in the 1970s and 1980s, they seem to miss some of the key features of more recent events, which are not easily attributable to the lack of fiscal and monetary discipline. Therefore, the second generation of models, originated from the contributions of Obstfeld (1986, 1996), qualifies crises as self-fulfilling events in the presence of multiple equilibria. In these models, the switch from the good to the bad equilibrium results from a (sudden) shift in investors' beliefs about the true state of the economy. As in the Keynesian beauty contest, what matters most in the eyes of international investors is not the true value of fundamentals, but what people think the true value is.[26]

In a typical balance-of-payments crisis of the Krugman–Flood–Garber (KFG henceforth) type, a small country fixes the exchange rate to that of a large foreign partner, and the domestic authorities are responsible for maintaining the parity. Both purchasing power parity (PPP) and uncovered interest parity (UIP) are assumed to hold continuously. Under the assumption of perfect capital mobility and perfect agents' foresight, a credible fixed exchange rate implies also perfect asset substitutability. Since money supply is composed of domestic credit and international reserves, under a fixed exchange rate, changes in expectations are reflected in changes in international reserves.

In a world where agents have perfect foresight, as long as the fixed exchange rate system is adopted, the authorities must keep the money supply fixed to maintain parity, accommodating changes in money demand with the stock of reserves. If the government decides to finance a deficit by expanding domestic credit, the domestic central bank will be forced to sell its international reserves. In this setting, no matter how high international reserves have been set initially and provided they have a lower limit, they will sooner or later be depleted, and the peg will become unsustainable. Indeed, equilibrium involves a speculative attack, which occurs before the authorities run out of reserves.

The lower limit of reserves does not need to be zero, and in reality the authorities often decide to abandon the peg well before all reserves have been compromised. Under multilateral agreements, the lower limit of reserves ultimately depends on the multilateral commitment to the agreement and its credibility. In the particular case of the ERM the weaker central bank had an unlimited borrowing facility from the stronger currency central bank (provided repayment of the debt occurred within a preset period of time). These arrangements clearly failed at the first difficulty (see Buiter *et al.* (1998) for a complete account of the events leading to the ERM crisis).

In first-generation models, the viability of the fixed exchange rate ultimately depends on the state of fundamentals, and the exhaustion of international reserves determines the regime collapse. This prediction is consistent with the 'unholy trinity' paradigm of monetary policy: a country cannot simultaneously maintain fixed rates, maintain an open capital market and pursue domestic monetary policy goals. The historical fragility of fixed exchange rates provides strong evidence in support of this theoretical result. However, a strong limitation of KFG models is the lack of consideration of the policy-maker incentives, the interaction between the policy maker and the private sector, and the speculators' coordination mechanism. This limitation makes them unable to explain important features of crises in the 1990s,[27] when speculative attacks often struck in countries where international reserves were sufficient to cope with a balance-of-payments deficit and fundamentals were generally considered sound.

However, the authorities' constraints to support the peg may have depended on less evident problems in the underlying economic structure. Defence ability could have been limited by the state of the business cycle, by borrowing limits imposed by foreign partners, by the debt maturity structure or by the state of the corporate sector.

While first-generation models combined linear behaviour rules assumed by both private agents (money demand) and the authorities (domestic credit expansion), which under perfect foresight resulted in the unique-attack equilibrium, second-generation models design a more complex role for economic agents, combining one or more non-linearities. The final result is that balance-of-payments crises can be the outcome of self-fulfilling expectations of a macro policy change in the presence of multiple equilibria. Expectations follow a self-fulfilling mechanism. If speculators believe that monetary policy will be loosened after the regime collapse and they are able to exhaust the remaining foreign reserves, and the authorities actually loosen monetary policy, they can cause the exchange rate depreci-ation they were looking for. This circular dynamic builds the potential for the crisis. However, the setting of policy-maker incentives becomes crucial, as the speculators' coordination problem changes depending on the distress of the authorities in the face of the attack. In turn, this distress varies with macroeconomic fundamentals, making a range of equilibria possible.

Obstfeld (1996) presents the problem in the form of a speculative game played by the monetary authority and speculators, where what matters is the level of commitment versus the size of the attack. The strategic inter-action between policy makers and speculators builds the case for multiple equilibria. The economy can sit indefinitely on the no-attack equilibrium or switch to the attack one. The speculative attack contains a self-fulfilling element embedded in the circular dynamic, and the run on the exchange rate depends on a shift in expectations. The potential for a run can be created by the knowledge that the policy maker has a constrained ability to defend the peg.

In this context, it is important to focus on the 'stark' choices faced by the authorities in the face of the attack, and second-generation models high-light the importance of government incentives to determine the potential for a speculative run. The resilience of exchange rate arrangements depends on the authorities' distress from the business cycle, which is endogenous to the model. While staying in the fixed system yields long-term benefits, opting out can provide a 'populist' solution to the shorter-term problems in the economy.[28]

Many authors have looked at this interaction within the standard frame-work proposed by Kydland and Prescott (1977) and Barro and Gordon (1983) of distortion effects of inconsistent monetary policies and have analysed the optimal choice between rules and discretion. The govern-ment's attempt to inflate the economy is punished by the private sector, cre-ating the potential for an inflation bias. During the 1990s, building a reputation for monetary stability has been a main concern, especially for those authorities which had previously made strong use of the monetary lever, and fixing the exchange rate provided the necessary anchor. A central bank with a low reputation may anchor its exchange rate to that of a more 'conservative' central bank (a concept due to Rogoff, 1985). For the case of the EMS, Giavazzi and Giovannini (1989) find empirical evidence that constraining the exchange rate had a significant inflation-reducing effect in those countries with a poor reputation in terms of price stability. This proposition is not necessarily welfare maximizing, especially if the economy is persistently hit by shocks. However, the result may be resuscitated when one allows for uncertainty in the central banker preferences (see, for example, Muscatelli, 1995, 1998). To achieve a welfare improvement there are two requirements: the economy must be relatively stable and society must be concerned with the social benefits from low inflation, compared to output stabilization. Obstfeld (1994) adapts the model to an open economy, assuming equality between the foreign and the domestic price level, where the dynamic policy inconsistency results in a 'Peso-problem'. Flood and Marion (1998) look directly at the net social benefits from depreciation and show how the rule is strictly better than discretion only when the economy is not hit by shocks. When a large shock hits the economy, society is better off with discretion. Since no regime is irrevocably fixed, the government should implement a rule with an escape clause. The escape clause carries a cost, but is also welfare enhancing, so that the government should choose the rule as long as the loss from the rule is lower than the loss from exercising discretion and pay the cost. The escape clause is implemented when the disturbance can be particularly disruptive and generally leads to devaluation. The policy implication is that rules with escape clauses are welfare enhancing, but also potentially destabilizing. In order to stabilize the system, the cost of abandoning must be set at such a high level that exercising discretion is never the preferred choice, i.e. adopt an irrevocably fixed exchange rate.

The circular dynamic intrinsic in the fulfilment of expectations makes the timing of the attack arbitrary, in contrast with the deterministic nature of crises in models of the KFG type. A credible regime may end in crisis because of minor events such as sunspots. Soros-type investors, rather than bad governments, can be held responsible for the crisis since under certain conditions they can create an ad hoc sunspot and trigger a major crisis. Within the framework, it is possible to conjugate optimizing models of realignment with the role of agents' preferences, and the impact of the uncertainty which originates from the potential dichotomy between the preferences of society and the central banker type. De Grauwe (1996) has provided a useful contribution to the identification of a broader definition of credibility. He traces back the origins of a speculative crisis to the dissolution of the consensus on the exchange rate commitment (De Grauwe,

1996: 26–7). The problem, then, becomes the identification of the basis of this consensus. According to De Grauwe, the first and fundamental source of this consensus is not endogenous to the country, but exogenous, or systemic. A fixed exchange rate system necessitates a systemic consensus, that is, a consensus among the participant nation states about the stance of monetary policy for the system as a whole, the so-called 'n−1 problem'. Consequently, it is the dissolution of this systemic consensus, represented by the rise of a conflict between the monetary policy objectives of the 'n−1 country' and the ones of the other participants in the system, which triggers the reaction of the markets and, eventually, the speculative crisis.

This approach leaves unsolved the problem of the identification and sources of the monetary policy objectives of both the 'nth' and the 'n−1' countries. However, even if at a subordinate level of explanation, De Grauwe considers also the endogenous sources of the dissolution or 'death' of consensus, identifying them in the conflict between a country's exchange rate commitment and its domestic economic objectives, the so-called 'adjustment problem' (De Grauwe, 1996: 59–60).

What this contribution tries to identify is exactly the basis of this domestic consensus on a certain level of fixed exchange rates. In other words, it looks for the sources of the objectives pursued by a country at the moment at which it commits itself to a fixed exchange rate, and the sources of the dissolution of this consensus. The credibility of a government's exchange rate commitment depends on the existence of a social 'consensus' to such a commitment within the domestic arena and, in particular, among the leading socio-economic groups (Eichengreen and Frieden, 1994). Therefore, credibility is linked to something 'more fundamental than the fundamentals', i.e. to the structure of capitalism itself and to the power relations between socio-economic groups at a certain historical moment. Of course, this interpretation of credibility needs a framework in which to analyse socio-economic behaviour. This framework is the subject of the next section of this chapter.

2 INTERESTS OR EXPECTATIONS? A POLITICAL ECONOMY ANALYTICAL FRAMEWORK TO THE CREDIBILITY OF EXCHANGE RATE COMMITMENTS

As detailed in the previous sections, economists and political scientists offer competing interpretations of exchange rate credibility. While political scientists focus primarily on a socio-political analysis aimed at tracing back the 'interests' underlying contextualized exchange rate commitments, economists tend to give importance to purely financial and economic variables as connected to the 'expectations' of the markets. However, more recently political scientists have sought to devote more attention to the issue from an integrated political economy perspective, which mainly focuses on the role of partisanship and governments' stability in influencing speculative behaviour (Leblang, 2002; Leblang and Bernard, 2000). Yet there remains considerable scope for speculation on the relation between socio-political and economic accounts of financial phenomena. There is, in other words, the possibility of finding a 'synthesis' of the two cognitive and interpretive models. Taken separately, economic and political perspectives can provide only a partial representation of reality.

The political economy approach to the credibility of the exchange rate proposed in this chapter challenges the belief that markets in general, and financial markets in particular, stand aside from history and society and behave independently of social and political considerations. The approach proposed here grounds financial market behaviour in the underlying political economy structure of capitalist economies, subordinating their expectations to the interests of the leading socio-economic groups (Gill, 1991). It challenges the assumption of the infallibility of the markets and of their independent 'inner rationality' and proposes an alternative political economy rationality which embeds markets' expectations into a given socio-economic structure. This political economy approach to the credibility of exchange rate commitments and of the rationality of financial market behaviour thus seeks to transcend ahistorical and abstract explanations without falling into the trap of historical or cultural relativism. It also provides the theoretical underpinnings for a rigorous analytical framework consisting of different levels of explanations structured in a clear-cut hierarchy. By introducing the crucial assumption that power relations are, eventually, the main heuristic tools in any attempts to explain socio-economic events, it inserts the notions of power and power struggles into the analysis. These power struggles are not, however, assumed to be confined to the state, but rather extend to the socio-economic groups which define the particular capitalist structure of a given nation state. Purely economic explanations or purely political ones are not, of course, discarded, but are situated within the analysis of the underlying political economy structure.

The political economy approach adopted in this chapter is based on three different levels of analysis, which correspond to three different levels of explanation. The first level of analysis might be called the 'political economy analysis'.[29] It is represented by an organic analysis of the domestic structure of capital and of power relations between the various socio-economic actors as historically developed. It represents the limits within which further developments must necessarily take place. This first level of analysis, then, allows for the identification of the power relations among the social forces under consideration within a given mode of production and historical conjuncture. It also provides a basis for comparison with different sets of power relations in different countries.

However, these kinds of structural considerations cannot in themselves account for the whole history of European monetary integration. Nor can they provide the basis for reliable predictions of future behaviour. Therefore, it is necessary to connect this first level of analysis to the more conjunctural analysis of the second and the third levels, in order to obtain a dynamic picture of the phenomenon under consideration. The second level of analysis, 'purely economic analysis', focuses on the identification of the concrete interest groups' preferences in a short-term time scale. It stresses the concrete struggle for economic power, and particularly the competition amongst interest groups to obtain favourable economic policies. It is at this level that classifications of socio-economic preferences towards exchange rates and regimes may be tested empirically.[30] Finally, the third level, 'purely political analysis', focuses, once again, on the short-term time scale: the day-to-day political struggles or the specific means by which economic interests become policies after having been processed through the political and institutional system. It is here that the political bargaining process, the role of political parties and leaders, and the incentive/disincentive mechanism are taken into consideration.

A comprehensive explanatory model requires a synthesis of each of these levels in order to provide the most reliable picture of the phenomenon under analysis. This reflects the fact that in the real world there are overlapping relationships of mutual reciprocity between the economic structure, the economic interests promoted by socio-economic groups, and the political and institutional life.

This analytical framework makes it possible to derive a 'phenomenology of credibility' of international economic commitments and, in particular, of exchange rate commitments. Credibility is not based on pure economic expectations, but rather on a more complex set of political economy considerations. In particular, it is possible to hypothesize that the more foreign economic commitments in general, and exchange rate policies in particular, are rooted in the interests of socio-economic actors, the more these commitments are credible. That is, in the case of fixed exchange rates or target zone commitments, the more they can count on the 'consensus' of the most powerful sections of society, the less likely they are to be challenged by the markets. Indeed, there is a dialectic relation between interests and expectations; expectations of the markets are deeply influenced by the interests and preferences of the leading socio-economic sectors of the country under consideration. Market expectations, and thus also markets' behaviour, are crucially affected by considerations about something 'more fundamental than the fundamentals': the economic structure and the way in which it is reflected in economic and political life. This definition is perfectly consistent with the political scientists' view that exchange rate commitments are international agreements and therefore need to be based on the existence of a domestic 'consensus' rooted in the 'interests' of domestic actors.

From the economists' standpoint, this approach to the credibility of exchange rate pegs could help in reconciling the two opposing theories on speculative attacks. The contemporary debate on exchange rate economics is in fact characterized by the opposition between 'fundamentalists', i.e. supporters of the thesis that real exchange rate fluctuations largely reflect changes in macroeconomic fundamentals, and those who believe that: 'Foreign exchange markets behave more like the unstable and irrational asset markets described by Keynes than the efficient markets described by modern finance theory' (Krugman, 1989: 61).

As underlined above, the latter approach assumes that speculative attacks are self-fulfilling or that, in a multiple equilibriums environment, the markets produce their own exchange rate expectations without any intelligible connection with fundamentals (De Grauwe, 1996). In turn, these expectations produce speculative attacks, which ultimately compel governments to abandon the exchange rate peg and to adopt ex-post softer monetary stances. A compromise approach has been proposed which allows for multiple equilibriums only within a certain range of fundamentals' performance. Alternatively, economists tend to overcome the problem by lifting the assumption of market participants' complete information on the performance of economic fundamentals (see section 1.2).

Here it is argued, however, that the failure of the 'fundamentals' to explain speculative attacks does not necessarily imply that exchange rate markets act 'irrationally' or 'inefficiently' or that they are constrained by the lack of information. It can also mean that the markets, in deciding which of the multiple equilibriums is more likely to be adopted by the government after a speculative attack, evaluate a wide range of events, including socio-political and structural ones. Thus the credibility of an exchange rate commitment is crucially dependent on the behaviour and interests of socio-economic actors at a particular historical moment.

Of course, this model is not static, and changes may occur at each level of analysis. At the first level of analysis, changes are certainly long-term ones and are represented by substantial transformation of the underlying structure of power. At the second level of analysis, the preferences of the socio-economic groups considered may vary from time to time and from country to country. Finally, at the third level, changes are linked to the decline of the leadership of given political parties or leaders.

This political economy approach to exchange rate credibility allows us to formulate the following testable hypotheses:

> Hypothesis 1: The higher the level of socio-economic consensus to an exchange rate agreement, the higher its level of credibility and the lower the possibility that it will succumb to speculative attacks.
> Hypothesis 2: The higher the level of support to an exchange rate agreement by the most powerful socio-economic groups, the higher its credibility and vice versa.

The two first hypotheses reinforce each other, which means that, if they both are met, the outcome should be stronger. However in the case that only one of the two is met, the authors identify a third hypothesis:

> Hypothesis 3: If only the most powerful socio-economic groups support an exchange rate agreement, the credibility of the exchange rate peg is higher than if only the other socio-economic groups support it and vice versa.

The next section reports on the empirical testing of this alternative political economy approach to exchange rate credibility.

3 EMPIRICAL INVESTIGATION: THE CREDIBILITY OF BRITISH AND ITALIAN COMMITMENT TO EXCHANGE RATE STABILITY, 1978–98

In order to provide some empirical grounding for the above discussion, an econometric exercise has been performed to test the above hypotheses on the Italian Lira and British Pound exchange rate experience during the period between January 1978 and December 1998. In particular, following the empirical literature on speculative attacks and currency crises, limited dependent variables regression techniques are used to estimate the probability of crisis on the basis of a set of fundamental controls and test the residual impact exercised by 'consensus' indicators. In the economic literature, the evidence on the fundamental determinants of currency crises can hardly be considered as conclusive.[31] For the purposes of the present research, the probability of a large exchange rate variation (depreciation) or that of a speculative attack is tested against some of the most likely suspects among the country's own fundamentals.

A further set of guidelines can be extracted from previous empirical work for this investigation. First, compared to speculative pressure episodes (both successful and unsuccessful) actual devaluation events seem to be easier to explain on the grounds of fundamentals. This result can be justified on the grounds that devaluations often stem from the unilateral decision of the monetary authorities on the basis of optimal social policy options, which in turn are more likely to depend on the state of fundamentals.

However, limiting the analysis to actual changes in the exchange rate regime would exclude all those situations where the central bank has successfully used its instruments to tackle a speculative run on the currency, and avoided an unwanted depreciation. Hence, a more thorough analysis of balance-of-payments crises requires a broader perspective on speculative pressure. In this study, monthly data are used in order to reach a compromise between the need to capture as much as possible of the underlying speculative pressure, and maintaining the ability to assess the role of fundamentals. However, this work departs from past empirical research in at least two ways. Contrary to past empirical research, which concentrated alternatively on episodes of devaluations or on speculative attacks, this work considers both of these 'crisis definitions' as through different degrees of speculative pressure.

3.1 Crisis Definition

A first important issue within the empirical investigation involves the choice of the appropriate crisis definition. Clearly, the answer to this question depends on the specific goal of the analysis. While early studies on balance-of-payments crises focused on actual crisis events, since Eichengreen, Rose and Wyplosz (ERW henceforth, 1994) researchers have underlined the importance of concentrating on both 'successful' and 'unsuccessful' attacks. In this investigation, two indices are applied in order to capture varying degrees of speculative pressure and let the data distinguish between crisis and non-crisis periods. This distinction may turn out to be particularly important, given the interest of this work in the interaction between the role of consensus from the private sector and the commitment of the policy maker. In order to perform a wider-spectrum analysis, a comparison between the two definitions is proposed.

The first of these measures is a sizeable depreciation of the exchange rate (defined in terms of the national currency unit for foreign currency, i.e. an exchange rate rise represents depreciation). We mark as 'relevant' any change in the nominal exchange rate greater than one and a half standard deviations above the mean. This threshold is a sensible answer to the need for capturing significant episodes, whilst avoiding too much noise from the indicator, i.e. 'normal' fluctuations of the exchange rate misunderstood for crisis episodes. This indicator takes the following form:

$$I_{EX} = \begin{cases} 1 \text{ if } \Delta s_t \geq \mu_{\Delta s} + 1.5\sigma_{\Delta s}, \\ 0 \text{ otherwise} \end{cases}$$

where s is the logarithm of the nominal exchange rate, μ and σ are, respectively, the mean and the standard deviation of the series of exchange rate monthly changes. Among the two proposed measures, this indicator is more likely to capture either successful attacks, as this definition will pick up all those cases where the exchange rate depreciates without the monetary authority using any of the instruments available for its defence, or unilateral violations of the 'rules of the game' from the authority.

The second crisis definition employed follows the approach to identifying speculative pressure suggested by ERW, who add to the above definition changes in the interest rate and international reserves. Their index of speculative pressure is therefore computed as the weighted average of exchange rate changes, interest rate changes, and the negative of reserve changes. The ERW measure has the following formulation:

$$ERW = \frac{\sigma_s}{\sigma_s + \sigma_i + \sigma_r}\Delta s_t + \frac{\sigma_i}{\sigma_s + \sigma_i + \sigma_r}\Delta i - \frac{\sigma_r}{\sigma_s + \sigma_i + \sigma_r}\Delta r,$$

where, as before, s_t is the exchange rate, i_t and r_t are, respectively, the interest rate and the level of international reserves expressed in logarithm and, again, μ and σ are the period mean and standard deviation.[32] Since the three series exhibit different degrees of variability, relative volatility weights are imposed to make them comparable. Whenever this index reaches values of 1.5 standard deviations above the mean, it signals a speculative attack, i.e.:

$$I_{ERW} = \begin{cases} 1 \text{ if } ERW_t \geq \mu_{ERW} + 1.5\sigma_{ERW}. \\ 0 \text{ otherwise} \end{cases}$$

These indices have been widely used in the literature in order to assess the impact of different economic indicators on the probability of crisis. Even though neither of the two can be considered as a perfect measure of exchange market pressure, they are still a useful tool for drawing inferences on currency crises and speculative attacks.

Clearly, as the left-hand side is a zero/one variable, the appropriate way to estimate the probability of crisis is to apply limited dependent variable econometric methods. Despite some limitations, this approach seems more appealing than others for a number of reasons. In particular, it allows the parametric estimation and significance testing of each indicator, together with the overall probability of crisis conditional on the joint contribution

of the different indicators, which can be broadly interpreted as the vulnerability of the country to a currency crisis at a particular point in time.
Moreover, Berg and Patillo (1999) have demonstrated that this method out-
performs the alternative semi-parametric approach proposed by Kaminsky
and Reinhart (1999, 2003) in terms of out-of-sample properties.[33]

The speculative pressure indices discussed above give a form to exchange
market pressure, a latent variable, and allow the identification of the
'events'. Hence, the probability of an event of 'excessive' exchange rate
market pressure (EMP) can be re-written as the probability that the event
will occur, $\Pr(I_{EMP}=1)$, in order to explain the probability of a speculative
attack.

In order to test the relevance of the political economy explanations for
exchange market pressure, a number of macroeconomic fundamentals,
usually associated by the economic literature to exchange rate weakness,
have been introduced as conditioning variables. These include the real interest rate (RIR) differential,[34] the ratio of domestic credit to gross domestic
product, the ratio of M2 to reserves, and industrial production.[35] A further
set of indicators designed to capture political 'consensus' have then been
included in the regression, representing the variables of 'interest'. The estimating equation becomes:

$$\Pr(I_{EMP} = 1) = \boldsymbol{\beta}' \mathbf{X}_{t-1} + \sum_i \delta_i (Consensus)_{it-1},$$

where $\Pr(I_{EMP}=1)$ is the above-defined probability of a crisis event, either
large depreciation or excessive market pressure, X is the matrix of fundamental controls, and $Consensus_i$ is a set of dummy variables designed to
capture the periods of consensus from different socio-economic groups.
Since the dependent variable is dichotomous, and the explanatory variables
enter the regression in lagged form, the fitted values can be interpreted as
the one-step-ahead probabilities of a crisis.

3.2   The Data on 'Consensus'

The data on consensus have been gathered through document analysis
and interviews with the representatives of the relevant socio-economic
groups between 1994 and 1999. They refer to the support afforded by
those groups to the adoption by the government of a pegged or fixed
exchange rate regime, like the ERM of the EMS between 1978 and 1992
and EMU thereafter. The related dummy variables built on the data
about consensus acquire a value of one if the group supports the exchange
rate commitment or a value of zero if there is not consensus on such a
commitment.

In particular, the following 'consensus' indicators have been introduced as variables of 'interest'. For Italy, three measures of consensus have been constructed. The first, *Unions' Consensus*, captures the support from the three main workers' unions (CGIL, CISL and UIL). The second, *Business Sector Consensus*, takes a value of one if the pegged rate is favoured by the main associations representing the production sector (Confindustria, API, IRI, INTERSIND), and the third measure, *Full Consensus*, is an indicator that joins the support from both Unions and the Business Sector.

For the United Kingdom, indicators for support are from the City of London, the Business Sector (represented by the CBI), the Unions (represented by the TUC) and both the Business and the Financial Sectors (City of London and CBI) together. Finally, again, a Full Consensus indicator has been considered.

3.3 The Results

Tables 1.1 to 1.8 present the probit and logit regressions. In every table, the introduction of the consensus dummies is compared to a benchmark regression including the fundamentals only. In Tables 1.1 and 1.2, estimates for the measure of large depreciation, denoted as 'events', in Italy are reported.

Table 1.1 Probit estimates for 'events' in Italy

	Benchmark	(1)	(2)	(3)	(4)
RIR differential	−0.089***	0.026	0.239***	−0.076**	0.104**
	(0.027)	(0.036)	(0.061)	(0.034)	(0.041)
M2/reserves	0.001	0.004	0.006*	0.003	0.005
	(0.001)	(0.003)	(0.003)	(0.002)	(0.003)
Domestic	0.001	0.002	0.007	0.001	0.004
credit/GDP	(0.004)	(0.006)	(0.005)	(0.006)	(0.005)
Industrial	0.001	0.006	0.003	0.007	0.005
production	(0.002)	(0.004)	(0.003)	(0.005)	(0.004)
Full Consensus		−0.301***			
		(0.033)			
Business Sector				−0.529***	−0.254***
Consensus				(0.059)	(0.084)
Unions'			−0.977***		−0.530***
Consensus			(0.127)		(0.149)
Observations	249	249	249	249	249

Notes: Robust standard errors in parentheses
* significant at 10%; ** significant at 5%; *** significant at 1%

Table 1.2   Logit estimates for 'events' in Italy

	Benchmark	(1)	(2)	(3)	(4)
RIR differential	−0.152***	0.040	0.472***	−0.176**	0.208*
	(0.051)	(0.082)	(0.146)	(0.070)	(0.108)
M2/reserves	0.002	0.008	0.014**	0.006	0.010
	(0.002)	(0.005)	(0.006)	(0.005)	(0.006)
Domestic credit/ GDP	0.002	0.004	0.013	0.002	0.006
	(0.007)	(0.013)	(0.010)	(0.012)	(0.012)
Industrial production	0.002	0.015*	0.006	0.017*	0.011
	(0.004)	(0.008)	(0.005)	(0.010)	(0.008)
Full Consensus		−0.578***			
		(0.076)			
Business Sector Consensus				−1.022***	−0.473**
				(0.144)	(0.212)
Unions' Consensus			−1.920***		−1.040***
			(0.300)		(0.382)
Observations	249	249	249	249	249

Notes: Robust standard errors in parentheses
* significant at 10%; ** significant at 5%; *** significant at 1%

A first point worth mentioning is the fact that fundamentals seem to be unable to explain the occurrence of large depreciations. Columns 1, 2 and 3 report on the introduction of each consensus dummy separately. These always enter the regressions with significant and negative signs, as expected. When Unions' and Business Sector Consensus are introduced simultaneously, in column 4, again both maintain their significance and their expected sign. The results are similar if probit or logit is used. During periods of support for the exchange rate peg, the probability of a large depreciation is smaller. As can be seen from Table A.1.1 in Appendix 1.1, when the Relogit methodology of King and Zheng (2001) is used estimates confirm this result.

In Tables 1.3 and 1.4, results are presented for regressions where the definition of crisis is switched from 'large depreciations' to that of excessive exchange market pressure.

Again Full Consensus, Unions' Consensus and Business Sector Consensus enter the regression with a negative sign and significantly at the 1 per cent level in both the probit and the logit regressions. Interestingly, however, when Full Consensus is separated into the Unions and the Production components, this last factor seems to retain both greater significance and a larger coefficient. Consensus from the Production Sector seems to reduce more greatly the probability of a crisis. As before, Relogit

Table 1.3   Probit estimates for 'speculative pressure' episodes in Italy

	Benchmark	(1)	(2)	(3)	(4)
RIR differential	−0.119***	−0.065*	0.043	−0.127***	−0.078*
	(0.029)	(0.033)	(0.036)	(0.034)	(0.043)
M2/reserves	−0.000	−0.000	−0.000	−0.001	−0.000
	(0.001)	(0.001)	(0.002)	(0.001)	(0.001)
Domestic credit/	0.001	0.002	0.004	0.001	0.002
GDP	(0.005)	(0.008)	(0.008)	(0.008)	(0.008)
Industrial	−0.000	0.000	0.000	0.000	0.000
production	(0.002)	(0.004)	(0.003)	(0.004)	(0.004)
Full Consensus		−0.233***			
		(0.022)			
Business Sector				−0.432***	−0.323***
Consensus				(0.042)	(0.059)
Unions' Consensus			−0.670***		−0.182*
			(0.067)		(0.101)
Observations	249	249	249	249	249

Notes: Robust standard errors in parentheses
* significant at 10%; ** significant at 5%; *** significant at 1%

Table 1.4   Logit estimates for 'speculative pressure' episodes in Italy

	Benchmark	(1)	(2)	(3)	(4)
RIR differential	−0.207***	−0.141**	0.061	−0.263***	−0.171**
	(0.055)	(0.068)	(0.072)	(0.070)	(0.085)
M2/reserves	−0.000	−0.001	−0.001	−0.001	−0.001
	(0.002)	(0.002)	(0.003)	(0.002)	(0.002)
Domestic credit/	0.002	0.008	0.008	0.007	0.008
GDP	(0.008)	(0.017)	(0.017)	(0.016)	(0.017)
Industrial	−0.000	−0.000	−0.000	0.001	0.000
production	(0.004)	(0.008)	(0.006)	(0.009)	(0.009)
Full Consensus		−0.430***			
		(0.051)			
Business Sector				−0.809***	−0.608***
Consensus				(0.104)	(0.120)
Unions' Consensus			−1.240***		−0.323*
			(0.149)		(0.174)
Observations	249	249	249	249	249

Notes: Robust standard errors in parentheses
* significant at 10%; ** significant at 5%; *** significant at 1%

estimates, presented in Table A.1.2 in Appendix 1.1, are in agreement and results are not qualitatively different for the variables of interest.[36]

In Tables 1.5 to 1.8 attention has been turned to the UK. As before, regressions compare consensus measures with benchmark equations, where only fundamentals have been included. Importantly, for the UK it is also possible to isolate the consensus expressed by the Financial Sector represented by City of London. As before, the evidence on the relevance of fundamentals is at best mixed for the large depreciation events and the speculative pressure episodes.[37] On the other hand, evidence on the importance of consensus is unequivocal. As can be seen from Tables 1.5 and 1.6, both the probit and logit regressions respectively show that, when introduced separately, consensus measures always enter significantly and with a negative sign. A particularly interesting result, however, is the fact that, differently from the Italian case, when the Unions' Consensus is introduced together with the Consensus from Business and the Financial Sectors, it loses its significance. Only the latter seems to have a role in reducing the probability of a large depreciation.

Estimates on the speculative pressure measure for the UK presented in Tables 1.7 and 1.8 seem on the other hand to assign a role to the Consensus expressed by the Unions, but this role emerges as less important than that of the Business and Financial Sector. Also, and very interestingly, the City of London seems to have the largest coefficient among the consensus measures. As can be seen from Tables A.1.3 and A.1.4 in Appendix 1.1, these results are validated when the Relogit methodology is used as a robustness check in place of probit and logit.

CONCLUSIONS

This chapter starts from a definition of the credibility of exchange rate agreements based on the synthesis between political science approaches and economic models, i.e. between socio-economic 'interests' and market 'expectations'. Its objective was to demonstrate empirically that financial markets, in deciding whether to attack a currency peg or not, base their considerations on something more fundamental than fundamentals, namely on the consensus of socio-economic groups and, in particular, of the most powerful ones. Here consensus is defined as the support to the currency peg afforded by the socio-economic groups in a given country at a given historical moment. In turn the strength of the socio-economic groups is measured in terms of their contribution to the national GDP or, for the trade unions, the number of members.

Applying this analytical model to the case of British and Italian exchange rate experience in the period between 1978 and 1998 it is possible

Table 1.5 Probit estimates for 'events' in the UK

	Benchmark	(1)	(2)	(3)	(4)	(5)	(6)
RIR differential	-0.038	0.053*	-0.008	0.082***	0.092***	-0.047	0.077**
	(0.028)	(0.030)	(0.029)	(0.030)	(0.031)	(0.030)	(0.031)
M2/reserves	-0.002	-0.003**	-0.003	-0.004**	-0.004**	-0.002	-0.003**
	(0.002)	(0.002)	(0.002)	(0.002)	(0.002)	(0.002)	(0.002)
Domestic credit/GDP	0.002	0.004	0.003	0.005*	0.006*	0.003	0.005
	(0.003)	(0.003)	(0.003)	(0.003)	(0.003)	(0.003)	(0.003)
Industrial production	-0.000	-0.000	-0.000	0.000	-0.000	-0.000	-0.000
	(0.001)	(0.002)	(0.002)	(0.002)	(0.002)	(0.001)	(0.002)
Full Consensus		-0.885***					
		(0.124)					
Unions' Consensus			-1.629***				-0.133
			(0.197)				(0.281)
City of London Consensus						-1.839***	
						(0.443)	
Business Sector Consensus					-1.681***		
					(0.164)		
Business and Financial Consensus				-1.480***			-1.395***
				(0.190)			(0.253)
Observations	252	250	250	251	251	251	250

Notes: Robust standard errors in parentheses
* significant at 10%; ** significant at 5%; *** significant at 1%

Table 1.6   *Logit estimates for 'events' in the UK*

	Benchmark	(1)	(2)	(3)	(4)	(5)	(6)
RIR differential	−0.063	0.100**	−0.012	0.138***	0.150***	−0.081	0.130***
	(0.048)	(0.048)	(0.048)	(0.049)	(0.050)	(0.052)	(0.049)
M2/reserves	−0.003	−0.006*	−0.004	−0.006**	−0.007**	−0.003	−0.006**
	(0.003)	(0.003)	(0.003)	(0.003)	(0.003)	(0.003)	(0.003)
Domestic credit/GDP	0.004	0.007	0.005	0.009*	0.009*	0.004	0.008
	(0.005)	(0.005)	(0.005)	(0.005)	(0.005)	(0.005)	(0.005)
Industrial production	−0.000	−0.001	−0.001	−0.001	−0.001	−0.001	−0.001
	(0.002)	(0.003)	(0.003)	(0.003)	(0.003)	(0.002)	(0.003)
Full Consensus		−1.674***					
		(0.271)					
Unions' Consensus			−2.903***				
			(0.425)				
City of London Consensus						−3.421***	
						(1.034)	
Business Sector Consensus					−2.947***		
					(0.332)		
Business and Financial Consensus				−2.671***			−2.499***
				(0.350)			(0.461)
Observations	252	250	250	251	251	251	250

Notes: Robust standard errors in parentheses
* significant at 10%; ** significant at 5%; *** significant at 1%

Table 1.7 Probit estimates for 'speculative pressure' episodes in the UK

	Benchmark	(1)	(2)	(3)	(4)	(5)	(6)
RIR differential	-0.147***	-0.062**	-0.103***	-0.056*	-0.046	-0.151***	-0.062*
	(0.033)	(0.031)	(0.032)	(0.030)	(0.030)	(0.035)	(0.032)
M2/reserves	0.001	0.002	0.002	0.002	0.002	0.001	0.002
	(0.002)	(0.002)	(0.002)	(0.002)	(0.002)	(0.002)	(0.002)
Domestic credit/GDP	-0.000	-0.001	-0.001	-0.001	-0.001	-0.001	-0.001
	(0.003)	(0.004)	(0.003)	(0.004)	(0.004)	(0.003)	(0.004)
Industrial production	0.000	0.001	0.001	0.001	0.001	0.000	0.001
	(0.001)	(0.002)	(0.002)	(0.002)	(0.002)	(0.001)	(0.002)
Full Consensus		-0.719***					
		(0.090)					
Unions' Consensus			-1.560***				
			(0.198)				
City of London Consensus						-1.868***	
						(0.466)	
Business Sector Consensus					-1.265***		
					(0.141)		
Business and Financial Consensus				-1.100***			-0.716***
				(0.139)			(0.201)
Observations	252	250	250	251	251	251	250

Notes: Robust standard errors in parentheses
* significant at 10%; ** significant at 5%; *** significant at 1%

Table 1.8 Logit estimates for 'speculative pressure' episodes in the UK

	Benchmark	(1)	(2)	(3)	(4)	(5)	(6)
RIR differential	-0.250***	-0.094*	-0.175***	-0.085*	-0.072	-0.266***	-0.096*
	(0.060)	(0.051)	(0.056)	(0.051)	(0.049)	(0.067)	(0.054)
M2/reserves	0.002	0.003	0.003	0.003	0.004	0.002	0.003
	(0.003)	(0.003)	(0.003)	(0.003)	(0.004)	(0.003)	(0.003)
Domestic	-0.001	-0.001	-0.002	-0.001	-0.001	-0.001	-0.001
credit/GDP	(0.006)	(0.007)	(0.006)	(0.008)	(0.008)	(0.006)	(0.006)
Industrial	0.000	0.001	0.001	0.001	0.001	0.000	0.001
production	(0.002)	(0.003)	(0.003)	(0.003)	(0.003)	(0.002)	(0.003)
Full Consensus		-1.283***					
		(0.182)					
Union's Consensus			-2.796***				
			(0.423)				
City of London						-3.527***	
Consensus						(1.057)	
Business Sector					-2.189***		
Consensus					(0.280)		
Business and Financial				-1.937***			-1.235***
Consensus				(0.268)			(0.365)
Observations	252	250	250	251	251	251	250

Notes: Robust standard errors in parentheses
* significant at 10%; ** significant at 5%; *** significant at 1%

to claim that the main hypotheses seem to be confirmed by the data. In particular, empirical evidence seems to suggest that both in the case of the UK and in the case of Italy, the probability of exchange rate instability is inversely related to the total consensus by the socio-economic groups. This, in turn, means that the higher the level of consensus to the currency peg, the higher the credibility of the governments' commitment to the exchange rate regime, if there were any. Moreover, in the case of both Italy and the UK, the most powerful groups, i.e. the Production Sector in Italy, and the City of London in the UK, seem to have the most relevant impact on the credibility of the exchange rate commitments.

NOTES

1. See Commission of European Communities (1990: 17): 'If the move to EMU were not to take place, given 1992, it is quite likely that either the EMS would become a less stable arrangement or capital market liberalization would not be fully achieved or maintained.' For further analysis of the economic mechanism, see Padoa-Schioppa (1988).
2. This is mainly due to the fact that a reduction of transaction costs and the elimination of hedging expenses are particularly appealing to the industrial sector, and mainly to those manufacturing companies particularly involved in intra-European trade. On the other hand, the financial sector, which, incidentally, has much to gain from the instability of exchange rates, is much more interested in keeping an independent monetary policy in an environment of loose regulatory constraints. Given the relevance of the financial sector for the British economy, and the declining importance of the manufacturing sector, it appears less puzzling why the UK could profit from the single market without being compelled to join EMU. For more detail on the subject see Talani (2000).
3. See Perez *et al.* (2006); Artis *et al.* (2002); Artis and Zhang (1997); Belo (2001); Bordo and Helbling (2003); Burns and Mitchell (1946); Hallett and Richter (2004); Kose *et al.* (2003); Mills and Holmes (1999); Mundell (1961); Rose (1999); Stock and Watson (2003); Vahid and Engle (1993); and Wynne and Koo (2000).
4. For a realist interpretation of the process leading to EMU see Baun (1996). See also Middlemas (1995).
5. See Andrews (1993, 1994).
6. See Moravcsik (1993).
7. See Moravcsik (1998: 387).
8. See Moravcsik (1998: 401).
9. The distinction between 'monetarists' and 'economists' emerged in the course of the discussions over the Werner Plan and referred to the strategy to be adopted during the transitional period. The 'monetarists' stressed the importance of achieving exchange rate stability through European institutional arrangements, while the 'economists' pointed out the necessity of policy coordination and, ultimately, convergence before agreeing on the adoption of a European fixed exchange rate regime or a currency union. For more details see Tsoukalis (1997).
10. See Allsopp (2002, 2006); and Carlin and Soskice (2005).
11. See Moravcsik (1998: 404).
12. For a very detailed account of the relation between EMU and labour market flexibility see Talani (2004), Ch. 6.
13. See Dyson (2000).
14. For the explanation of the hegemonic role of Germany in the ERM of the EMS see De Grauwe (1996), Ch. 3.

15. See Moravcsik (1998: 411).
16. In fact, the real exchange rate can be expressed as the relationship between the price of non-tradable goods and that of tradable ones: P\P*xe. By assumption, the price of tradables, P*, is set on world markets and cannot be changed, in foreign currency terms, by national policy. Depreciation makes tradables relatively more expensive in domestic currency terms, while non-tradables become relatively cheaper; appreciation has the opposite effect.
17. This, in turn, has been measured in a variety of ways. See, for example, Fratianni and Artis (1996); and Rose and Svensson (1994).
18. Opposite evidence has been found by Bordo and MacDonald for the Gold Standard, where even temporary violations of the 'rules of the game' were possible. See Bordo and MacDonald (1997, 2003).
19. Indeed, the rate of return of a foreign investment after 'τ' months (R_t, τ) depends on both the current (S_t) and the future spot exchange (S_t,τ) according to the following relation:

$$R_t, \tau = [(1 + i^*_t, \tau) . (S_t, \tau / S_t)] - 1$$

Therefore, if the spot exchange rate (S_t) can fluctuate between a minimum (S_t) and a maximum ($\overline{S}_t$) the rate of return (R_t,) will also fluctuate between a minimum (R_t,) and a maximum ($\overline{R}_t$).
20. The expected spot exchange rate is then defined according to uncovered interest rate parity as:

$$eS_t, \tau = S_t (1 + i_t, \tau / 1 + i^*_t, \tau)$$

where 'eS_t,τ' is the expected spot exchange after 'τ' months, 'S_t' is the spot exchange rate, 'i_t, τ' is the domestic interest rate after 'τ' months and 'i^*_t, τ' is the foreign interest rate after 'τ' months.
21. The total rate of expected depreciation ($E_t(\Delta s_t) / \Delta t$) can be separated into two parts:

$$E_t(\Delta s_t) / \Delta t \equiv E_t (\Delta x_t) / \Delta t + E_t (\Delta c_t) / \Delta t$$

where x_t denotes the deviation of the spot rate from the central parity (c_t).
   The object of interest is the expected rate of change of the central parity $E_t (\Delta c_t) / \Delta t$, which can actually be measured by using the interest rate differential (δ_t) under the assumption that $E_t (\Delta x_t) / \Delta t = 0$. However, economists have devised a number of methods to measure the drift. See Lindberg *et al.* (1991); Rose and Svensson (1994); and Svensson (1991).
22. This method is the so-called 'drift adjusted method' and the drift can be measured in different ways. See Fratianni and Artis (1996); and Rose and Svensson (1994).
23. Fratianni and Artis propose the following testable equation:

$$i_{j,t} - i_{d,t} = f(A(L) \pi_{j,t}, B(L) \pi_{d,t}, C(L)y_{j,t}, D(L)y_{d,t})$$

where π stands for the rate of inflation, y for the deviation of output from the trend, L for the lag operator, and A, B, C and D for functional operators.
24. See Major (1990).
25. Yet we shall argue that this is not true and that, however paradoxical this claim may seem, British commitment to the ERM was less credible than the Italian one. Of course, the definition of credibility on which this claim is based is different from the economic ones given so far.
26. The Asian crisis, however, has inspired the development of a 'third generation' of currency and financial crisis models, where moral hazard, bank runs and balance-sheet effects interact with the exchange rate to determine the crisis outcome. Ultimately, as commented by Krugman (2001), 'each wave of crisis seems to elicit a new style of model,

one that makes sense after the fact'. Each family of models seems to set a different role for public and private agents, gives different predictions regarding the crisis outcome, and proposes different policies for crisis prevention and crisis management.

27.   The most notable of these crisis events include, aside from the breakdown of the ERM in 1992–93, the Mexican 'Tequila hangover' in 1994–95, the Asian meltdown of 1997–98, the Rouble debacle of 1998, and the Brazilian Real collapse in 1999.

28.   Under uncovered interest parity, the strong incentive to devalue means that expectations cause interest rates to rise, increasing the pressure to realign. Raising interest rates can be costly if unemployment is already high. Ozkan and Sutherland (1998), for example, consider the case where the currency crisis is triggered by an optimizing policy maker who decides to abandon the fixed exchange rate in response to an adverse demand shock, such as the one produced by German unification before the EMS crisis. Similarly, the authorities may face the harsh choice between keeping interest rates at excessively high levels and endangering an already weak financial sector, or devaluing and increasing the probability of a debt default due to balance-sheet effects. Expectations can also influence forward-looking wage contracts and cause a further reduction of the competitiveness of the economy. In both cases, the fixed rate represents a limitation to offsetting adverse shocks, and apparently viable regimes may be attacked and turn out to be fragile. Fiscal weakness can be another constraint to support the peg, limiting the ability of the country to credibly borrow reserves and buy back the high-powered money supply. In all these cases, the complex choice between alternative policy options creates the potential for the crisis. In models of the KFG type, the state of fundamentals followed either long-run compatibility or incompatibility with fixed exchange rates. In Obstfeld (1994, 1996) the same prediction applies only for extreme values of fundamentals. Within an intermediate range, fundamentals are not sound enough to deter the attack, but not so weak as to make it a sure bet.

29.   Similar testing can be found in Eichengreen *et al.* (1995); and Leblang (2002).

30.   See, for example, Frieden (1991, 1994, 1998).

31.   See Goldstein *et al.* (2000) for a rather exhaustive review of the indicators used in empirical studies to predict currency crises.

32.   Given that these parameters will ultimately depend on the monetary policy regime, the period under consideration has been separated in two sub-samples, before and after 1990.

33.   As usual for binary choice models, the presence of a latent variable y* is assumed such that:

$$y_t^* = \beta'X_t + \varepsilon_t,$$

where X is a vector of explanatory variables at time t, β is the vector of coefficients to be estimated, and ε_t is the error term, which is assumed to be normally distributed. Then we observe:

$$y_t = \begin{cases} 1 \text{ if } y_t^* > 0 \\ 0 \text{ if } y_t^* \leq 0 \end{cases}$$

Now:

$$Pr(y_t = 1) = Pr(y_t^* > 0) =$$

$$Pr(\beta'X_t + \varepsilon_t > 0) = Pr(\varepsilon_t > -\beta'X_t)$$

Since the distribution is symmetric:

$$Pr(y_t^* > 0) = Pr(\varepsilon_t < \beta'X_t) = \Phi \beta'X_t),$$

where Φ is the standard normal distribution. As a robustness check, however, two alternative sets of regressions have been performed. In the first variation the logistic distribution is adopted in place of the normal distribution, i.e.:

$$\Lambda(X) = \frac{e^{\beta'X}}{1 + e^{\beta'X_i}}.$$

The second variation applies the method proposed by King and Zheng (2001) that corrects for the bias arising from the fact that the left-hand-side variable will in general contain many more zeros than ones.

34. Defined as the short-term interest rate (money market rate or equivalent) less inflation.
35. All of these variables enter the estimating equation as yearly percentage changes (yearly log differences) and with a period lag. Other specifications have been attempted, but with no significant change to the basic results.
36. The only difference pertains to the fundamentals, with the real interest rate differential turning significant.
37. Only for the latter, the real interest rate differential seems to enter the regression significantly and with a negative sign.

BIBLIOGRAPHY

Allsopp, C. (2002), 'The Future of Macroeconomic Policy in the European Union', Bank of England, External MPC Unit Discussion Paper No. 7, accessed on-line on 22 August 2006, http://www.bankofengland.co.uk/publications/externalm pcpapers/extmpcpaper 0007.pdf.

Allsopp, C. (2006), 'Inter-country Adjustment in EMU: Are There Lessons for the New Member States?', Presentation, Chatham House, London, 11 July.

Andrews, D.M. (1993), 'The Global Origins of the Maastricht Treaty on EMU: Closing the Window of Opportunity', in A. Cafruny and G.G. Rosenthal, *The State of the European Community: The Maastricht Debate and Beyond*, Boulder, CO and London: Lynne Rienner Publishers.

Andrews, D.M. (1994), 'Capital Mobility and State Autonomy: Toward a Structural Theory of International Monetary Relations', *International Studies Quarterly*, **38**: 193–218.

Angeloni, I. and L. Dedola (1999), 'From the ERM to the Euro: New Evidence on Economic and Policy Convergence among EU Countries', Working paper 4, ECB.

Artis, M. and W. Zhang (1997), 'International Business Cycles and the ERM: Is There a European Business Cycle?', *International Journal of Finance and Economics*, **2**: 1–16.

Artis, M., H. Krolzig and J. Toro (2002), 'The European Business Cycle', Working paper 2242, CEPR.

Barro, R. and C. Gordon (1983), 'Rules, Discretion and Reputation in a Model of Monetary Policy', *Journal of Monetary Economics*, **12**(1): 101–21.

Baun, M.J. (1996), *An Imperfect Union: The Maastricht Treaty and the New Politics of European Integration*, Boulder, CO: Westview Press.

Belo, F. (2001), 'Some Facts about the Cyclical Convergence in the Euro Zone', Working paper 7-01, Banco de Portugal.

Berg, A. and C. Patillo (1999), 'Predicting Currency Crises: The Indicators Approach and an Alternative', *Journal of International Money and Finance*, **18**: 561–86.

Bordo, M. and T. Helbling (2003), 'Have National Business Cycles Become More Synchronized?', Working paper 10130, National Bureau of Economic Research, Cambridge, MA.

Bordo, Michael D. and Ronald MacDonald (1997), 'Violations of the "Rules of the Game" and the Credibility of the Classical Gold Standard, 1880–1914', Working paper 6115, National Bureau of Economic Research, Cambridge, MA.

Bordo, Michael D. and Ronald MacDonald (2003), 'The Inter-war Gold Exchange Standard: Credibility and Monetary Independence', *Journal of International Money and Finance*, Elsevier, **22**(1), February: 1–32.

Buiter, W.H., M.G. Corsetti and P.A. Pesenti (1998), 'Interpreting the ERM Crisis: Country-Specific and Systemic Issues', *Princeton Studies in International Finance*, **84**.

Burns, A. and W. Mitchell (1946), 'Measuring Business Cycles', Working paper, National Bureau of Economic Research, Cambridge, MA.

Carlin, Wendy and David Soskice (2005), 'The 3-Equation New Keynesian Model: A Graphical Exposition', UCL Economics Discussion Paper 05-03.

Commission of European Communities (1990), 'One Market, One Money', *Economic Papers*, **44**.

Crouch, C. (2000), *After the Euro*, Oxford: Oxford University Press.

De Grauwe, P. (1996), *International Money*, Oxford: Oxford University Press.

Dyson, K. (2000), *The Politics of the Euro-Zone*, Oxford: Oxford University Press. Scholarship Online, 66http://www.oxfordscholarship.com/oso/public/content/politicalscience/0199241651/toc.html.

Eichengreen, B. and J. Frieden (1994), *The Political Economy of European Monetary Union*, Boulder, CO: Westview Press.

Eichengreen, B., A. Rose and C. Wyplosz, (1994), 'Speculative Attacks on Pegged Exchange Rates: An Empirical Exploration with Special Reference to the European Monetary System', CEPR Discussion Paper Series No. 1060.

Eichengreen, B., A. Rose and C. Wyplosz (1995), 'Exchange Market Mayhem: The Antecedents and Aftermaths of Speculative Attacks', *Economic Policy*, **21**: 249–312.

Engelmann, D., H.J. Knopf, K. Roscher and T. Risse (1997), 'Identity Politics in the European Union: The Case of Economic and Monetary Union', in P. Minkkinen and H. Potomaki (1997), *The Politics of Economic and Monetary Union*, Dordrecht: Kluwer Academic Publishers.

Evans, P.B., H.K. Jacobson and R.D. Putnam (1993), *Double-Edged Diplomacy: International Bargaining and Domestic Policy*, Berkeley: University of California Press.

Flood, R.P. and P. Garber (1984), 'Collapsing Exchange Rate Regimes: Some Linear Examples', *Journal of International Economics*, **17**: 1–17.

Flood, R.P. and N.P. Marion (1996), 'Speculative Attacks: Fundamentals and Self-Fulfilling Prophecies', Working paper 5789, National Bureau of Economic Research, Cambridge, MA.

Flood, R.P. and N. Marion (1998), 'Perspectives on the Recent Currency Crisis Literature', IMF Working Paper 98/130.

Fratianni, M. and M. Artis (1996), 'The Lira and the Pound in the 1992 Currency Crisis: Fundamentals or Speculation?', *Open Economies Review*, **7**: 573–89.

Frieden, J. (1991), 'Invested Interests: The Politics of National Economic Policies in a World of Global Finance', *International Organization*, **45**, Autumn.

Frieden, J. (1994), 'The Impact of Goods and Capital Market Integration on European Monetary Politics', Preliminary version, August.

Frieden, J. (1998), *The New Political Economy of EMU*, Oxford: Rowman & Littlefield.

Garret, G. (1993), 'The Politics of the Maastricht Treaty', *Economics and Politics*, **5**(2).

Giavazzi, F. and A. Giovannini (1989), 'The Role of the Exchange Rate Regime in a Disinflation: Empirical Evidence on the European Monetary System', in F. Giavazzi and A. Giovannini (eds), *Managing Exchange Rate Flexibility: The European Monetary System*, Cambridge, MA: MIT Press.

Gill, S. (1991), 'Historical Materialism, Gramsci and International Political Economy', in C.N. Murphy and R. Tooze (1991), *The New International Political Economy*, Boulder, CO: Lynne Rienner Publishers.

Goldstein, M., G.L. Kaminsky and C.M. Reinhart (2000), *Assessing Financial Vulnerability: An Early Warning System for Emerging Markets*, Washington, DC: Institute for International Economics.

Haas, E.B. (1968), *The Uniting of Europe: Political, Social and Economic Forces*, 2nd edn, Stanford, CA: Stanford University Press.

Hallett, A. and C. Richter (2004), 'A Time-Frequency Analysis of the Coherences of the US Business Cycle and the European Business Cycle', Discussion paper series 4751, CEPR.

Kaminsky, G.L. and C.M. Reinhart (1999), 'Bank Lending and Contagion: Evidence from the Asian Crisis', www.puaf.umd.edu/papers/reinhart.htm.

Kaminsky, G.L. and C.M. Reinhart (2002), 'The Center and the Periphery: Tales of Financial Turmoil', Unpublished manuscript, George Washington University.

Kaminsky, G.L. and C.M. Reinhart (2003), 'The Center and the Periphery: The Globalization of Financial Turmoil', NBER Working Papers 9479, National Bureau of Economic Research.

King, G. and L. Zheng (2001), 'Logistic Regression in Rare Events Data', http://gking.harvard.edu/files/0s.pdf.

Kose, M., E. Prasad and M. Terrones (2003), 'How Does Globalization Affect the Synchronisation of Business Cycles?', *American Economic Review Papers and Proceedings*, **93**: 57–62.

Krugman, P. (1979), 'A Model of Balance-of-Payment Crises', *Journal of Money Credit and Banking*, **11**(3): 311–25.

Krugman, P. (1989), 'The Case for Stabilising Exchange Rates', *Oxford Review of Economic Policy*, **5**: 61–72.

Krugman, P. (1991), 'Target Zones and Exchange Rate Dynamics', *The Quarterly Journal of Economics*, **106**(3), August: 669–82.

Krugman P. (2001), 'Crises: The Next Generation?', draft paper prepared for Razin Conference, Tel Aviv University, 25–26 March, http://sapir.tau.ac.il/papers/sapir_conference/krugman.pdf.accessed 19 November 2007.

Kydland, F.E. and C.E. Prescott (1977), 'Rules rather than Discretion: The Inconsistency of Optimal Plans', *Journal of Political Economy*, **85**(3): 473–91.

Leblang, D.A. (2002), 'The Political Economy of Speculative Attacks in the Developing World', *International Studies Quarterly*, **46**(1), March: 69–93.

Leblang, D. and W. Bernard (2000), 'The Politics of Speculative Attacks in Industrial Democracies', *International Organisation*, **54**(2), Spring: 291–324.

Lindberg, H., L. Svensson and P. Soderlind (1991), 'Devaluation Expectations: The Swedish Krona 1981–1991', IIES Seminar Paper 495.

Lindberg, L.N. and S.A. Scheingold (1970), *Europe's Would-Be Polity: Patterns of Change in the European Community*, Englewood Cliffs, NJ: Prentice-Hall.

McNamara, K. (1998), *The Currency of Ideas: Monetary Politics in the European Union*, Ithaca, NY: Cornell University Press.

Major, J. (1990), 'Inflation Pressures Beginning to Ease', *Financial Times Weekend*, 6/7 October.

Martin, L. (1993), 'International and Domestic Institutions in the EMU Process', *Economics and Politics*, **5**(2).

Middlemas, K. (1995), *Orchestrating Europe*, London: Fontana Press.

Mills, T. and M. Holmes (1999), 'Common Trends and Cycles in European Industrial Production: Exchange Rate Regimes and Economic Convergence', *Manchester School*, **67**(4): 507–87.

Moravcsik, A. (1993), 'Preferences and Power in the EC: A Liberal Inter-governmentalist Approach', *Journal of Common Market Studies*, **31**(4), December: 474.

Moravcsik, A. (1998), *The Choice for Europe: Social Purpose and State Power from Messina to Maastricht*, London: UCL Press.

Mundell, R. (1961), 'A Theory of Optimal Currency Areas', *American Economic Review*, **51**.

Muscatelli, V.A. (1995), 'Delegation versus Optimal Inflation Contracts: Do We Really Need Conservative Central Bankers?', University of Glasgow Discussion Papers in Economics No. 9511.

Muscatelli, V.A. (1998), 'Optimal Inflation Contracts and Inflation Targets with Uncertain Preferences: Accountability through Independence?', *Economic Journal*, **108**(447): 529–42.

Obstfeld, M. (1986), 'Rational and Self-Fulfilling Balance-of-Payment Crises', *American Economic Review*, **76**(1): 72–81.

Obstfeld, M. (1989), 'Competitiveness, Realignment and Speculation: The Role of Financial Markets', in F. Giavazzi and A. Giovannini (eds), *Managing Exchange Rate Flexibility: The European Monetary System*, Cambridge, MA: MIT Press.

Obstfeld, M. (1994), 'The Logic of Currency Crises', Working paper series No. 4640, National Bureau of Economic Research, Cambridge, MA.

Obstfeld, M. (1996), 'Models of Currency Crises with Self-Fulfilling Features', *European Economic Review*, **40**(3–5): 1037–47.

OECD (1991), *Economic Outlook*, **50**, December.

Ozkan, G. and A. Sutherland (1998), 'A Currency Crisis Model with an Optimising Policymaker', *Journal of International Economics*, **44**: 339–64.

Padoa-Schioppa, T. (1988), 'The European Monetary System: A Long Term View', in F. Giavazzi S. Micossi and M. Miller (1988), *The European Monetary System*, Cambridge: Cambridge University Press, pp. 373–76.

Padoa-Schioppa, T. (1994), *The Road to Monetary Union in Europe: The Emperor, the Kings and the Genies*, Oxford: Clarendon Press.

Perez, P.J., D.R. Osborn and M.J. Artis (2006), 'The International Business Cycle in a Changing World: Volatility and the Propagation of Shocus in the G-7', *Open Economics Review*, **17**, July: 255–80.

Risse, T. (1998), 'To Euro or Not to Euro: The EMU and Identity Politics in the European Union', ARENA Working Paper 98/1, http://www.arena.uio.no/publications/wp98_1.htm.

Rogoff, K. (1985), 'The Optimal Degree of Commitment to an Intermediate Monetary Target', *Quarterly Journal of Economics*, **100**(4): 1169–89.

Romer, D. (1993), 'Rational Asset-Price Movements without News', *American Economic Review*, **83**(5): 1112–30.

Rose, A. (1999), 'One Money, One Market: Estimating the Effect of Common Currencies on Trade', Discussion paper 2329, CEPR.

Rose, A.K. and E.O. Svensson (1994), 'European Exchange Rate Credibility before the Fall', *European Economic Review*, **38**: 1185–1216.

Sandholtz, W. (1993), 'Choosing Union: Monetary Politics and Maastricht', *International Organization*, **47**: 1–39.

Stock, J. and M. Watson (2003), 'Understanding Changes in International Business Cycle Dynamics', Working paper 9859, National Bureau of Economic Research, Cambridge, MA.

Svensson, L. (1990), 'The Simplest Test of Target Zone Credibility', IMF working paper, WP/90/106.

Svensson, L. (1991), 'Assessing Target Zone Credibility: Mean Reversion and Devaluation Expectations in the EMS', Institute for International Economic Studies, Seminar Paper 493.

Talani, L.S. (2000), *Betting for and against EMU*, London: Ashgate.

Talani, L.S. (2004), *European Political Economy: Political Science Perspectives*, London: Ashgate.

Tsoukalis, L. (1997), *New European Economy Revisited*, Oxford: Oxford University Press.

Vahid, F. and R.F. Engle (1993), 'Common Trends and Common Cycles', *Journal of Applied Econometrics*, **8**(3): 341–60.

Wooley, J.T. (1993), 'Linking Political and Monetary Union: The Maastricht Agenda and German Domestic Politics', *Economics and Politics*, **5**(2).

Wynne, M. and J. Koo (2000), 'Business Cycles under Monetary Union: A Comparison of the EU and the US', *Economica*, **67**: 347–74.

Between growth and stability

APPENDIX 1.1

Table A.1.1   Relogit estimates for 'events' in Italy

	Benchmark	(1)	(2)	(3)	(4)
RIR differential	−0.149***	0.027	0.420***	−0.166**	0.156
	(0.050)	(0.081)	(0.143)	(0.068)	(0.105)
M2/reserves	0.002	0.007	0.013**	0.005	0.009
	(0.002)	(0.005)	(0.006)	(0.005)	(0.006)
Domestic	0.001	0.004	0.013	0.002	0.006
credit/GDP	(0.007)	(0.013)	(0.010)	(0.012)	(0.012)
Industrial	0.001	0.015*	0.005	0.017*	0.011
production	(0.004)	(0.008)	(0.005)	(0.010)	(0.008)
Full Consensus		−0.526***			
		(0.075)			
Business Sector				−0.938***	−0.452**
Consensus				(0.142)	(0.207)
Unions'			−1.748***		−0.864**
Consensus			(0.294)		(0.373)
Observations	249	249	249	249	249

Notes: Robust standard errors in parentheses
* significant at 10%; ** significant at 5%; *** significant at 1%

Table A.1.2   Relogit estimates for 'speculative pressure' episodes in Italy

	Benchmark	(1)	(2)	(3)	(4)
RIR differential	−0.202***	−0.136**	0.053	−0.251***	−0.171**
	(0.054)	(0.067)	(0.071)	(0.069)	(0.083)
M2/reserves	−0.000	−0.001	−0.000	−0.001	−0.001
	(0.002)	(0.002)	(0.003)	(0.002)	(0.002)
Domestic	0.002	0.008	0.007	0.007	0.008
credit/GDP	(0.008)	(0.017)	(0.017)	(0.016)	(0.017)
Industrial	−0.000	−0.000	−0.000	0.000	−0.000
production	(0.004)	(0.008)	(0.006)	(0.009)	(0.008)
Full Consensus		−0.405***			
		(0.050)			
Business Sector				−0.764***	−0.590***
Consensus				(0.102)	(0.117)
Unions'			−1.173***		−0.267
Consensus			(0.146)		(0.170)
Observations	249	249	249	249	249

Notes: Robust standard errors in parentheses
* significant at 10%; ** significant at 5%; *** significant at 1%

Table A.1.3 Relogit estimates for 'events' in the UK

	Benchmark	(1)	(2)	(3)	(4)	(5)	(6)
RIR differential	-0.061	0.094**	-0.011	0.131***	0.142***	-0.079	0.122**
	(0.047)	(0.047)	(0.047)	(0.048)	(0.049)	(0.051)	(0.048)
M2/reserves	-0.003	-0.005*	-0.004	-0.006**	-0.007**	-0.003	-0.006**
	(0.002)	(0.003)	(0.003)	(0.003)	(0.003)	(0.003)	(0.003)
Domestic credit/GDP	0.003	0.007	0.005	0.008*	0.009*	0.004	0.008
	(0.005)	(0.005)	(0.005)	(0.005)	(0.005)	(0.005)	(0.005)
Industrial production	-0.000	-0.001	-0.001	-0.001	-0.001	-0.001	-0.001
	(0.002)	(0.003)	(0.003)	(0.003)	(0.003)	(0.002)	(0.003)
Full Consensus		-1.601***					
		(0.266)					
Unions' Consensus			-2.794***				
			(0.417)				
City of London Consensus						-2.918***	
						(1.014)	
Business Sector Consensus					-2.826***		
					(0.325)		
Business and Financial Consensus				-2.558***			-2.330***
				(0.343)			(0.450)
Observations	252	250	250	251	251	251	250

Notes: Robust standard errors in parentheses
* significant at 10%; ** significant at 5%; *** significant at 1%

Table A.1.4 Relogit estimates for 'speculative pressure' episodes in the UK

	Benchmark	(1)	(2)	(3)	(4)	(5)	(6)
RIR differential	−0.244***	−0.090*	−0.168***	−0.082*	−0.068	−0.259***	−0.092*
	(0.059)	(0.050)	(0.055)	(0.050)	(0.048)	(0.066)	(0.053)
M2/reserves	0.002	0.003	0.002	0.003	0.004	0.002	0.003
	(0.002)	(0.003)	(0.003)	(0.003)	(0.003)	(0.003)	(0.003)
Domestic credit/GDP	−0.001	−0.001	−0.002	−0.001	−0.001	−0.001	−0.001
	(0.006)	(0.006)	(0.006)	(0.008)	(0.008)	(0.006)	(0.006)
Industrial production	0.000	0.001	0.001	0.001	0.001	0.000	0.001
	(0.002)	(0.003)	(0.003)	(0.003)	(0.003)	(0.002)	(0.003)
Full Consensus		−1.236***					
		(0.179)					
Unions' Consensus			−2.687***				−1.324**
			(0.415)				(0.548)
City of London Consensus						−3.021***	
						(1.036)	
Business Sector Consensus					−2.119***		
					(0.274)		
Business and Financial Consensus				−1.871***			−1.164***
				(0.263)			(0.356)
Observations	252	250	250	251	251	251	250

Notes: Robust standard errors in parentheses
* significant at 10%; ** significant at 5%; *** significant at 1%

APPENDIX 1.2 – MACRO DATA

All macroeconomic data have been collected from the International Financial Statistics of the International Monetary Fund (CD-Rom, 2005).
Exchange rate: Italian Lira (line AE) and British Pound exchange (line AG) rate with respect to the Deutsche Mark (line AE)
International reserves: line 1L
Short-term interest rate: line 60B
Real interest rate: short-term interest rate (line 60B) minus inflation (yearly percentage changes in the consumer price index) (line 64)
M2: Italy (line 39M), United Kingdom (line 35L)
Domestic credit: line 32
Gross domestic product: line 99B
Industrial production: line 66

2. Is the SGP crisis also the crisis of the EU? Assessing the EMU from a structural, transatlantic perspective[1]

Alan Cafruny and Magnus Ryner

Scholarship on the EU has been overtaken by events. The 'non's' and 'nee's' on the Constitutional Treaty, two decades of economic stagnation in 'core Europe', welfare state retrenchment, the increased propensity of Europeans to vote for populist mavericks, the inability of political elites to respond credibly to these phenomena, and the failure of the common foreign and security policy as exemplified by the Iraq War contradict euphoric academic assessments.

EU studies have consistently sung the praises of the Union and its project of a common currency. The EMU is widely seen as spearheading a 'European challenge' to the United States. For Kupchan, 'Europe is arriving on the global stage. Now that its single market has been accompanied with a single currency, Europe has a collective weight on matters of trade and finance comparable to that of the United States.'[2] Others see the EMU as part of a successful 'self-transformation' of the 'European social model' (Hemerijck, 2002; Rhodes, 2002). But when the 'basic force' and formalistic assumptions about power are abandoned, and when a structural conception is adopted, different conclusions emerge.[3] The EU's aspiration to build a monetary union to promote competitiveness, sustained growth, regional autonomy and social cohesion is self-limiting because the Maastricht design of the EMU is inherently connected to a neo-liberal transnational financial order that displaces socio-economic contradictions from the US to other parts of the world, including Europe. Europe's subordinate participation within this order pre-empts the possibility of resolving structural problems of post-industrial, or as we prefer post-Fordist, society in a manner consistent with Europe's social and Christian-Democratic social accords. Economic stagnation, uneven development, and the widening gap between new forms of economic governance and social citizenship amplify legitimation problems and political conflicts, with adverse effects on the EU's political ability to mobilize as a counterweight to the US.

In this chapter we adopt a structural approach to account for EMU's embedding in American minimal hegemony. We then demonstrate the lack of correspondence between the design of the EMU and European long-term growth prospects (although this is not to say that policies do not serve the interests of particular – and powerful – European class fractions and regions). Finally, we outline the attendant socially disintegrative implications. Focusing on France and Germany – EMU's core states – we account for a crisis of representation resulting from a politics of welfare state retrenchment that is counterproductive in its objective to revive growth in the European economy.

1   THE TRANSATLANTIC DIMENSION OF EMU: A STRUCTURAL APPROACH

According to Leonard Seabrooke, the origin of US structural power lies in the advantages that the Dollar's *numeraire* status gave US international banks in the Bretton Woods period. This offered these banks the opportunity to monopolize the issue of dollar-denominated liabilities with zero exchange risk, increasingly demanded on the commercial loan, investment services and foreign exchange markets because of the expansion of international trade (Seabrooke, 2001: 48). At the same time, in sharp contrast to the situation in most European states, the more market-oriented Fordist settlement in the US encouraged the development of a securitized domestic financial market (encouraging 'ordinary' Americans to invest in the stock market and to take on personal debt). Significantly, the US government created incentives for US banks to set up foreign subsidiaries in order to exercise control over domestic monetary policy whilst providing reserve currency for international trade and also to ensure US control over the emerging transnational financial networks (Seabrooke, 2001: 60). Consequently, US banks came to dominate the Euro-dollar markets, which made it possible to expand Dollar-denominated assets on a sufficient scale to facilitate international trade without imposing adjustment constraints on the US economy (Seabrooke, 2001: 64, 66–70). This created the infrastructure which made it possible for the US to exercise minimal hegemony when the Bretton Woods system collapsed. The uncertainties of exchange rates and interest rates favoured the US economy in part because the Dollar remained the world's reserve currency and in part because market uncertainties promoted direct financing (hence favouring the US economy, which had the 'deepest' and most capitalized domestic financial market). Deep market capitalization also had a social base in the US which was lacking in European states, given their social accords. Nevertheless, America's highly capitalized market also progressively became an attractive place for Japanese and European banks, given the exchange- and interest-rate risks associated with the Debt Crisis. Asian and European corporations were progressively attracted towards the US stock market as a source of finance, as an alternative to their traditional house-bank links at home (Seabrooke, 2001: 73–106, 111–18).[4]

In this context, US assets are seen as less risky. From the large government deficits of Reagan to the massive expansion of private debt during Clinton, and even greater governmental deficits under Bush II, capital accumulation has been sustained, despite relatively low yields on capital invested in the US compared to the return of US investments abroad,[5] and despite the credit crises in Latin America, the former Communist states and East Asia. Indeed, the American-centred system has managed to turn these crises into strengths by extending their control over and progressively subsuming disintegrated and weakened particularistic domestic systems (Grahl, 2001: 23–47).

The EMS operated within these structures. In the absence of seignorage privileges, and with radically different 'bank-centred' domestic financial systems and with savings collectivized in welfare state institutions (e.g. pension systems), floating exchange rates and mobile transnational financial markets posed significant problems in Europe. The failure of French Keynesianism under Mitterrand expressed the impasse of the 'overdraft economy', based on 'the consensual refusal of the state, the trade unions, and the employers to control nominal changes in incomes and prices', unlimited credit and periodic external adjustment (Loriaux, 1991: 10–11). Subsequently, France has searched for pan-European agreement to reconstitute its growth model from a position of weakness (Clift, 2003). Germany's dilemma was different. In the early 1970s the Schmidt administration was no longer willing to import US inflation via the fixed rates of the Bretton Woods and allowed the appreciation of the German Mark, which in any case served to contain costs of oil and other imports and helped facilitate the acquiescence of organized labour and social market imperatives. However, floating exchange rates *within* Europe posed a threat of competitive devaluations, and Germany promoted an EMS on its own terms in exchange for conditional support of other currencies through German foreign reserves (Lankowski, 1982).

Yet these attempts to create a European 'zone of stability' were ultimately undermined by Europe's collective vulnerability to US monetary unilateralism, chronic uneven development among, and increasingly within, the member states, and the persistence of defensive labour strength, which made it impossible to maintain sufficient discipline or 'internal adjustment'. Prior to EMU, imbalances between Germany and the rest of

Europe meant that the German Mark was a powerful magnet for international capital seeking a safe, non-inflationary haven. The 1992 collapse of the ERM exemplified this tendency (Seabrooke, 2001: 163). As long as European economies were expanding, ERM members were able to raise their interest rates in order to maintain parity with the rising Mark. Reunification, however, precipitated a crisis both for Germany and for the EU as a whole, when the Bundesbank raised interest rates to historically unprecedented levels, ushering in a period of sustained economic stagnation into the fledgling single market. In terms of broad socio-economic trends, the EMS was a consistent drag on the expansion of aggregate demand and served to foreclose post-Fordist alternatives based on social democratic and corporatist principles. The post-unification boom and bust decisively ended a whole range of embryonic developments to that effect (Lipietz, 1989, 1997).

To be sure, the EMU was supposed to address the instabilities of the EMS. A common currency eliminates exchange rate risks and the need to hedge against such risks. The composition of the European Central Bank (ECB) also countered German unilateralism. However, as optimal currency area theory suggests, exchange rates are not only sources of instability for economic policy, but also shock absorbers. The abandonment of national currencies has served to displace the instabilities to other areas of economic policy. More fundamentally, the Maastricht design of the EMU amounts more to a continuation of the EMS regime than a fundamental break. It does not challenge the US-centred financial structures as described above. If anything, the plethora of reforms of European financial systems is likely to consolidate the subordinate convergence of European finance to these structures (Story and Walter, 1997).

The authority and terms of reference of the European Central Bank as laid down in the Treaty of Maastricht also confirm the continuation of the principles of disciplinary neo-liberal norms and macroeconomic austerity (Dyson, 2000; Gill, 1998). ECB independence was legally codified in the Maastricht Treaty (Articles 105 and 107) and can only be altered through a unanimous decision by member states. Hence, policy making is 'locked into' a monetarist framework to an unprecedented degree. The ECB enjoys organizational independence from political processes to pursue its primary objective of price stability, as defined by itself (TEU Article 3a and 105[1]). The ECB seeks to develop a policy that is 'credible' (Chapters 1 and 3) in the financial markets that determine the extension of liquidity and credit. Interest rate setting endows the ECB with considerable power to shape the terms for other apparatuses in implicit policy coordination.[6] Policies that contradict ECB conceptions of price stability – and indirectly, it should be underlined, productivity – are construed as entailing higher inflation risks,

resulting in upward pressure on interest rates via credibility gaps in
financial markets. The most important asymmetry is between the supra-
national monetary policy and intergovernmental fiscal policy. There is no
meaningful EU 'fiscal-federal' budget and transfer-payment system. (To
dispel any ambiguity on this point, the ECB is forbidden to lend directly to
EU institutions and member states. CAP and regional policy, while important in specific sectors and regions, have little aggregate effect.) Instead, the
Stability and Growth Pact had the opposite effect. Constructed on the tem-
plate of the initial Maastricht convergence criteria, it sought to preclude
attempts by individual member states to 'free-ride' on policy credibility by
pursuing expansionary fiscal policies without running the risk of a proportional rise of interest rates (as in the EMS). Employment policy has
become a benchmarking process emphasizing 'supply-side measures' for
employability. While its efficacy can be debated, it is clearly configured in
the disciplinary neo-liberal mould (Tidow, 2003: 77–98). This feeds into
wage policy, which in the context of non-accommodating macroeconomic
policy forces European trade unions into 'competitive corporatist' concession bargaining, ensuring wage increases below rates of productivity
growth (Bieling and Schulten, 2003: 239–47).

The foregoing suggests why, in view of the claims that EMU constitutes
a fundamental challenge to US monetary hegemony, the response from
Washington and Wall Street was initially cautious but eventually muted.
American official and semi-official commentary on the Euro during the
1990s replicated the response towards the single market a decade earlier.
Opposition to a perceived French-inspired 'fortress Europe' evaporated
when it became clear that the single market would actually promote
Atlantic integration. Granted, Washington's 'benign neglect' of EMU had
numerous proximate causes, including widespread scepticism, Britain's
decision to remain outside the Euro-zone, and the preference of the US to
influence monetary policy through domestic policy and unilateral action
rather than multilateral negotiations. More fundamentally, however, EMU
as presently constituted is subordinated to the 'Wall Street/Dollar regime'.[7]

2   EMU AND EUROPE'S FAILED POST-FORDIST TAKE-OFF

The effects of the different positions of the US and the EU with regard to
transnational financial structures, via macroeconomic expansion in the
former, and EMS and EMU transmitted restriction in the latter, are consistent with OECD statistics. These verify a sustained period of output and
productivity growth stagnation and low employment rates in the Euro-zone,

in marked contrast with the US situation.[8] Of course, explaining this stagnation partially in terms of 'demand-side' effects, as we do, is not uncontroversial. More conventional explanations attribute employment and
growth problems to a lack of 'flexibility' and 'competitiveness'. But this is
spurious.[9] The same is the case with the often related 'post-industrial
dilemma' thesis inspired by the work of Baumol (Pierson, 2001: 80–104). If
'post-industrial' societies with large service sectors are assumed inherently
to suffer from low productivity growth, rendering high labour cost
economies untenable, especially when age-dependency ratios are high, then
why do growth and productivity rates vary so dramatically, with the US
achieving rates similar to the Fordist 'golden age', and with Sweden and
Finland reaching even higher levels despite being close to full capacity uti-
lization?[10] Especially the latter two cases, with high degrees of decommodi-
fication on the labour market, falsify the axiom that economic stagnation
can be reduced to a lack of market conformity in industrial relations and
social policy (Mahon, 2007: 79–85). The OECD's own analysis casts doubts
on such supply-side reductionism when it attributes the disappointing slowdown of 2000–02 to:

> domestic demand . . . act[ing] to break growth momentum. Stock building has
> contributed negatively to growth since the start of 2001; business demand
> adjusted to bleak demand prospects . . . [and] private consumption decelerated
> sharply as growth in disposable income was hit. [This is despite] some policy
> stimulus to counteract these tendencies by a series of cuts in interest rates.
> (OECD, 2003: 22)

This survey also identified the 'downside risks' to be on the demand side,
namely a 'further reduction of consumer confidence' and, interestingly, 'the
fiscal tightening implied by France and Germany attempting to honour the
Stability and Growth pact'. Finally, any further appreciation of the Euro
in relation to the Dollar was identified as a major (subsequently realized)
downside risk (OECD, 2003: 22, 27).

The survey not only lent credence to the contention that the main
problem of the Euro-zone economy is demand-led. Its warnings against
attempts to redress this through fiscal stimulus also support our contention
that the Euro-zone suffers from a self-limiting lock-in: fiscal expansion
would have a negative impact on 'confidence' in financial markets, which
would neutralize any positive fiscal policy effects (OECD, 2003: 22–3, 27).
Euro-zone GDP has been consistently 1 per cent below its potential
GDP, which contrasts with the situation in the United States, where actual
GDP has been on par with potential GDP (OECD, 2004, Table 10). This
is arguably central to the increased divergence between the 'potential
GDPs' of the US and the Euro-zone, as it is pre-empting positive

Kaldor–Verdoorn effects, where expanding demand facilitates productivity growth through adequate investment levels and a stable environment in which firms are willing and able to experiment in the application, development, and diffusion of new technology through 'learning by doing'.[11] As regulation theory warned already in the early 1990s, in the context of such a macroeconomic stance, the single market was likely to engender a 'defensive' restructuring of the European economy, based on mergers of existing transnational corporations consolidating surplus capacity and resulting in capital-intensive labour shedding.[12] The essentials of this self-limitation are captured by Albo's term 'competitive austerity': '[A situation when] each country reduces domestic demand and adopts an export-oriented strategy of dumping its surplus production [by keeping wages below productivity growth and pushing down domestic costs], for which there are fewer consumers in its national economy' (Albo, 1994: 147).

What is more, there are good reasons to suspect that the defensive and market-conforming structural transformation that competitive austerity generates, now further enhanced through the National Action Plans of the Lisbon Agenda, has adverse effects on macroeconomic stabilization policy too. This is because of the negative impact on 'automatic stabilizers' of tax and benefit systems 'reforms' (Mabbett and Schelkle, 2007). In a generally stagnant economic environment where countries have surrendered stabilization instruments, these policies produce political fragmentation and conflict as exemplified by the 2003–04 crisis of the Stability and Growth Pact (Chapters 3 and 4). The depreciation of the Euro after 1999 ameliorated the dampening effect of the Stability and Growth Pact. But as the Euro began to appreciate against the Dollar after 2002 it became clear that the pact no longer accorded with the interest of Germany, France and Italy. During the decade following the signing of the Maastricht Treaty in 1992 Germany's unemployment rate rose from 4.5 to 11 per cent. Given the importance of the German economy (31 per cent of EU GDP), low growth greatly impacted the French economy and rippled throughout the Euro-zone. The pressure even compelled convinced monetarists such as German Finance Minister Eichel to suggest that the constraints of the Stability Pact should be abandoned in favour of targets on public spending (Ryner, 2003: 201–30). Though Chancellor Schroeder overruled him after protests from the ECB, opposition continued to mount at the very core of the Euro-zone. Commission President Prodi proclaimed the Stability Pact 'stupid'. France, Germany and Italy violated the deficit rules, and the Stability Pact was finally *de facto* abandoned in November 2003.[13] Consequently, financial markets have become even more dependent on a monetarist ECB to maintain the value of the Euro. Even under the terms of the Stability Pact, despite very high unemployment, the ECB has less flexibility than the

Federal Reserve Board, which in 2001 cut interest rates 11 times even as the US current account deficit exceeded $400 billion. Europe's cyclical 'recovery' of 2006, including growth in both France and Germany, does not mean that the problems of stagnation and dependence have been overcome. In comparison to previous upturns, the present upturn is soft; since the mid-1980s recovery cycles have become progressively more shallow. Even limited Euro-zone recovery is highly susceptible to a slowdown in the US (and hence global) economy.[14]

The EMU, then, is self-limiting because it does not provide necessary institutional and political foundations for sustained growth. The virtual absence of a Union budget does not allow for the transfer payments required to minimize uneven development by compensating weaker regions and economies that have lost the option of devaluation. Current EU revenues are 1.3 per cent of member-state GNP, much less even than the 10 per cent viewed as the minimum necessary budget called for in the McDougall Report of 1977.[15] Unless the Union budget increases substantially and a European fiscal policy is developed, the realities of uneven national development will threaten the stability of an integrated market with a monetary union.

The failure to activate sustainable economic growth should be seen with reference to more or less viable strategies to address the crisis of Fordism and attempts to launch new paradigms of production and capital accumulation. Here it is pertinent to link Seabrooke's work to that of David Harvey. According to Harvey, the transition from the Fordist crisis to 'post-Fordism' in the US has depended on a 'temporal displacement' of values in defunct Fordist enterprises to ventures in new sectors. This was made possible through 'the explosion of new financial instruments and markets coupled with the rise of highly sophisticated systems of financial coordination on a global scale' and a more tightly tied relationship between consumer, corporate and governmental debt (Harvey, 1990: 182–3, 194–5). Resting on these sophisticated structures, US military Keynesianism has sustained transnational capital accumulation, but it has done so in a way that systematically favours the United States, as outlined in section 1.

On the basis of such financial power, the United States has pursued a 'flexible liberal' 'post-Fordism', institutionally compatible with its social settlement as reorganized since the Reagan administration. This has entailed elimination of collective bargaining rights, individualized contracts, incentives, threats and 'numerically flexible' wages, all used to deepen the 'enterprise corporate' culture. Whilst the attendant wage cost reduction has a tendency to reduce aggregate demand, this is compensated through an intensified consumption by the middle class and a reduction of turnover time of this consumption, particularly in the service sector. This consumption has typically been debt financed against the collateral of wealth accumulated in the increased values of the stock and property markets. The financial sector also plays an important role in employment expansion (Sassen, 1991).

One can interpret not only the EMU, but also the Lisbon Process and the Financial Services Action Plan (FSAP) *inter alia*, as an attempt to implement US-style finance in the EU (Bieling, 2003: 203–24). But a successful copying *presupposes* the economic growth that the US enjoys due to its dominant role in transnational finance. Also, financial liberalization is undermining the financial institutions of European national systems of innovation and the capacities of European corporations to mediate between long-term competitiveness and social cohesion through 'own resource'.[16] Moreover, European economic integration has proceeded through mutual recognition between different domestic systems rather than through positive creation of a single European system. Consequently, while short-term commercial capital is mobile in Europe and world-wide, bond and especially stock markets and high-tech venture capital markets remain nationally segmented in the Euro-area, and stand in a hub-and-spoke relationship with the primary-tier markets of New York and London. Whilst the FSAP may result in further integration, there is a large difference between *de jure* aspirations and *de facto* mergers of various European stock markets. Furthermore, the EU is still a far way off from possessing the kind of retail banking sector that forms part of the US system. The realization of this would entail a much deeper challenge to the European social settlements.[17] Current attempts to reform pensions are a step in that direction, but social conflicts accounted for in section 3 demonstrate that such reforms are compounding legitimation crisis tendencies. These are not eased by the absence of substantive economic growth.

All this suggests that the present EU reform package, consisting of a strict macroeconomic policy stance, anglo-saxonization of finance and a retrenched but still recognizably social- and Christian-democratic social settlement, is not a stable constellation. This is, of course, also what the EU's neo-liberal policy establishment maintains in the efforts to pursue further reforms. It is our point, however, that in the absence of America's privileged position in world financial markets, and with Europe's vastly different systems of innovation, this is unlikely to be a successful strategy.

These macroeconomic and political factors are not thematized in the EU's policy discourse, which rather emphasizes potential economies at the macro- and meso-levels. But to reiterate, the evidence of their case is weak. Research into labour processes has consistently shown that coordinated bargaining and co-determination regimes such as those in Scandinavia and the Germanic countries are highly conducive to the development of skilled, functionally flexible, high-productivity post-Fordist production (Freyssenet, 1998: 91–117). Where active labour market policy is used, it has proven to be an adequate substitute for numerical flexibility as an inducement to 'external' flexibility. Indeed, in contrast to the Bundesbank under the EMS, the ECB cannot rely on the stability provided by the *quid pro quo* 'encompassing' coordinated wage bargaining, as in Germany in the 1980s (Crouch, 2000; and Chapter 4). Given the difficulties entailed in copying the Anglo-Saxon financial system, it could be argued that publicly induced investments, more along the lines of traditional 'bank-centred coordinated' or 'Rhineland' lines on a continental scale, would represent a more appropriate response to Fordist crisis (this would be closer to Etienne Davignon's concept of restructuring, which was abandoned by European business and elites in the latter part of the 1980s). It is more likely that this would generate propitious Kaldor–Verdoorn effects and provide for an expansion of welfare services and service employment in the 'reproductive sector', and perhaps in ecological investments, which in turn would increase employment and reduce the age-dependency ratio (Lipietz, 1996; Ryner, 2002).[18] But this would require a remarkable mobilization of collective action, which is not prevented merely by some neo-liberal false consciousness, but also by uneven development, spurred on by the effects of the EMU.

Uneven development under competitive austerity generates divisions over the extent and content of the 'social dimension' of the EU, and greatly limits the extent to which 'negative' market integration is counteracted with supranational 'positive integration' (Scharpf, 1996: 58–83). For example, the highly entrenched 'social capitalist' Netherlands managed in the 1990s to boost employment growth and achieve fiscal balance while engaging in a limited form of welfare state retrenchment. Its 'Polder Model' was based on negotiated concession bargaining and wage segmentation, the creation of a two-tier social insurance system, and active labour market policies (Visser and Hemerijck, 1997). This was done while adopting a highly orthodox stance on the EMU and the Stability and Growth Pact. But this was a niche strategy that could not have been sustained without fortuitous circumstances such as the Dutch location as a European transport hub, independent energy in the form of North Sea gas, and its location in relation to Germany, which allowed the Netherlands to just undercut German social costs in wage competition (Becker, 2000; Ryner, 2002). These conditions mitigated the contradictions between flexible liberal change and the 'social market'. Similar conditions obtained in Denmark (Torfing, 1999), and later Sweden and Finland, which were even more successful in mediating between macroeconomic balance, flexibility and welfare state provision.

As already discussed, the critical importance of niche strategies, and the differential conditions of growth models, is underlined by the experience of West Germany under the EMS. But, together with the stagnation of the European economy as a whole, developments over the last decade in Germany demonstrate the limitations implied in niche strategies. In Germany, contradictions between a disciplinary neo-liberal macroeconomic policy and the social market are mounting. One largely ignored dimension of the success of Germany's export-oriented 'strong Mark' policy was the extent to which it depended on the validation of its production, not only through the US 'locomotive effect' but also on imports from France, depending on the looser and more inflationary stance of France during the EMS (Deubner *et al.*, 1992). As the OECD's 1993 Economic Survey of Germany pointed out, contraction of French aggregate demand – the effect of French copying of Bundesbank monetarism – played a crucial role in the stagnation of German growth, which was compounded by the drag of German reunification on any stimulation effects from export orientation (OECD, 1993). Furthermore, cost-cutting and new outsourcing strategies of German business, leading to wage increases lagging behind productivity growth, undermined the mechanisms that transmitted demand stimuli to the domestic economy via the wage relation (Ganssman, 1997). In addition, the polarization between regions such as Baden-Württemberg, which continue to do well within this pattern of uneven growth, and North-Rhine Westphalia, not to mention the former GDR, underlines the distributive tensions within as well as across EU member states (Dunford, 2005: 149–76). Again, conventional analysis would rather reduce German problems to high labour costs preventing the growth of a service sector. But these analyses ignore the fact that the source of German stagnation is squarely on the demand side, and that reductions of benefits intended to reduce labour costs become counterproductive as they encourage precautionary savings.[19] The most intelligent statements of the 'post-industrial dilemma' thesis recognize this problem, as well as the fact that, in principle, an expansion of public services along Scandinavian lines is just as viable a response to Germany's 'post-industrial dilemma'. But again, EMU-induced austerity closes off such alternatives: '[T]he first priority for the Federal Government is *balancing* its budget, not *expanding* it. The main criterion by which the performance of the Finance Minister is publicly judged year by year is whether his budget meets the targets of the Maastricht stability pact' (Streeck and Trampusch, 2005: 22). This brings home the point that competitive austerity is a zero-sum game that restricts the prospects of a dynamic take-off of the European economy as a whole.

3 THE LIMITS OF EURO-LEGITIMACY

EMU, embedded within US-centred transnational financial structures, has failed to institute an adequate post-Fordist mode of regulation for the Single European Market (SEM). The result has rather been economic stagnation and uneven development, resulting from a continuation of competitive austerity. This is a consequence of a neo-liberal concept of economic governance. It is also a cause thereof, as the response to the problems continues to be further and deeper neo-liberal reform in a process of self-limitation. In this section we link this dynamic to the problems of legitimacy. The basic point here is that, despite the neo-liberal nature of the SEM and the EMU, these projects have been represented to large segments of European civil societies in a much more composite and hybridic way. They have more often than not been presented in mass-popular discourse as compatible with the essentials of the social welfare accords that underpin these civil societies. This is not to rule out the possibility of further neo-liberal deepening in Europe. However, consistent with our definition of crisis, such deepening now threatens the very identity of these social accords, and a resolution is not possible unless *either* these identities are changed *or* the US-led neo-liberal direction is reversed.

3.1 EMU and Welfare State Retrenchment

One needs to be careful of economic reductionism and of inferring too linear a relation between the economic and the political. This would be to assume away, rather than explain, the complex mechanisms that characterize the relationship between the two 'spheres'. Some influential analysts also assert that European welfare systems and social accords can 'weather the storm' or even that the EMU contributes positively to the revitalization of these accords under new conditions. Rhodes points to the 'remarkable continuity' of social expenditure levels and contends that the empirical evidence does not justify the fear of 'social dumping' where economic competition from less developed welfare states in southern (and now also eastern) Europe would compel the northern European welfare states to 'retrench' in a 'race to the bottom' (Rhodes, 2002: 311–12). He argues that there is evidence of a 'race to the top' insofar as the southern welfare states – notably Portugal – have extended coverage to more groups who previously were not protected (Rhodes, 2002: 319–20). The EMU and the SGP have also increased the *need* and the *scope* for strengthening the corporatism and industrial relations regimes. The need has increased because this is one of the few ways in which nation states can recover economic policy autonomy. The scope has simultaneously increased since the reduction of policy tools under the formal discretion of the state has reduced the distributive conflict agendas. The conclusion of 'social pacts' also mushroomed in the 1990s throughout the EU, after a decade of corporatist decline in the 1980s (Rhodes, 2002: 324, 327).

According to Rhodes, Maastricht-induced fiscal consolidation was largely met through reduced interest payments, caused by reduced risk premiums that could be 'imported' to previous high-inflation countries from the low-inflation countries in the EMU core through the common currency backed by the credibility of the SGP. This even had positive demand-side effects. Also, fiscal consolidation was largely secured on the revenue side and not only because of privatizations. Whilst corporate taxation rates and employers' contributions were reduced, tighter write-off rules for corporate taxes and the switching from payroll surcharges to general taxation increased the tax base (Rhodes, 2002: 317–18).

Hence, the relationship between the EMU and welfare state retrenchment is not linear, but rather highly complex. For one, the welfare state is an institution that is, as argued above, intertwined with, and constitutive of, the very being of modern European social order. Hyperbolic claims of an outright 'end' of the welfare state are out of order. It is also possible in some locales to maintain at existing levels or even expand the welfare state. Yet, the implications for *social citizenship* conveyed by these indicators are highly misleading. As Esping-Andersen (1990, p. 19) put it in a memorable turn of phrase, it is hard to find any instance where social forces have struggled for spending as such. What matters is, rather, *effective entitlements* and the extent to which they correspond to the norms of distributive justice and legitimacy that are contained in social citizenship accords.

When thus considered, the stability of social expenditure levels may actually be an indicator of significant welfare state retrenchment. From the point of view of *unchanged* social citizenship norms about entitlements there are good grounds to suppose that there should be an *increase* of claims. First, ageing populations and early retirement have increased markedly the number of pensioners ready to make claims on programmes they see themselves as having contributed towards in their working lives. Second, divorce rates have increased and there has also been a significant increase in the number of single parents. These factors, along with the efforts to increase employment rates and the aspiration of women to become full economic citizens, have increased the demand for family services. It is no wonder, then, that Rhodes's more disaggregated figures point to a marked shift of resources towards areas such as these (Rhodes, 2002: 312–13). Given the increased demand and claims of these programmes despite fixed resources, there has indeed been significant retrenchment. Korpi, drawing on the unparalleled database of the Stockholm Institute of

Social Research, finds a marked reduction of the net replacement rates for benefits received during sickness, work accidents and unemployment in Europe.[20] This is confirmed by the 'social reforms database' of the Fondazione Rodolfo Debenedetti.[21] But above all, Hemerijck, Rhodes and other proponents of the 'new politics of retrenchment' literature forget that the end of the full employment commitment, and the understanding of employment in terms of 'a right to work' at a certain standard, is *in and of itself* a crucial indicator of welfare state retrenchment (Korpi, 2003: 592, 593–4, 596). Furthermore, unemployment is the major mechanism through which ECB-led austerity is transmitted towards welfare state retrenchment, as it increases claims on expenditure, deprives social insurance systems of revenue and excludes people from the systems in the first place, compelling state managers to cut back entitlements.

Hence, it is not surprising that inequality increased in the 1990s, nor that there were serious cutbacks to public services in relation to demand (Clayton and Pontusson, 1998: 67–98). Nor, looking at the matter in a slightly longer time scale, is it surprising that the almost perfect proportionality of social wage and GDP growth has been broken, indicating that the wage relation is increasingly defined as a 'market variable' as opposed to a means to disseminate the 'fruits of progress' (Boyer, 1990). It is also doubtful whether the corporatist bargains of the 1990s really represent continuity or even 'self-transformation'. Whereas corporatism used to contain price increases at full employment, negotiations are now to secure wage settlements below rates of productivity growth at high unemployment levels. Unions have acquiesced to these policies from a position of exceptional weakness in order to increase the probability – but not guarantee – that this will boost employment. This puts serious strain on the 'moral economy' that makes workers join unions in the first place, as unions are seen to contain rather than increase wages, and as these policies attenuate internal representative structures within unions at the expense of peak-level concertation. These strains are exacerbated when the policies *fail* to boost employment because they are contributing to the dynamic of competitive austerity (Bieling and Schulten, 2003: 251–4).

Considering matters at this more disaggregated level of entitlement, Rhodes also concedes that there has been significant retrenchment. The point he makes, though, is that changes are 'necessary', and the EMU has engendered this necessary retrenchment in order to put European welfare states on a more secure footing. It is in this sense that the EMU has been 'good' for the European welfare state.

There are two problems with this argument. First, welfare state restructuring is understood in the extremely deterministic way of a 'post-industrial dilemma', critiqued at the beginning of section 2. The second problem,

related to the notion of a successful 'self-adjustment', pertains to the
definition of 'self'. At what point does retrenchment challenge the very
quality and identity of the social citizenship accords? This question cannot
be answered *in abstracto*. It depends on the extent to which reforms can be
rendered compatible with the terms of legitimacy in mass civil societal political culture. The next subsection discusses the tensions that are generated in
the mechanisms and channels that link civil and political society.

3.2   Strains in the Politics of Mediation

The welfare state is intimately connected to the rise of social citizenship,
redeeming the equality of status as required by political and civic citizenship in a capitalist society and hence with *substantive legitimacy*.[22] The
welfare state reproduces social accords and distributive coalitions that lie
at the heart of the European social order. These coalitions are connected
to political society through mass parties and their competition and cooperation.[23] In almost the entire Euro-zone, where Christian Democracy has
been hegemonic in the definition of the 'national-popular' after World War
II, reproduction and change take place through a *politics of mediation* – 'a
religiously inspired, ideologically condensed and politically practiced con-
viction that conflicts of interests can and must be reconciled politically in
order to restore the natural and organic harmony of society' (van
Kersbergen, 1995: 2). Successful political and electoral strategies of mass
parties have been based on the management of the various dimensions
of socio-political cleavages (especially of class, religion and language).
However, as economic growth slows and as welfare state retrenchment proceeds, the scope of such politics of mediation is restricted, thereby reducing the range of social forces that can be integrated into the political
mainstream. This in turn requires a change in the politics of mediation
itself. Parties are compelled either to redefine the terms of the redistribu-
tive coalitions, or to change the politico-economic framework, or sometimes both. Here we show how this political dynamic has unfolded in
Germany and France.

   It is exceedingly difficult to implement the abstract and uncompromising
neo-liberal reforms of 'flexibility' (Boyer, 2000: 24–89). Such reforms con-
travene the very nature of compromise and mediation, and threaten highly
entrenched status groups as well as the claims of social protection of the
most vulnerable in society. Electorally, implementing these reforms is a
hazardous exercise for political movements whose success has been based
on constructing complex and composite coalitions such as the SPD and,
quintessentially, the CDU in Germany (Schmid, 1998; Ryner 2002). French
presidentialism seems to give the state more 'executive authority' to take

'hard decisions'. However, there are powerful countertendencies: the 'dual executive' nature of the French system; electoral laws that encourage the formation of composite coalitions; and the semi-autonomous status given to professional groups and unions in the management of French social insurance, connected to the 'Jacobin' tradition of street protests when the executive goes 'too far'. As the emblematic mass demonstrations of 1995 and 2005, and indeed April 2006, show, French unions and other social movements have developed skills in strategically harnessing such outbursts (*'greviculture'*) (Palier, 2000).

Since the 1983 Mitterrand 'U-turn', French politics has been characterized by a series of neo-liberalization and welfare retrenchment thrusts that have provoked organized resistance, which has in turn led to reversals, symbolic calls for a compensatory 'social dimension' to European restructuring and a European 'economic government', and more cautious retrenchment by stealth.[24] This cycle has produced some rather spectacular phenomena, including periodic mass demonstrations, Jospin's surprise election as prime minister in 1997, his equally surprising ousting in the first round presidential elections in 2002 and the 'non' in the referendum on the EU Constitution. The politics of austerity and retrenchment has made *Front Nationale* a mainstay in French political society, with strong support in the white French working class, and it has fragmented the Left. France has returned to a political economy of stagnation, where neo-liberal reform is resisted by strong social groups, but the commitments of the EMU and the impossibility of economic nationalism prevent demand-led recovery. It is against this backdrop that France breached SGP rules (by refusing to finance tax cuts through a reduction of expenditure), and together with Germany essentially rendered the SGP inoperative.

France has always had an ambivalent and difficult relationship with monetarism, EMS and the EMU because of the difficulties of mediating its economic rationality with social and political legitimacy. French monetary politics is often characterized in terms of a 'long game', where France acquiesces to monetarist integration pragmatically from a defensive position of weakness, in order to push for further integration in a more interventionist direction at opportune moments (Clift, 2003: 173–200). But this 'long game' affirms a sort of post-modern neo-liberalism, where the promise of a 'social Europe' remains forever absent and affirms its opposite. The outcome of the referendum on the constitutional treaty may indicate an exhaustion of this process.

Germany had a much less problematic relationship with the EMS and the EMU. However, since the late 1990s the German mass parties have found it increasingly difficult to pursue successful electoral and governance strategies that reproduce their coalitions. The CDU and the SPD have continuously fought over the allegiance of east German voters, still in the throes of post-socialist restructuring, and white-collar middle classes, both of which value their social benefits, protections and pensions, but also support 'economic competence'. Hence, the parties have tried to appeal to these groups together with their core constituencies (the blue-collar working class in the case of the SPD and market-oriented business groups, 'value conservatives' and Catholic workers in core regions in the case of the CDU). The cutbacks of transfer payments by Kohl in 1996 and 1997, as Germany faced pressures to meet the Maastricht convergence criteria, enabled the SPD to win the votes of the latter groups in 1998. However, the abandonment of Lafontaine's Keynesianism effectively deepened Kohl's retrenchment.[25] The SPD lost power even in its 'safest' state of North Rhine-Westphalia and suffered massive losses of party membership, interrupted only temporarily by Schröder's tactical opposition to the US invasion of Iraq. Nostalgia for stability and the 'competence factor' propelled the CDU into tenuous leadership of a grand coalition, which promises continuing retrenchment. It is important to underline that the Grand Coalition is a sign of weakness, not strength. It is the very competitiveness of the party system that is central to the legitimacy of mass liberal democratic political societies, since it 'helps set the national system of government *above* any particular office holders' (Lipset and Rokkan, 1990: 92). The formation of a grand coalition represents a major attenuation of this principle, where the legitimacy of the system as such becomes much more intimately connected with the success of the office holders. It would be particularly damaging if the coalition were to fail to restore economic growth and stabilize the economy and welfare system – a scenario that seems all too likely since it is unlikely to challenge the socio-economic framework that precludes a take-off of growth in Europe.

The fragmentation in Germany and France appears to be part of a broader trend away from the established parties. (Examples abound in Austria, the Netherlands, Denmark and of course Italy.) No doubt, electoral studies and political sociologists correctly identify broad structural determinants to these phenomena. However, we hypothesize that more immediate causes are constituted by welfare state retrenchment compelled by EMU-imposed austerity.

CONCLUSION

The crisis of EMU arises from two fundamental contradictions. First, the political and economic imperatives of EMU as presently constituted undermine essential features of European welfare capitalism. Second, EMU is incompatible with the further development of European solidarity and, hence, the establishment of a common fiscal policy, and more broadly a polity that can provide social and political cohesion. Far from promoting greater integration, as its architects predicted, EMU serves to intensify conflict among and within member states by accelerating uneven development, dramatizing regional and international inequalities, and – less than five years after its inception – provoking demands in some quarters for the re-nationalization of monetary policy.

Europe's inability to generate a stable growth trajectory from within implies continuing dependence on the United States. Europe's economic fortunes remain hostage to the American 'growth locomotive' and monetary and fiscal policies that reflect the vagaries of American priorities. The ultimate impact of these policies on Europe remains uncertain and potentially profoundly destabilizing. Despite the size, depth and centrality of US capital markets it may not be possible to finance the massive American trade and budget deficits indefinitely. A prolonged US recession could send shockwaves throughout the world economy, presenting Europe with novel dangers, but lacking the internal cohesion required to adequately address these dangers.

NOTES

1. This is a revised version of 'Monetary Union and the Transatlantic and Social Dimensions of Europe's Crisis', *New Political Economy*, **12**(2) (2007), http://www.informaworld.com.
2. See Kupchan (2003: 22). See also Rifkin (2004); Haseler (2004); Reid (2005); and Leonard (2005).
3. Assumptions of basic force relations between the economics and politics also permeate historical materialist analyses, for example Wallerstein (2003: 27–35); and Arrighi (2005), **32**, pp. 23–80 and **33**, pp. 83–116. For a critique, see Panitch and Gindin (2005: 101–23). As they argue, the fallacy of the former analyses is caused by a regress back to a base-superstructure conception and hence a failure to adequately theorize the structural relation between the economy and the state in capitalism.
4. Initially, US dominance was primarily due to the dominant role of American banks in transatlantic arbitrage operations – an advantage that was multiplied by the oil crisis and the need to 'recycle' the 'petro-Dollars'. However, the 'indebted innovation' during the Reagan presidency added deeper structural dimensions to US power. Whilst Washington initially considered regulating the Euro-dollar market in 1978 amidst concerns about the control of the domestic money supply, by the early 1980s – certainly by the time of Reagan's Economic Recovery Tax Act of 1981 – it was decided that the best way to deal with the Euro-dollar markets was to 'internalize aspects of them within the US domestic financial system'. This internalization came in the form of a further commitment to highly capitalized, disintermediated, 'direct-financing' capital markets as a way to deal with foreign exchange and interest rate uncertainties, and eventually also the Debt Crisis. In the 1980s, financial innovation within the US increased the capacity of the financial system to deal with higher levels of both personal and government debt. Money mutual funds expanded their operations. Futures trading on stock market indices started, and a

broad range of options and derivatives were introduced. US commercial banks came to rely increasingly upon operations of debt securities (such as bonds and shares) rather than deposits ('off balance-sheet activities'). Significantly, the 1984 Secondary Mortgage Market Enhancement Act created a market for mortgage-based securities. CMOs (collateralized mortgage obligations) allowed 'homeowners to draw against a line of credit supported by the appreciated value of their homes'. In turn, commercial banks could sell the package of these loans on to investment banks to create asset-backed securities to be sold on as bonds to various investors as the basis for further investment ventures. Thus, increased home ownership provided investment banks with a steady supply of debt capital. Between 1980 and 1985, total US credit market debt increased from $4.7 trillion to $8.2 trillion and non-financial sector debt increased from $3.9 trillion to $6.9 trillion. Household indebtedness increased by 69 per cent. This did not lead to economic stagnation, but rather provided tremendous capacities for the US to manipulate time and space as it restructured its capital accumulation regime along neo-liberal post-Fordist lines.

5. Processing data from the French state and the Federal Reserve, Dumenil and Levy (2004: 664–5) show that yields on US direct investments abroad are about three times larger than the yield on foreign direct investments in the US. With regard to total holdings, the yield on the holdings of the US to the rest of the world is more than twice that on the holding of the rest of the world in the US. Consistently with our argument, they attribute this asymmetry to the United States being 'at the centre of a system in which capital is simultaneously exported and imported, to and from the rest of the world . . . Agents of other countries may want to protect their holdings from national risk or constraints . . . Such investments are seen as risk free and liquid, but are remunerated at comparatively low rates' (p. 665).

6. Holman (2004: 714–35); the ECB's chief economist states bluntly a doctrine amounting to asymmetrical regulation through *ex post* policy coordination in Issing (2002: 435–58).

7. Longer-range US concerns include the loss of seignorage. While the Euro will displace the Dollar in eastern Europe, it is doubtful that, in the absence of a generalized global economic crisis, the overall impact on the Dollar would be large. Another concern is the protectionist potential of the EMU. Between 1999 and 2002 the Euro declined by 25% against the Dollar, benefiting German and French export interests (see Talani, 2005: 204–31). While a strategy of 'neo-liberal mercantilism' is consistent with Franco-German interests, it does not provide a basis for the Euro to mount a challenge to the Dollar. Transatlantic economic integration has accelerated dramatically over the last 25 years and Europe's growth remains heavily dependent on the US economy (see *inter alia* Quinlan, 2003; Cafruny, 2003: 285–306).

8. OECD (1999), Table 3.1; OECD (2004), Tables 1, 12 and 20. The 2.5 per cent average annual real GDP growth rate of the Euro-zone since the 1990s should be compared to the 5.1 per cent over the period 1960–73, 2.7 per cent 1973–79 and 2.2 per cent 1980–89. By contrast, US growth figures returned almost to the same level as during the 'Golden Age' in the later part of the 1990s (3.8 per cent between 1994 and 2000 as opposed to 4 per cent 1960–73). In 2005, growth for the Euro-zone was 1.4 per cent and for the US 3.6 per cent (OECD, 2005). Average annual growth of business sector labour productivity 1994–2003 was 1.15 per cent in the Euro area and 2.11 per cent in the US, reversing by one-fifth the tendency towards a European 'catch-up' in the post-World War II period. See also Gordon (2002). The Euro-zone employment rate in 2002 was 63.9 per cent, compared to 71 per cent in the US.

9. OECD (2000); Nickell (1997: 55–74); Buchele and Christiansen (1998: 117–36); Glyn (2001: 629–46); Eurostat (2001); and Andersen (2007: 71–8).

10. See, for example, the European Commission's own analysis (2003).

11. Boyer (1996: 18–69, 2000); and Boyer and Petit (1991). Data from the European Commission supports this interpretation. The Commission finds that the EU's lower productivity growth, compared to the US, is due to inadequate investment and innovation outside the non-ICT sectors of the economy (inadequate diffusion). European Commission (2003). For more 'mainsteam' analyses that also point to adverse effects of

macroeconomic austerity for productivity enhancing structural policy, see IMF (2004: 48, 58).

12. Boyer (1990: 109–42); Ramsie (1995); and Lipietz (1997: 23–4).
13. ECOFIN reached an agreement to 'amend' the pact on 21 March 2005. (See Council of the EU, Improving the Implementation of the Stability and Growth Pact 7423/05 UEM 97 ECOFIN 104; European Commission, Proposal for a Council Regulation: Amending Regulation (EC) No. 1466/97 on the Strengthening of the Surveillance of Budgetary Positions and the Surveillance and Coordination of Economic Policies, 20.4.2005 COM (2005) 154 final; Proposal for a Council Regulation: Amending Regulation (EC) No. 1466/97 on Speeding Up and Clarifying the Implementation of the Excessive Deficit Procedure, 20.4.2005 COM (2005) 155 final.) Whilst the amendments were presented as an 'improvement', there can be no doubt that they represent a radical retraction of the objectives initially set for the GSP. They represent a belated admission of the trade-off between macroeconomic 'balance' in the medium term and growth. As such the amended pact is often represented as more 'intelligent' than the previous version. But it is questionable whether it can be considered a pact at all. The amended version is full of general clauses, inviting ad hoc, arbitrary and discretionary interpretations. First, the call for a differentiated assessment of Medium-Term Objectives (in light of structural policies pursued and potential growth rates) opens up considerable room for interpretation, disagreement and conflict. The same is the case for 'exceptional' and 'temporary' deficits 'close' to the reference value. But the most notable general clause is the one stating that 'due consideration will be given to any other factors, which in the opinion of the nation state concerned are relevant in order to comprehensively assess in qualitative terms the excess over the reference value. In that context, special consideration will be given to budgetary efforts towards increasing, or maintaining at a high level financial contributions, international solidarity and to achieving European policy goals, notably the unification of Europe if it has a detrimental effect on the growth of fiscal burden of a Member State' (Council of the EU, Improving the Implementation of the Stability and Growth Pact, p. 15). The latter opens up tremendous room for interpretation and it should be seen against the backdrop of Germany's invocation of its exceptional burden of financing German reunification and France's invocation of its expenditure on defence as a contribution to the Common Foreign and Security Policy (CFSP) during the negotiations leading up to the amendments. During these negotiations, according to Euro-12 Chairman Jean-Claude Juncker: 'views were expressed . . . with a vehemence that amazed me' (quoted in George Parker, 'EU Attempts to Reform Stability Pact Breaks Down', *Financial Times*, 9 March 2005).
14. Munchau (2006: 9).
15. McDougall (1977).
16. See Grahl (2001: 30–32, 39), who summarizes the pressure posed on European productive capital from the intertwining with Anglo-Saxon-centred financial capital: 'To summarise the shareholder value agenda, one can look at matters from the point of view of capital market itself – that is, in terms of the reallocation of capital resources. This market would see, on the one hand, over-capitalised enterprises situated in slow growth sectors, perhaps with high earning streams but with relatively limited possibilities of accumulation. To the extent that they escape pressures from shareholders as principals, these "cash cows" may have acquired complex networks of insider coalition partners, representing stakeholder interests. To such a company, the shareholder value agenda is all too familiar. Pressures for productive adjustment will involve downsizing, disposal of peripheral, under-performing divisions, stripping-out of cushioned managerial layers and so forth. Financial reorganisation will include higher distribution ratios, equity buy-backs and increased gearing through the bond finance of assets that provide adequate collateral. In effect, shareholders are saying: "there is no such thing as internal resources, everything is ours". Companies on which this programme has been imposed will provide higher returns on a possibly diminished equity base. This will correspond to higher risk for equity holders, but today's fund managers are confident that they can diversify those risks.'

17. Watson (2001: 504–23). Making the distinction between *de jure* and *de facto* developments, Watson is much more sceptical than Bieling that regional integration of stock markets will take place as a result of Lisbon. They both agree with Grahl, however, on the negative impacts on European systems of innovation.
18. See, for example, Lipietz (1996: 377–8); and Ryner (2002), Chapter 2.
19. Munchau (2004).
20. Korpi (2003: 597). These indicators are more transparent, since changes in the likes of pensions only have an effect after a long time lag (though reforms, such as those in the French pension system, will affect future replacement rates; see for example Palier, 2000, pp. 113–36).
21. http://www.frdb.org/documentazione/centro_doc.php, accessed 4 April 2005, cited in Mabbett and Schelkle (2007).
22. Marshall (1950); Unger, (1976: 193–200).
23. Hausler and Hirsch (1989: 306).
24. As a result of low growth rates and increased unemployment since 1973, the autonomous, professionally specific, social security funds (*caisses*) that constitute the bulk of France's income replacement system have suffered recurring deficit problems. Until the early 1990s, these problems were typically resolved through increased contributions (though the indexation method for family allowances shifted from wages to prices). However, in the wake of the 1993 recession that came in the context of the EMS crisis and the effort to meet the Maastricht Convergence Criteria, retrenchment took on another quality. The *Allocation Unique Dégressive* (AUD) was introduced, which consolidated the unemployment insurance programmes into one, significantly reduced the incomes replacement principle over time, and increased reliance on means testing. In the private sector, a pension reform increased the qualification period for full pensions from 37.5 to 40 years, and the reference salary of calculation of benefits was extended to the best 25, as opposed to the best 10, years. The attempt to extend a similar reform to the public sector triggered the strikes of 1995. This same 'Juppe Plan' also exerted increased state control over the budget of the health *caisses*. In addition, means-tested programmes, such as the RMI (*Revenu Minimum d'Insertion*) and the CMU (*Couverture Maladie Universelle*), have been introduced to cover the increased stratum of long-term unemployed and precariously employed, expressing a tendential qualitative move away from income replacement towards residualism. In addition, a less well-publicized side of the Socialist 35-hour week labour law is that it has also increased significantly the scope and practice of individualized and numerically flexible employment (see Palier, 2000).
25. Retrenchment of the Schröder government included a shift towards more regressive taxation (consumption taxes), pension reform increasing the role of private finance and actuarianism, and most recently the Agenda 2010 reforms, with radically reducing the incomes replacement principle. See Martin Seeleib-Kaiser (2003); Siegel (2004: 103–25).

BIBLIOGRAPHY

Albo, Gregory (1994), ' "Competitive Austerity" and the Impasse of Capitalist Employment Policy', in R. Miliband and L. Panitch (eds), *The Socialist Register*, London: Merlin Press.
Andersen, Jorgen Goul (2007), 'Citizenship Politics: Activation, Welfare and Employment in Denmark', *New Political Economy*, **12**(1).
Arrighi, Giovanni (2005), 'Hegemony Unravelling', *New Left Review*, **32** and **33**.
Becker, Uwe (2000), ' "A Dutch Model': Employment Growth by Corporatist Consensus and Wage Restraint: A Critical Account of an Idyllic View', *New Political Economy*, **6**(1).

Bieling, Hans-Jurgen (2003), 'Social Forces in the Making of the New European Economy: The Case of Financial Market Integration', *New Political Economy*, **8**(2).

Bieling, Hans-Jurgen and Thorsten Schulten (2003), ' "Competitive Restructuring" and Industrial Relations within the European Union: Corporatist Involvement and Beyond', in A. Cafruny and M. Ryner (eds), *A Ruined Fortress?*, Lanham, MD: Rowman & Littlefield.

Boyer, Robert (1990), 'The Impact of the Single Market on Labour and Employment: A Discussion of Macroeconomic Approaches in Light of Research in Labour Economics', *Labour and Society*, **15**(2).

Boyer, Robert (1996), 'Capital–Labour Relations in OECD Countries: From the Fordist Golden Age to Contested National Trajectories', in J. Schor and J.-I. You (eds), *Capital, the State and Labour: A Global Perspective*, Cheltenham, UK and Lyme, USA: Edward Elgar.

Boyer, Robert (2000), 'The Unanticipated Fallout of European Monetary Union: The Political and Institutional Deficits of the Euro', in C. Crouch (ed.), *After the Euro*, Oxford: Oxford University Press.

Boyer, Robert and Pascal Petit (1991), 'Technical Change, Cumulative Causation and Growth', in F. Chesnais (ed.), *Technology and Productivity: The Challenge of Economic Policy*, Paris: OECD.

Buchele, Robert and Jens Christiansen (1998), 'Do Employment and Income Security Cause Unemployment? A Comparative Study of the United States and E-4', *Cambridge Journal of Economics*, **22**(1).

Cafruny, Alan (2003), 'Europe, The United States, and Neoliberal (Dis)Order: Is There a Coming Crisis of the Euro?', in Alan Cafruny and Magnus Ryner (eds), *A Ruined Fortress? Neoliberal Hegemony and Transformation in Europe*, Lanham, MD: Rowman & Littlefield.

Clayton, Richard and Jonas Pontusson (1998), 'Welfare State Retrenchment Revisited: Entitlement Cuts, Public Sector Restructuring, and Inegalitarian Trends in Advanced Capitalist Societies', *World Politics*, **51**(1).

Clift, Ben (2003), 'The Changing Political Economy of France: *Dirigisme* under Duress', in Alan Cafruny and Magnus Ryner (eds), *A Ruined Fortress? Neoliberal Hegemony and Transformation in Europe*, Lanham, MD: Rowman & Littlefield.

Crouch, Colin (2000), 'National Wage Determination and Economic and Monetary Union', in C. Crouch (ed.), *After the Euro*, Oxford: Oxford University Press.

Deubner, Christian, Udo Rehfeld and Frieder Schlupp (1992), 'Franco-German Relations within the International Division of Labour: Interdependence, Divergence or Structural Dominance?', in William Graf (ed.), *The Internationalization of the German Political Economy: Evolution of a Hegemonic Project*, New York: St Martin's Press.

Dumenil, Gerard and Dominique Levy (2004), 'The Economics of US Imperialism at the Turn of the 21st Century', *Review of International Political Economy*, **11**(4).

Dunford, Mick (2005), 'Old Europe, New Europe and the USA: Comparative Economic Performance, Inequality and Market-Led Models of Development', *European Urban and Regional Studies*, **12**(2).

Dyson, Kenneth (2000), *The Politics of the Euro-Zone: Stability or Breakdown?*, Oxford: Oxford University Press.

Esping-Andersen, Gosta (1990), *The Three Worlds of Welfare Capitalism*, Cambridge: Polity Press.

European Commission (2003), *European Economy*, **6**, Brussels: Office for the Official Publications of the EC.

Eurostat (2001), *Structural Indicators: Labour Productivity*, 11 December, Brussels: Eurostat.

Freyssenet, Michel (1998), ' "Reflective Production": An Alternative to Mass Production and Lean Production?', *Economic and Industrial Democracy*, **19**(1).

Ganssman, Heiner (1997), 'Soziale Sicherheit als Standortsproblem', *Prokla*, **106**.

Gill, Stephen (1998), 'European Governance and New Constitutionalism: Economic and Monetary Union and Alternatives to Disciplinary Neo-Liberalism in Europe', *New Political Economy*, **3**(1).

Glyn, Andrew (2001), 'Inequalities of Employment and Wages in OECD Countries', *Oxford Bulletin of Economics and Statistics*, **63**(1).

Gordon, Robert (2002), 'Why Was Europe Left at the Station when America's Productivity Locomotive Departed?', Working paper 10661, National Bureau of Economic Research, Washington, DC.

Grahl, John (2001), 'Globalized Finance: The Challenge to the Euro', *New Left Review*, **8**, March/April.

Harvey, David (1990), *The Condition of Postmodernity*, London: Blackwell.

Haseler, Stephen (2004), *Superstate: The New Europe and its Challenge to America*, London: I.B. Tauris.

Hausler, Jurgen and Joachim Hirsch (1989), 'Political Regulation: The Crisis of Fordism and the Transformation of the Party System in West Germany', in M. Gottdiener and N. Komninos (eds), *Capitalist Development and Crisis Theory*, New York: St Martin's Press.

Hemerijck, A. (2002), 'The Self Transformation of the European Social Model(s)', *International Politics and Society*, **4**.

Holman, Otto (2004), 'Asymmetrical Regulation and Multidimensional Governance in the European Union', *Review of International Political Economy*, **11**(4).

International Monetary Fund (IMF) (2004), 'Euro Area Policies: Selected Issues', *IMF Country Report*, 04/234, Washington, DC.

Issing, Otmar (2002), 'On Macroeconomic Policy Coordination and the EMU', *Journal of Common Market Studies*, **40**(2).

Korpi, Walter (2003), 'Welfare State Regress in Western Europe: Politics, Institutions, Globalization and Europeanization', *Annual Review of Sociology*, **29**.

Kupchan, Charles (2003), *The End of the American Era: US Foreign Policy and the Geopolitics of the 21st Century*, New York: Vintage.

Lankowski, Carl (1982), 'Model Deutschland and the International Regionalization of the West German State', in A. Markovits (ed.), *The Political Economy of West Germany: Modell Deutschland*, New York: Praeger.

Leonard, Mark (2005), *Why Europe Will Run the 21st Century*, London: Fourth Estate.

Lipietz, Alain (1989), 'The Debt Problem, European Integration and the New Phase of World Crisis', *New Left Review*, **178** (old series).

Lipietz, Alain (1996), 'Social Europe: The Post-Maastricht Challenge', *Review of International Political Economy*, **3**(3).

Lipietz, Alain (1997), 'The Post-Fordist World: Labour Relations, International Hierarchy and Global Ecology', *Review of International Political Economy*, **4**(1).

Lipset, Seymor-Martin and Stein Rokkan (1990), 'Cleavage Structures, Party Systems and Voter Alignments', in P. Mair (ed.), *The West European Party System*, Oxford: Oxford University Press.

Loriaux, Michael (1991), *France after Hegemony: International Change and Financial Reform*, Ithaca, NY: Cornell University Press.

Mabbett, Deborah and Waltraud Schelkle (2007), 'Bringing Macroeconomics back into the Political Economy of Reform: The Lisbon Agenda and the "Fiscal Philosophy" of EMU', *Journal of Common Market Studies*, **45**(3).

McDougall, D. (1977), *Report of the Study Group on the Role of Public Finance in European Integration*, Brussels: European Commission.

Mahon, Rianne (2007), 'The Swedish Model Dying of Baumol's Disease?', *New Political Economy*, **12**(1).

Marshall, T.H. (1950), *Citizenship and Class and Other Essays*, Cambridge: Cambridge University Press.

Munchau, Wolfgang (2004), 'Europe Needs Retail Therapy', *Financial Times*, 9 May.

Munchau, Wolfgang (2006), 'Fairy Tale of the Eurozone Goldilocks Recovery', *Financial Times*, 21 August.

Nickell, Stephen (1997), 'Unemployment and Labor Market Rigidities: Europe vs. America', *Journal of Economic Perspectives*, **11**(3).

OECD (1993), *Economic Surveys: Germany*, Paris: OECD.

OECD (1999), *Historical Statistics*, Paris: OECD.

OECD (2000), *Employment Outlook*, Paris: OECD.

OECD (2003), *Economic Surveys: Euro Area 2003*, Paris: OECD.

OECD (2004), *Economic Outlook*, **75**, Paris: OECD.

OECD (2005), *Economic Outlook*, **76**, Paris: OECD.

Palier, Bruno (2000), '"Defrosting" the French Welfare State', *West European Politics*, **23**(2).

Panitch, Leo and Sam Gindin (2005), 'Superintending Global Capital', *New Left Review*, **35**.

Pierson, Paul (2001), 'Post-Industrial Pressures on the Mature Welfare States', in P. Pierson (ed.), *The New Politics of the Welfare State*, Oxford: Oxford University Press.

Quinlan, J.P. (2003), *Drifting Apart or Growing Together? The Primacy of the Transatlantic Economy*, Baltimore, MD: Paul H. Nitze School of Advanced International Relations, Johns Hopkins University.

Ramsie, Harvie (1995), 'Le Defi Europeen: Multinational Restructuring, Labour and EU Policy', in Ash Amin and John Tomaney (eds), *Behind the Myth of European Union*, London: Routledge, pp. 174–97.

Reid, T.R. (2005), *The United States of Europe: The Superpower No-One Talks About*, New York: Penguin.

Rhodes, Martin (2002), 'Why the EMU Is – or May Be – Good for European Welfare States', in K. Dyson (ed.), *European States and the Euro*, Oxford: Oxford University Press.

Rifkin, Jeremy (2004), *The European Dream: How Europe's Vision of the Future Is Quietly Eclipsing the American Dream*, Cambridge: Polity Press.

Ross, George (2004), 'Monetary Integration and the French Model', in A. Martin and G. Ross (eds), *Euros and Europeans*, Cambridge: Cambridge University Press.

Ryner, Magnus (2002), *Capitalist Restructuring, Globalisation and the Third Way: Lessons from the Swedish Model*, London: Routledge.

Ryner, Magnus (2003), 'Disciplinary Neoliberalism, Regionalization and the Social Market in German Restructuring', in Alan Cafruny and Magnus Ryner (eds),

A Ruined Fortress? Neoliberal Hegemony and Restructuring in Europe, Lanham, MD: Rowman & Littlefield.

Sassen, Saskia (1991), *The Global City: New York, London and Tokyo*, Princeton, NJ: Princeton University Press.

Scharpf, Fritz (1996), 'Negative and Positive Integration in the Political Economy of European Welfare States', in G. Marks *et al.* (eds), *Governance in the European Union*, New York: Sage.

Schmid, Josef (1998), 'Wandel der Konsensstrukturen', in G. Simonis (ed.), *Modell Deutschland nach der Wende*, Opladen: Neue Politikstrukturen.

Seabrooke, Leonard (2001), *U.S. Power in International Finance: The Victory of Dividends*, Basingstoke: Palgrave Macmillan.

Seeleib-Kaiser, Martin (2003), 'Continuity or Change? Red-Green Social Policy after 16 Years of Christian-Democratic Rule', *ZeS-Arbeitspapier*, 3, Bremen: Bremen Zentrum für Sozialpolitik.

Siegel, Nico (2004), 'EMU and German Welfare Capitalism', in A. Martin and G. Ross (eds), *Euros and Europeans*, Cambridge: Cambridge University Press.

Story, Jonathan and Ingo, Walter (1997), *The Political Economy of Financial Integration in Europe: The Battle of the Systems*, Cambridge, MA: MIT Press.

Streeck, Wolfgang and Christine Trampusch (2005), 'Economic Reform and the Political Economy of the German Welfare State', Working paper No. 2, Max Planck Institut für Gesellschaftsforschung, Cologne.

Talani, Leila S. (2005), 'The European Central Bank: Between Growth and Stability', *Comparative European Politics*, 3(2).

Tidow, Stephan (2003), 'The Emergence of European Employment Policy as a Transnational Political Arena', in H. Overbeek (ed.), *The Political Economy of European Unemployment*, London: Routledge.

Torfing, Jacob (1999), 'Workfare within Welfare: Recent Reforms of the Danish Welfare State', *Journal of European Social Policy*, 9(1).

Unger, Roberto M. (1976), *Law in Modern Society*, New York: Free Press.

van Kersbergen, Kees (1995), *Social Capitalism: Study of Christian Democracy and the Welfare State*, London: Routledge.

Visser, Jelle and Anton Hemerijck (1997), '*A Dutch Miracle': Job Growth, Welfare Reform and Corporatism in the Netherlands*, Amsterdam: Amsterdam University Press.

Wallerstein, Immanuel (2003), 'Entering Global Anarchy', *New Left Review*, 22, July/August.

Watson, Matthew (2001), 'Embedding the "New Economy" in Europe: A Study in the Institutional Specificities of Knowledge-Based Growth', *Economy and Society*, 3(4).

3. A dead Stability and Growth Pact and a strong Euro: there must be a mistake!

Leila Simona Talani

INTRODUCTION

In November 2003, the Stability and Growth Pact died at the hands of its father and mother, Germany and France.[1] Yet, contrary to all expectations the Euro did not plunge. Indeed, it remained stronger than ever and the markets did not even think about speculating on the lack of credibility of a post-SGP EMU.[2] Here a fundamental paradox arises: how can a currency strengthen in the midst of a serious crisis of fiscal rule?

This counterintuitive phenomenon raises a set of fundamental questions concerning the European macroeconomic regime after the establishment of EMU. On what is the credibility of exchange rate commitments grounded? What kind of considerations induce financial markets to keep or withdraw confidence in a currency? Is fiscal stability in any way related to exchange rate credibility?

In political science there is considerable disagreement among various interpretations of these events, ranging from intergovernmentalism to neo-constructivism.[3] At the same time, economists continue to dominate the debate about both the credibility of exchange rates and fiscal coordination in a monetary union.[4] This chapter seeks to explain the paradox within the framework of a revised, 'embedded' version of intergovernmentalism based on Andrew Moravcsik's liberal intergovernmentalism (Moravcsik, 1993a).

Intergovernmentalists would predict that, as applied to the working of the SGP, the interests of the most powerful member states prevail over those of smaller states in the ECOFIN decision-making process. Embedded inter-governmentalism traces the interests of the most powerful Euro-zone member states in the macroeconomic preferences of their leading socio-economic sectors (Talani, 2005). This means that the relaxation of the fiscal rules corresponded to the needs of the dominant socio-economic sectors in both Germany and France. However these were the same actors which had supported a strict interpretation of the fiscal rule as a founding principle of economic and monetary union through the adoption of the Maastricht requirements and of the Stability and Growth Pact. Indeed, the credibility of the monetary enterprise had been grounded on the adoption of a rigid interpretation of an anti-inflationary fiscal policy, particularly by Germany, with the full support of its leading economic elites (Moravcsik, 1998). What changed in 2003? Did the relaxation of fiscal policy indicate a lack of commitment to an anti-inflationary EMU by the most powerful European states and their leading interest groups?

This chapter claims that the shift of emphasis from strict fiscal policy to a more relaxed one implicit in the new version of the SGP (see Chapter 5) did not detract from the credibility of the member states' commitment to EMU and, therefore, did not produce a speculative attack against the Euro. This is why, after the decision by the ECOFIN not to impose sanctions on France and Germany, financial markets did not bet on a depreciation of the Euro, whose value kept on increasing vis-à-vis the Dollar. Neither did financial operators ask for higher interest rates to keep assets denominated in Euros. This chapter employs a definition of credibility of EMU rooted in the consensus of the most powerful socio-economic actors (see Chapter 1). Here, credibility derives primarily from structural considerations relating to the institutionalization of a set of favourable macroeconomic policies following from this particular form of monetary union (Gill, 1997). Adopting a tripartite distinction of the levels of analysis (Talani, 2000a), 'political economy' analysis, 'purely economic' analysis and 'purely political' analysis (see Table 3.1), it is argued here that, at the political economy, structural level, the leading socio-economic actors continued to support the set of anti-inflationary and supply-side policies that were enshrined in EMU. Indeed, it was precisely because at the purely economic level and at the purely political level the SGP had turned into an obstacle for the implementation of those same policies that its stricter constraints were abandoned for the time being by Germany and France. The second level of analysis, 'purely economic' analysis, focuses on the identification of the concrete interest groups' preferences in a short-term time scale. It is at this level that is possible to trace back changes in the attitude of socio-economic groups in relation to their macroeconomic preferences. In the context of this analysis, the economic interests of the French and German business sectors, previously relying on the devaluation of the Euro, now focused on a reduction of taxes and on the implementation of structural reforms to improve their competitiveness in the global economy (Crouch, 2002; Talani, 2007). In turn, at the political level of analysis, the adoption of structural reform in a neo-corporatist system had still to rely on the consensus of the trade unions. This means that when the external,

Table 3.1   Three-level analysis of the demise of the SGP

	Prevailing socio-economic interests in most powerful Euro-zone member states	Consequences
Political economy level	EMU credibility based on structural reforms	The crisis of the SGP provokes no reactions by financial markets
Purely economic level	Increase business competitiveness through competitive devaluations in the short term and structural reforms in the medium term	Benign neglect of the depreciation of the Euro by the ECB – the SGP becomes a straitjacket for business
Purely political level	Obtain consensus of trade unions to structural reforms	The need for tax cuts to pass structural reforms brings about the crisis of the SGP

international conditions cannot be modified by their previous institutional referents, such as the ECB, socio-economic groups and the governments supporting their interests may modify their policy preferences and decide to target other referents, such as, in this case, the ECOFIN.

On the basis of similar considerations it is possible to explain why, from 2002 onwards, given the unlikelihood that the ECB could reverse or even slow down the depreciation of the Dollar, the most powerful member states, namely Germany and France, sought to obtain a relaxation of the macroeconomic policy framework, much needed by their economic domestic actors, by loosening the grip of the SGP. The exact timing of the crisis, in turn, was defined by the political needs of the German government, which in November/December 2003 was involved in the final stages of a tough negotiation with both the opposition and the trade unions for the approval of a package of structural reforms denominated Agenda 2010 (see Chapter 4). As noted above, however, the demise of the SGP did not signify an abandonment of the EMU project, but only a short-term, contingent shift of the economic interests of the most powerful Euro-zone states. Therefore the credibility of their commitment to EMU remained intact, and the markets did not feel the need to attack the Euro in the aftermath of the abandonment of the fiscal rule or to bet against the stability of EMU asking for higher yields. In brief, the credibility of the EMU project was still rooted in structural considerations, while the decision to relax the fiscal rule was justified by a change of macroeconomic preferences by the leading socio-economic groups at the 'purely economic' and at the 'purely political' level of analysis.

Summing up, the chapter finds out, on the basis of empirical evidence, that:

● The credibility of the EMU was not undermined by the collapse and reform of the SGP.
● Financial markets hardly budged at the news of the collapse of the SGP.
● The German and French commitment to the fiscal rule of the SGP was relaxed as a consequence of the need to obtain the consensus to the structural reforms of the social partners.
● The abandonment of the SGP was often related to the strength of the Euro in domestic debates.
● The leading socio-economic sectors in the big Euro-zone countries welcomed the relaxation of the fiscal rule.

The chapter is divided into three sections. The first section reviews different theories explaining the collapse and reform of the SGP, with a particular focus on international/European political economy ones. It proposes an embedded intergovernmentalist approach to the explanation of the paradox arising from the collapse of the SGP and sets out the theoretical foundations to explain it. The second section introduces some empirical evidence. It explores the reaction of financial markets to the freezing of the SGP in November 2003 and traces back the domestic economic considerations at the roots of German and French failure to stick to the fiscal rule. It also highlights the shift of opinion of the leading socio-economic sectors in France and Germany towards the fiscal straitjacket, which the two countries had previously strongly supported. The chapter concludes by assessing the validity of various theoretical interpretations of the collapse of the SGP. It proposes an 'embedded' intergovernmentalist explanation to account for the paradox of the lack of reaction by the markets to the death of fiscal coordination in the Euro-zone.

1   THEORIZING THE DOMESTIC POLITICS OF FISCAL COORDINATION IN EUROPE

The subject of fiscal policy in EMU is still dominated by economists.[5] Recently, however, political scientists have proposed some useful analytical frameworks to explain key developments in the Euro-zone. For example, Amy Verdun has applied a neo-constructivist approach to the formation and collapse of the SGP (Heipertz and Verdun, 2004). She argues that the SGP was possible owing to a convergence in basic ideas about the relationship between monetary and fiscal policies held by experts in ministries of finance, central banks and the Commission, as well as in academia and international organizations. However, ideational convergence provided only the basis for a political compromise. The final decision to adopt it was possible thanks to the prominent position of Germany in the intergovernmental talks leading to the approval of the SGP and the creation of a convergence of interests with France in a typical power-politics fashion (Heipertz and Verdun, 2004: 1–2). However, as Verdun rightly states, 'designing rules is one thing, applying them another' (Heipertz and Verdun, 2005: 16).

In seeking to explain the (non-) application of the SGP Verdun presents an eclectic mixture of four theoretical approaches: intergovernmentalist, neo-functionalist, domestic politics and ideationalist approaches (Heipertz and Verdun, 2005: 2). The neo-functionalist and the ideationalist approaches, however, are applied mainly to the questions relating to the making of the SGP, which is out of the scope of this discussion, although Verdun acknowledges that the adoption of the SGP was conditional on an agreement between France and Germany, as intergovernmentalists would predict. As regards the implementation or non-implementation of the SGP, Verdun retains the intergovernmentalist perspective in asserting that 'France and Germany while no longer holding the same degree of influence over specific outcomes, were still able to shape events according to their national interest' (Heipertz and Verdun, 2005: 3).

Finally, Verdun utilizes a domestic politics approach to scrutinize the internal situation of the relevant governments in their respective countries: again Germany and France. Adopting a neo-institutionalist/neo-constructivist account of the role of domestic actors in the making of EMU (Dyson and Featherstone, 1996; McNamara, 1994; Martin, 1994; Sandholtz, 1993; Young, 1999) Verdun identifies as the most relevant domestic actors all political parties (in government and opposition) and the central banks. Other actors (parliaments, trade unions, etc.) were only influential on EMU and the SGP insofar as they succeeded in influencing public opinion and the national governments (Heipertz and Verdun, 2005: 10).

Thus, in seeking to explain the decision to suspend the implementation of the excessive deficit procedure (EDP) on 25 November 2003 Verdun emphasizes the desire of the French and German governments to respond to their electorates, mainly by cutting tax and therefore abandoning their fiscal pledges. This was despite the fact that in neither case were the elections close and that promises to cut tax had been broken before, particularly in France. Verdun argues here that, having broken his promises about tax cuts before, Chirac this time decided to go ahead with them, arguing that they were a necessary complement to pension reform. For Schröder, the application of the SGP in November 2003 would have implied a loss of face domestically and put oil on the fire of the opposition. Potential sanctions could have eventually become a concrete possibility in 2006, which would be an election year (Heipertz and Verdun, 2005: 15). But why did Chirac decide to cut tax in November 2003? Why was Schröder so worried about losing face with the electorate in 2003 when the elections would not be till 2006? Who wanted to cut taxes? Was the tax cut so necessary as to jeopardize the SGP that France and Germany had wanted so much? Was the cut in tax the only reason why Germany and France could not stick to the fiscal rule? And what about the credibility of EMU after this decision?

In sum, what is debatable in Verdun's analysis is whether the only relevant actors were institutional ones. The exclusive focus on governments, parties and central banks risks resulting in a rather descriptive account of the domestic politics of formal decisions, while from a more analytical point of view it would be important to ask why those decisions were taken by investigating their distributional effects. In other words, it is worth asking who wins and who loses from the making of certain decisions, and which socio-economic interests were at play. In particular, it is necessary to understand the distributive effects of the fiscal rule on socio-economic sectors.

David McKay has addressed the issue of the impact of fiscal coordination on the behaviour of domestic political actors (McKay, 2002). He identifies three dimensions of the EU fiscal policy: fiscal federalism, fiscal coordination through the implementation of the SGP, and fiscal harmonization. For each of these dimensions, he proposes hypotheses relating to the effects of fiscal policy on domestic politics. Leaving aside the questions relating to fiscal federalism and fiscal harmonization, which are outside the scope of this analysis, it is worth recalling the implications of the SGP for the domestic structure. One obvious consequence, often emphasized in the literature (Crouch, 2002; McKay, 2002; Talani, 2004), is that budgetary constraints would imply a reform of the domestic labour market structure, activating the key socio-economic domestic actors: trade unions and the employers' organizations. The rationale, in its simplified form, is that, lacking other tools to react to asymmetric shocks, Euro-zone member states would have to revert to labour market flexibility to solve their economic unbalances (Talani, 2004). What is relevant for McKay, however, is what kind of response the structural reforms brought about by the SGP will have on the electorate once it recognizes that labour market practices are being abandoned and social benefits are being reduced as a consequence of the implementation of this particular form of EMU. While some political scientists address this issue in terms of legitimization crisis (Verdun and Christensen, 2000; Weale, 1996), McKay is interested in how single countries would react to these developments. From his point of view, reactions will be different in different countries, and might produce, in times of recession, a breach of the fiscal rules adopted through the SGP. Indeed this prediction is in line with those of many economists who had forecast that the SGP would not hold in many circumstances (Eijffinger and de Haan, 2000: 92–3). And indeed, this is exactly what happened with the crisis of the SGP in November 2003. What however McKay failed to realize is that this would not have major consequence for the Euro, the ECB or indeed the EMU project. His idea was that: 'Unchallenged fiscal recidivism on the part of some members would damage the euro on the foreign exchanges, and, via imported inflation, might undermine the whole project' (McKay, 2002: 84).

But this is exactly what did not happen. Other domestic politics approaches might help to explain this seeming paradox. Colin Crouch (2002) provides an analysis of the impact of EMU and the budgetary constraints of the SGP on labour markets and trade unions. He focuses on the ways in which national governments will react to the lack of competitiveness of their labour markets in the absence of the possibility of competitive devaluations. In particular, he identifies three phases in the development of an EU industrial relation system as a consequence of the establishment of EMU: the short term, the medium term and the long term. Leaving aside the long term in which the possibility of the creation of a transnational, European collective bargaining system is envisaged (Crouch, 2002: 297), Crouch focuses particularly on the short and the medium term. In the short term, the devaluation of the Euro is considered the means by which nation states have addressed the lack of competitiveness of their industrial sectors. In this context, the policy of benign neglect towards the devaluation of the Euro, implemented by the ECB in the first years of activity (Talani, 2004), should be regarded as a short-term surrogate of the national competitive devaluations lost with the establishment of EMU. As a consequence, it was accepted with great enthusiasm by the socio-economic sectors of the main members of the Euro-zone hoping for an export-orientated growth of their economies (Crouch, 2002: 282). It is important to note that according to Crouch this policy was perfectly in line with the previous behaviour of Germany, which had relied on a weak although stable currency for most of the 1970s (Crouch, 1994; Streeck, 1994). It is also consistent with the intergovernmentalist view that Germany decided to enter EMU to guarantee a stable but slightly less strong currency to its industrial sector (Moravcsik, 1998).

Crouch argues, however, that the Euro-devaluation strategy could not be sustained for too long, and would be substituted in the medium term by social pacts and labour market reforms. What is particularly important here is that, according to Crouch, structural reforms in the Euro-zone member states would take place in a neo-corporatist fashion (for similar arguments see Boyer, 2000; Marsden, 1992; Pochet, 1998). Neo-corporatism is defined more as action coordination amongst social partners than institutionalization of corporatist practices. It can take various forms, including organized decentralization, which is defined as 'a shift away from centralised bargaining managed by employers' organisations and trade unions' (Crouch, 2002: 293). In turn, the relationship between the government and the social partners is one of mutual dependence, as the government needs consensus of the social partners to ensure smooth acceptance by the electorate of the structural, welfare policy reform, while social partners, particularly trade unions, need neo-corporatism to keep being involved in the decision-making process (Crouch, 2002: 285). This is true, according to Crouch, for the great majority of western European countries, excluding only the UK. Also according to Martin Rhodes (2002), the reform of the labour markets and of the welfare state would not happen in a deregulatory fashion, but through a neo-corporatist strategy or, better, as he calls it, 'competitive corporatism' (Rhodes, 1997). Paradoxically, EMU, instead of decreasing the power of social partners, increases their role in the welfare and wage bargaining processes. For our purposes it is important to note that these neo-corporatist practices entail that structural reforms need to rely on the consensus of the social partners. Indeed, as Dyson points out (2002: 182), Schröder, his economic adviser Klaus Gretshmann, finance minister Hans Eichel, economics minister Werner Muller and labour and social affairs minister Walter Riester all agreed that the way for Germany to improve its competitiveness was 'managed capitalism'. Managed capitalism required cooperation, coordination in wage bargaining, dialogue with the social partners and consensus in managing supply-side reforms. Consensus was indeed the main principle of managed capitalism and was deeply entrenched in both the political and the economic German systems (Dyson, 2002). By the same token, France's recipe to combat the loss of competitiveness attached to globalization implied a short-term reliance on competitive devaluation and a medium-term consensus by the social partners to structural reforms (Crouch, 2002). It is true that, since Mitterrand's decision in 1983 to keep the Franc in the ERM, the process of European monetary integration had been seen as a tool to reinforce domestic economic reform. However, particularly after German re-unification, the constraints of EMU were increasingly blamed for the French economic crisis (Howarth, 2002). Indeed, the substantial decline of the Euro in relation to the Dollar and the Yen suited French preferences. Throughout the 1990s the French government had argued that European currencies were overvalued in relation to the Dollar (Howarth, 2002). My interpretation is that in both Germany and

France consensus to structural reform in the absence of the possibility of a devaluation of the Euro would mean relaxing the adherence to the SGP budgetary constraints. However, this would not reduce the credibility of the EMU project because it would signal a change of preferences of the socio-economic groups only at the level of purely economic or purely political interests, and not at the political economy level.

2   A DEAD STABILITY AND GROWTH PACT AND A STRONG EURO: IS THERE A MISTAKE?

'Refrigerated', 'hospitalised', 'dead':[6] these were the adjectives the press used to describe the SGP on the eve of the historical ECOFIN decision not to impose sanctions on the delinquent French and German fiscal stances. The fate of the SGP was settled in the early hours of 25 November 2003 in what was a true institutional crisis between the European Commission and the ECB on one side, demanding that the rules be applied, and the inter-governmentalist ensemble of the Euro-zone finance ministers rejecting the application of sanctions to the leading EU member states.[7]

The positions were clear: Romano Prodi, the European Commission president, and Jean-Claude Trichet, the European Central Bank president, led demands for the rules to be applied. Smaller countries, led by Gerrit Zalm, the Dutch finance minister, claimed Germany was exporting its excessive budget deficit to other countries through higher interest rates.[8] Hans Eichel, the German finance minister, refused to accept the Commission recommendation, backed by the threat of sanctions, to make a further €6 billion ($7billion, £4.2 billion) of budget cuts in 2004.[9] France, overshooting the 3 per cent deficit to GDP rule for the second time in a row,[10] supported Germany, as did Italy, holder of the rotating EU presidency. The Italian EU presidency pushed through a political declaration asking France and Germany to bring their deficits within the 3 per cent limit by 2005, but lifting the threat of fines if they failed. Eventually, the Italian compromise proposal, put forward by Giulio Tremonti, chair of the meeting, was approved by the ECOFIN. Only Austria, the Netherlands, Finland and Spain voted against this political declaration to suspend the operations of the Stability Pact for Germany and France.

The atmosphere after the meeting was heated. Nervous ministers and EU leaders raged over the decision to freeze the pact. Yet all of this *Sturm und Drang* contrasted with the reaction of the markets, which accepted the decision calmly and did not budge at the news of the collapse of the pact, and this despite the fact that economists and financial experts had warned on many occasions, even on the day of the crisis,[11] that Euro-zone states should take into consideration the reaction of financial markets before deciding to scrap the European fiscal rule.

Markets were supposed to have a disciplinary effect on member states. Cassandras proclaimed that a departure from fiscal discipline by a particular government was supposed to trigger a run on the Euro and reduce investments in the whole area. A reduced demand for bonds denominated in Euros would have meant higher yields and higher borrowing costs.[12] Indeed, in the immediate aftermath of the pact's suspension the ECB indicated that the collapse of the pact could force up Euro-zone interest rates. Gerrit Zalm, the Dutch finance minister and one of the fiercest critics of the deal, warned of higher long-term interest rates.[13]

What happened to financial markets after the crisis of 25 November? How did foreign exchange markets react to the bad news coming from Brussels? How did bond yields move as a consequence of the loss of creditworthiness of the Euro-zone fiscal straitjacket? Surprisingly enough, hardly anyone in the financial markets mourned the death of the SGP.[14] The Euro slipped less than half a cent, from about $1.181 at the opening to about $1.177 in the late afternoon on 25 November, but the following day it had already recovered to $1.828, to continue rising happily vis-à-vis the Dollar thereafter (Figure 3.1).

The reaction in the bond markets was similar: interest rates on European government bonds relative to US Treasuries barely twitched. By the close,

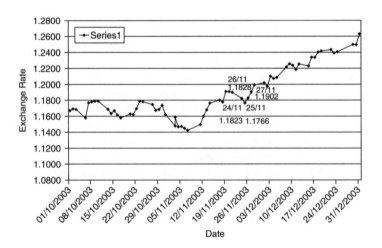

Source: ECB

Figure 3.1   Euro-dollar daily nominal exchange rates, October/November 2003

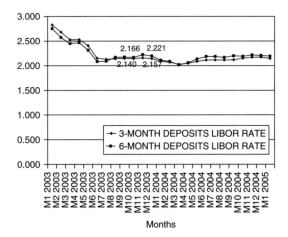

Source: IFS on-line

Figure 3.2 Euro LIBOR, 2003–05

the FTSE Eurotop 300 index was virtually unchanged untroubled by the suspension of the European Union's Stability Pact.[15] Both the 3 months and the 6 months Euro LIBOR deposit rates remained substantially stable (Figure 3.2). Yields (interest rates) on German and Italian long-term bonds actually decreased by about one basis point (0.01 percentage point) from 25 November 2003 to 26 November 2003.[16] In sum, markets reacted calmly. Yields on German government bonds, for example, rose less than US Treasury yields from their low in June 2003. The concerns expressed by the ECB that the crisis would necessarily bring about an increase of the Euro area repurchasing rates failed to impress the financial sector.

Perhaps even more strikingly, the Euro-zone was the place to invest in 2003. Since the start of the year, equity markets in Germany, France, Italy and Spain rose by 33 per cent, 14 per cent, 17 per cent and 25 per cent respectively. Americans had even more reason to buy European assets. With the 20 per cent appreciation of the Euro, the Dollar return on investing in German equities was some 57 per cent, far higher even than investing in the soaring Nasdaq index.[17] Overall, the decision by European finance ministers to freeze the mechanics of the Euro-zone's Stability and Growth Pact was expected to underpin the economic recovery.[18]

'Our view is that it is not that big a deal,' declared Ben Broadbent of Goldman Sachs.

'It's a good thing that the stability pact in its strictest interpretation is dead . . its interpretation is moving in the direction of allowing more

Table 3.2   Exports to US, quantity of goods (100 kg)

Month	Ratio over same month previous year			
	Germany	Euro-zone	France	Italy
July03/July02	95	94	111	92
Aug 03/Aug 02	64	87	101	117
Sept03/Sept02	101	98	105	90
Oct03/Oct02	66	83	73	73
Nov03/Nov02	79	81	80	70
Dec03/Dec02	102	90	91	62
AVG	85	89	93	84

Source: Eurostat

cyclical leeway for budget deficits during economic downturns, and that is something that we think should have been there from the beginning.'[19] Michael Hartnett, strategist for Merrill Lynch, proclaimed that: 'In the medium term, anything that boosts growth expectations in Europe is positive for the euro.'[20] The relaxation of the pact was intended by the financial community as a means for Europe's leading countries to introduce tax cuts and spending that will give their economies a boost. 'A bit of fiscal stimulus is really needed in Europe to get these economies going,' in the words of Karen Olney, strategist at Dresdner Kleinwort Wasserstein. Hartnett added that 'Markets have been concerned for some time about the growth potential in Europe and one of the concerns has been about the handcuffs of the inflation target and the stability and growth pact.'[21] In fact, investors had also been focusing much more on the US economy and the direction of the Dollar than on the Euro-zone. For example, Bear Stearns strategists had made it explicit in a note to clients that there would not be a better time to bury the Stability Pact. 'The eyes of the world are on the fragility of the dollar and this has provided the perfect smokescreen to pull the teeth out of the stability pact without the euro screaming', the broker claimed.

The behaviour of the financial operators clearly supports the initial suspicion that the crisis and collapse of the Stability and Growth Pact had little to do with the lack of credibility of the European monetary union, which remained substantially unquestioned by the markets. Instead, it was rooted in purely economic and purely political considerations, regarding mainly the capacity of France and Germany to emerge from their economic crisis without impairing the achievement of structural reforms. The markets simply knew that, with a depreciating Dollar and an impotent ECB, the only way for the biggest Euro-zone countries to pull out of the

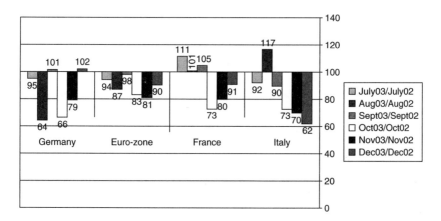

Source: Eurostat, elaboration of the author

Figure 3.3 Exports to US (quantity) (ratio over same month previous year)

economic crisis was to relax their fiscal policy, allowing for tax cuts and some increase in expenditure. This, in turn, was what socio-economic actors were asking in exchange for the implementation of structural reforms. And this is why no one in the financial world mourned the death of the SGP from the hands of its father and mother, France and Germany.

The financial sector had already warned on many occasions that the strength of the Euro was not helping the economic revival of the Euro-zone. Indeed, in May 2003 the level of exports from Euro-land had decreased by 5.3 per cent with respect to the same month of the previous year, and in June the fall was 8.6 per cent.[22] Of course, the fall was particularly worrying in the bilateral trade with the US and the biggest EU economies (Table 3.2).

On average, Germany lost 15 per cent of its exports in goods to the US over the previous year between July and December 2003, France 7 per cent, Italy 16 per cent and the Euro-zone overall 11 per cent (Eurostat) (Figure 3.3).

Given that in 2002 the US absorbed 17 per cent of exports from the Euro-zone (Eurostat), those figures were considered relevant.[23] Moreover, the fiscal straitjacket was increasingly deemed unsustainable by both financial markets and domestic actors.[24]

The difficulties of the three biggest Euro-zone countries in sticking to the pact were indeed well known. When the pact was frozen for Germany, the country had already breached the 3 per cent deficit-to-GDP rule for the third time. The government's deficit for the year 2003 amounted to €43.4 billion, more than twice the €18.9 billion figure originally envisaged.[25] The

German finance minister, Eichel, asked for a relaxation of the fiscal rule on the basis that the economic situation of the country would not be able to sustain further subsidy cuts to cover a shortfall in the following year's budget of €6 billion ($7.1 billion, £4.2 billion). Commentators noticed that such an amount, measured against a planned €22 billion tax cut for the following year, hardly seemed insurmountable. 'With federal and regional governments accounting for just under half of Germany's GDP of about €2,000 billion, you would think they could have found €6 billion', noted Elga Bartsch, a Morgan Stanley economist, in an interview to the FT.[26]

What was really at stake in the internal debate in Germany? The main point was that, for the economy to grow faster, structural reforms, including the labour law, tax and social security reforms, had to be adopted. However, as pointed out above, this would require a strong socio-economic consensus. Indeed, the crisis of the SGP happened in the midst of the talks over Agenda 2010. The talks were expected to last until mid-December, and the government was trapped between the opposition-dominated upper House of Parliament and the necessity to keep social consensus on the hard set of measures the reform entailed. In this context the Social Democratic government feared a loss of bargaining power if it was seen by the social actors as unable to control the country's fiscal policy.[27] The German chancellor, in an interview to *La Repubblica* in August 2003,[28] had already anticipated that the German government attached great importance to an interpretation of the SGP focusing on growth more than stability and that the objectives of the structural and fiscal reform made it necessary to adopt a more flexible interpretation of the pact. Hans Eichel reiterated, in an interview to the *FT* on 17 November, that the problem for Germany was not so much stability as growth.[29]

Germany was a stronghold of price stability. At 1.2 per cent, the German inflation rate was the lowest in the EU. The crucial challenge for Germany was to promote sustainable growth. The means by which the German government had planned to increase growth was Agenda 2010. This entailed undertaking far-reaching reforms in the social system. At the same time, the measure had to be accompanied by bringing forward the third stage of tax reform to 2004. Again, it was clear that an adaptable interpretation of the SGP was the price to pay to obtain the necessary consensus to Agenda 2010.

When the reform package was approved, in mid-December 2003, then the negotiating positions of the social actors were clearly revealed.[30] The adoption of the bills, in an unprecedented voting marathon by parliamentarians, marked the end of nine months of often strident talks since the chancellor had unveiled Agenda 2010 on 14 March. German chancellor Gerhard Schröder had struck a landmark political deal on economic reforms with opposition leaders, but was forced to compromise on the volume of tax cuts for the year 2004. In June the German chancellor decided that a €15.6 billion ($19.2 billion, £11 billion) tax cut that should have started in 2005 would be brought forward by a year, to be financed largely by new debt. The tax cut had been the price trade unions wanted in exchange for very tough labour and social security reforms.[31] The latter included new exclusions from Germany's strict job protection rules for companies with up to ten employees, and sharp cuts in unemployment benefits for the long-term unemployed. Jobless people would in future also be forced to accept jobs below local wage levels.

The CDU withdrew demands for a law to increase collective bargaining flexibility at the local level, settling instead for a joint declaration that this would be necessary in a year's time if such flexibility was not achieved on a non-regulatory basis. Heinrich Oberreuter, politics professor at Passau University, commented that compromises arose because both sides could ill afford failure: the chancellor because his political reputation hung on implementing his Agenda 2010 programme, and the opposition because it feared a popular backlash if it blocked the tax cuts.[32]

The DGB trade union federation welcomed the tax cuts but complained that the relaxation of job protection rules would leave 5.3 million employees without this protection. The agenda was welcomed by business as an important first step towards broader structural reforms.[33]

It was paradoxical that trade unions and the left-wing parties had supported tax cuts, while the CDU had fought to reduce them. That was an entirely political decision taken by Angela Merkel, CDU leader, which was not supported by business. The CDU withheld its support to tarnish the government's reputation for implementing reforms and to further undermine the SPD's poor poll ratings.[34] In sum, the tax cuts, and the related breach of the 3 per cent deficit to GDP for the following year, could count on the support of all the relevant socio-economic sectors in Germany.[35]

Equally broad was societal support to French abandonment of the Stability and Growth Pact. When Paris defaulted on the deficit-to-GDP ratio in November 2003, it was the second time in a row, and the excessive deficit procedure had been started already in 2002.[36] Given the economic downturn, the Commission had granted France an extra year to comply with the 3 per cent rule. In 2003 the Commission expected a French deficit of 4.2 per cent of GDP based on a real annual growth rate of 0.1 per cent. The deficit was forecasted to fall to 3.8 per cent the following year, assuming a growth rate of 1.7 per cent. This was judged insufficient to a return to below 3 per cent in 2005. Therefore the Commission asked for an additional 0.4 per cent cut in the cyclically adjusted budget deficit on top of the cuts already included in the budget.[37]

The French government argued that the Commission's plan would destabilize the economy and refused to comply with the request. In turn, French economic difficulties were explicitly related to the performance of the Euro.[38] A strong Euro was a problem for the French government, not only because it impaired the recovery of the French economy, but, most importantly, because it represented a potentially explosive subject in both the internal and the external debate in France.[39]

In May 2003, when the Euro was valued 1.15 to a Dollar, Jean-Pierre Raffarin defined this level as 'préoccupant' (worrying). The opponents of the strong Euro had to be found amongst the same groups who had opposed the policy of the 'Franc fort' (the strong Franc).[40] The ECB was accused of being unable to guarantee the competitiveness of the Euro-zone.[41] Moreover, it would have been necessary for the ECB to explain why an average deficit GDP of 2.6 per cent in the Euro-zone should be considered a bigger inflationist threat than a deficit to GDP of 5 per cent in the US or 7 per cent in Japan.[42] Therefore, the decision of the ECOFIN not to impose any sanction on France and Germany was welcomed in the French internal debate as a legitimate re-nationalization of the economic policies.[43]

As far as Italy was concerned, Silvio Berlusconi, the Italian prime minister, had called on many occasions for a looser interpretation of the rules of the SGP.[44] He also indicated that the ECB should loosen its monetary policy in view of Europe's difficult economic situation. In October 2003 he claimed that: 'The main remit of the ECB is to combat inflation, but combating inflation obviously has to be reviewed when the economy is stagnating.'[45] This comment was one of the strongest pleas by a European head of government for the ECB to focus more on helping revive economic growth in the Euro-zone. Berlusconi proposed that the 3 per cent should not be taken as an absolute value beyond discussion and might be adjusted down by one or two percentage points or up to 4 or 5 per cent in the case of economic stagnation. Besides, the Stability Pact, the EU and the Euro were to be blamed for the economic stagnation of Italy.[46]

Did Berlusconi's position reflect the opinion of the leading Italian socio-economic actors? Mr D'Amato, then leader of Confindustria, in the course of the debate over the approval of the budget in September 2003, had reminded the government that it should not sacrifice stimulating growth to the SGP objective of controlling the deficit. This basically meant that, despite the restraints imposed by the SGP, the government should keep the fiscal level low and should allow for investment-related expenditure and public investments, including research and development.[47] In his words: 'The Stability Pact is becoming a cage of over-regulation and high taxes which does not protect but threatens its goods.'[48] Of course, cuts had to focus on the health care system and, more controversially, on the planned reform of the pension scheme. And of course the trade unions, CGIL, CISL and UIL, strongly opposed similar cuts and were organizing, in autumn 2003, a general strike against the proposed change of the pension law (the so-called 'Dini law'). With regard to the SGP, the general secretary of the CGIL asserted that keeping the debt-to-GDP ratio stable implied a de facto reduction in social expenditure.[49]

It was therefore not surprising that, when the pact was eventually suspended for France and Germany, the Italian political elite, as well as societal groups, did not mourn its death for too long, if at all.[50] Only Romano Prodi, then president of the EU, and Carlos Azeglio Ciampi, the Italian president, were left defending the fiscal rule. The whole Italian government, instead, expressed its consensus to the decision of the ECOFIN, which was publicly defined as wise and responsible.[51]

As far as the social partners were concerned, the president of Confindustria underlined that if the constraints of the Stability Pact could be justified at the onset of EMU, in the light of the latest events they had to be reinterpreted, discussed and redefined.[52] According to Savino Pezzotta, leader of the CISL, the pact was not a totem to which to sacrifice everything, but an agreement amongst sovereign states. For Guglielmo Epifani of CGIL, the rules had to be changed for everyone, not only for France and Germany.

CONCLUSIONS: AN ALTERNATIVE DOMESTIC POLITICS ACCOUNT OF THE DEMISE OF THE SGP

Were the markets mistaken in failing to react to the demise of the SGP in November 2003? What was the market rationale behind their somewhat surprising display of coolness and *sang-froid* in the aftermath of the failure of Germany and France to respect the fiscal rule? This chapter sought to answer these questions by adopting an embedded intergovernmentalist perspective to the suspension of the SGP in 2003, based on the assumption that the credibility of exchange rate regimes is dependent on the consensus to it by the leading socio-economic groups of the most powerful member states.

In November 2003 this commitment was not put in doubt by the failure of Germany and France to respect the fiscal constraints of the SGP. Financial markets knew this, and did not question either the credibility of the Euro or the survival of the monetary union. Some scholars have explained this paradox by claiming that the economic pact of the governments with the markets remained intact and therefore the markets did not react.[53] This however leaves open the question of the reasons why the crisis happened at the end of November 2003, and not later or before. Indeed, what was put in doubt by the leading socio-economic groups in Germany was the necessity of sticking to the 3 per cent deficit-to-GDP rule at a precise historical moment. This happened because their contingent macro-economic preferences, what have been termed in the theoretical context their 'purely economic interests', as well as, particularly in the case of Germany, their political needs, changed and required the abandonment of the pact for the time being.

What were those purely economic interests and purely political needs that provoked the German decision to throw all its weight in the ECOFIN to avoid imposition of sanctions and made France and Italy and many others follow suit? In the case of Germany the answer is that at precisely the same time when the EDP was being put into question, Chancellor Schröder was involved in the very late stages of very delicate negotiations over the approval of the structural reform package denominated Agenda 2010. The reform was crucial to the interests of the business sector, which actively supported it but needed the approval of the trade unions, and because part of the electoral constituency of the Social Democratic government coincided with the pool of organized workers and pensioners who would be hit hard by the programmed structural reforms. And the trade unions required, in exchange for their consensus to Agenda 2010, a wave of tax cuts and increase in expenditures hardly compatible with the fiscal rule. This interpretation of the timing of the crisis is indeed consistent with all analyses dealing with the new involvement of trade unions in a neo-corporatist, managed capitalist or competitive corporatist fashion in the restructuring of the labour markets and in their flexibilization. In turn, the business sector not only was actively supporting structural reforms in Germany, but was also pleased by the fiscal reform, which was opposed only by Mrs Merkel in an attempt to gain some political traction by placing the blame for the failure of the agreement on the chancellor. Indeed, following Crouch, it can be argued that the most relevant worry of the Continental European industrial sector, and, given the nature of the capitalist structure of France and Germany, also of the banking sector (Dyson, 2002), was to improve their competitiveness. The standard tool that Germany, France and Italy, for that matter, had traditionally reverted to in order to increase competitiveness was devaluation. And in the short term the devaluation of the Euro within EMU appeased the business sectors' worries. However, as the Euro started rising again vis-à-vis the Dollar, the French and the Italian business sectors started showing signs of hostility towards the fiscal constraints. When the occasion came, the mighty German economy, for reasons explained above, decided that the pact could be put on ice. The French and the Italian socio-economic actors were more than happy to help.

In conclusion, consensus on the broader project of EMU did not weaken and the markets had no reasons to attack the Euro or to bet against the stability of the Euro by asking higher yields to assets held denominated in Euros. What had changed were the short-term, contingent economic and political preferences of the leading socio-economic sectors and that provoked a suspension of the pact which appeared to the financial markets as an entirely 'natural' outcome.

NOTES

1. For a very thorough account of the role of France and Germany in the making of the SGP see Heipertz and Verdun (2005).
2. See section 2 of this chapter.
3. See Chapter 1 of this book.
4. For the most recent literature see Allsopp and Artis (2003); Annett *et al.* (2005); Artis (2002); Artis and Buti (2000); Balassone and Franco (2000); Balassone *et al.* (2004); Begg and Schelkle (2004); Buti and Franco (2005); Eijffinger (2005); Wren-Lewis (2003); and Wyplosz (2002, 2005).
5. For the most recent literature see Allsopp and Artis (2003); Annett *et al.* (2005); Artis (2002); Artis and Buti (2000); Balassone and Franco (2000); Balassone *et al.* (2004); Begg and Schelkle (2004); Buti and Franco (2005); Eijffinger (2005); Wren-Lewis (2003); and Wyplosz (2002, 2005).
6. See George Parker, 'Europe's Stability Pact: Ministers Conduct Late-Night Burial for EU Fiscal Framework', *Financial Times*, 26 November 2003.
7. See Heipertz and Verdun (2004).
8. See George Parker and Bertrand Benoit, 'Europe: France and Germany May Escape EU Fines', *Financial Times*, 25 November 2003.
9. In 2001, Germany was coming close to the reference value with a budget deficit of 2.8 per cent of GDP. With the budget deficit reaching 3.5 per cent of GDP for 2002, ECOFIN was forced to issue a recommendation to Germany in January 2003. Initially, the German government seemed determined to tackle the deficit head on and bring it back below the 3 per cent threshold. However, as German economic growth continued to decline, the government was unable to abide by its commitment and ran a deficit of 3.8 per cent of GDP in 2003.
10. France's 2002 fiscal deficit was 3.2 per cent of GDP. It increased to 4.1 and 3.7 per cent of GDP in 2003 and 2004, respectively.
11. See Lorenzo Codogno, 'Comment: The Eurozone Cannot Escape Market Discipline', *Financial Times*, 25 November 2004.
12. See Codogno *et al.* (2003); and Dornbusch (1997).
13. See 'Prodi Calls for EU Economic Governance Plan', *Financial Times*, 25 November 2003.
14. See Ed Crooks, 'Europe's Stability Pact: EU May Yet Feel the Bite of Paper Tiger', *Financial Times*, 26 November 2003.
15. See Michael Morgan, 'FT Markets: Indices Unmoved by "Exceptional" Figures', *Financial Times*, 26 November 2003.
16. See Leblond (2005).
17. See 'Leader: Europe's Challenge', *Financial Times*, 20 December 2003.
18. See Deborah Hargreaves, 'Market Insight: A Kickstart for the Eurozone?', FT.com, 25 November 2003.
19. See Ed Crooks, 'Europe's Stability Pact: EU May Yet Feel the Bite of Paper Tiger', *Financial Times*, 26 November 2003.

20. See Ed Crooks, 'Europe's Stability Pact: EU May Yet Feel the Bite of Paper Tiger', *Financial Times*, 26 November 2003.
21. See Ed Crooks, 'Europe's Stability Pact: EU May Yet Feel the Bite of Paper Tiger', *Financial Times*, 26 November 2003.
22. See 'Export e disoccupazione i punti deboli di Eurolandia', *La Repubblica*, 8 August 2003.
23. In 2003 it was 15.76 per cent and in 2004 15.07 per cent. See http://epp.eurostat. cec.eu.int/extraction/retrieve/en/theme6/et_ybk/maintot_ez?OutputDir=EJOutputDir_ 1463&user=unknown&clientsessionid=F5685B86525321A6FF705C7198E21971.extra ction-worker-1&OutputFile=maintot_ez.htm&OutputMode=U&NumberOfCells=6& Language=en&OutputMime=text %2Fhtml&.
24. See 'Export e disoccupazione i punti deboli di Eurolandia', *La Repubblica*, 8 August 2003.
25. See Bertrand Benoit and Tobias Buck, 'Europe: Berlin to Breach Deficit Rules in 2004', *Financial Times*, 24 October 2003.
26. See George Parker and Bertrand Benoit, 'Europe: France and Germany May Escape EU Fines', *Financial Times*, 25 November 2003.
27. See George Parker and Bertrand Benoit, 'Europe: France and Germany May Escape EU Fines', *Financial Times*, 25 November 2003.
28. See Andrea Tarquini, 'Schroeder: giustizia sociale, non solo mercati', *La Repubblica*, 27 August 2003.
29. See Hans Eichel, 'Comment: The Stability Pact Is Not a Blunt Instrument', *Financial Times*, 17 November 2003.
30. See Bertrand Benoit, 'Europe: German Economic Reform Package Passed at Last', *Financial Times*, 20 December 2003.
31. For a very detailed account of the reasons why trade unions wanted tax cuts see Marzinotto (2005).
32. See Bertrand Benoit, 'Europe: German Economic Reform Package Passed at Last', *Financial Times*, 20 December 2003.
33. See Bertrand Benoit, 'Europe: German Economic Reform Package Passed at Last', *Financial Times*, 20 December 2003.
34. See Bertrand Benoit, 'Europe: German Economic Reform Package Passed at Last', *Financial Times*, 20 December 2003.
35. See Hugh Williamson, 'Europe: Tax Cuts Threaten to Undermine a "Positive" Compromise', *Financial Times*, 16 December 2003.
36. See Leblond (2005).
37. See Charles Wyplosz, 'Le pacte de stabilité, machine infernale', *Le monde*, 8 November 2003.
38. See 'Un nouveau dossier brûlant pour Jean-Pierre Raffarin', *Le monde*, 10 December 2003.
39. See 'Un nouveau dossier brûlant pour Jean-Pierre Raffarin', *Le monde*, 10 December 2003.
40. See 'Un nouveau dossier brûlant pour Jean-Pierre Raffarin', *Le monde*, 10 December 2003.
41. See 'Le pacte des hypocrites', *Le monde*, 4 December 2003.
42. See 'Le pacte des hypocrites', *Le monde*, 4 December 2003.
43. See 'UE: la victoire des égoïsmes nationaux', *Le monde*, 16 December 2003.
44. See Raphael Minder, 'International News: Berlusconi Calls for Easing of Stability Pact', *Financial Times*, 23 October 2003.
45. See Raphael Minder, 'International News: Berlusconi Calls for Easing of Stability Pact', *Financial Times*, 23 October 2003.
46. See 'Il premier parla a un convegno della Confindustria Europea', *La Repubblica*, 14 November 2003.
47. See 'Per viale dell'Astronomia la manovra correttiva per il 2004 rischia di essere più ampia di quella prevista dal governo', *La Repubblica*, 10 September 2003.
48. See 'Il premier parla a un convegno della Confindustria Europea', *La Repubblica*, 14 November 2003.

49. See Riccardo de Gennaro, 'Slitta la manovra, governo diviso su condono e pensioni', *La Repubblica*, 24 September 2003.
50. See 'Il presidente della Commissione Ue prende ancora le distanze sul blocco delle sanzioni per Francia e Germania', *La Repubblica*, 27 November 2003.
51. See 'Il presidente della Commissione Ue prende ancora le distanze sul blocco delle sanzioni per Francia e Germania', *La Repubblica*, 27 November 2003.
52. See 'Il presidente della Commissione Ue prende ancora le distanze sul blocco delle sanzioni per Francia e Germania', *La Repubblica*, 27 November 2003.
53. See Leblond (2005).

BIBLIOGRAPHY

Allsopp, C. and M. Artis (2003), 'The Assessment: EMU Four Years On', *Oxford Review of Economic Policy*, **19**(1): 1–29.

Annett, A., J. Decressin and M. Deppler (2005), 'Reforming the Stability and Growth Pact', *IMF Policy Discussion Paper*, PDP/05/2.

Artis, M.J. (2002), 'The Stability and Growth Pact: Fiscal Policy in the EMU', in F. Breuss, G. Fink, and S. Griller (eds), *Institutional, Legal and Economic Aspects of the EMU*, New York: Springer.

Artis, M.J. and M. Buti (2000), 'Close to Balance or in Surplus: A Policy Maker's Guide to Implementation of the Stability and Growth Pact', *Journal of Common Market Studies*, **38**(4): 563–92. Edited version in Buti and Franco (2005).

Balassone, F. and D. Franco (2000), 'Public Investment, the Stability Pact and the Golden Rule', *Fiscal Studies*, **21**(2): 207–29. Edited version in Buti and Franco (2005).

Balassone, F., D. Franco, and R. Giordano (2004), 'Market Induced Fiscal Discipline: Is There a Fallback Solution for Rule-Failure?', mimeo, Banca d'Italia: 389–426, available at www.ceistorvergata.it/conferenze&convegni/mondragone/XVI_papers/Paper-balassone-franco-giordano(06.04)pdf, accessed 19 November 2007.

Begg, I. and W. Schelkle (2004), 'The Pact is Dead: Long Live the Pact', *National Institute Review*, **189**: 86–98.

Boyer, R. (2000), 'The Unanticipated Fall Out of the European Monetary Union: The Political and Institutional Deficit of the Euro', in C. Crouch (ed.), *After the Euro: Shaping Institutions for Governance in the Wake of European Monetary Union*, London: Oxford University Press.

Buti, M. and D. Franco (2005), *Fiscal Policy in EMU: Theory, Evidence and Institutions*, Cheltenham, UK and Northampton, MA, USA: Edward Elgar.

Codogno, L., C. Favero and A. Missale (2003), 'Yield Spreads on EMU Government Bonds', *Economic Policy*, October

Crouch, C. (1994), 'Incomes Policies, Institutions and Markets: An Overview of Recent Developments', in R. Dore, R. Boyer and Z. Mars (eds), *The Return to Incomes Policies*, London: Pinter.

Crouch, C. (2002), 'The Euro, and Labour Markets and Wage Policies', in K. Dyson (ed.), *European States and the Euro*, London: Oxford University Press.

Dornbusch, R. (1997), 'Fiscal Aspects of Monetary Integration', *American Economic Review*, **87**(2): 221–3.

Dyson, K. (2000), *The Politics of the Euro-zone*, Oxford: Oxford University Press, Scholarship Online.

Dyson, K. (2002), 'Germany and the Euro: Redefining EMU, Handling Paradox and Managing Uncertainty and Contingency', in K. Dyson (ed.), *European States and the Euro*, London: Oxford University Press.

Dyson, K.H.F. and K. Featherstone (1996), 'Italy and EMU as Vincolo Esterno', *Journal of South European Society and Politics*, **2**(3): 272–99.

Eichengreen, B., A. Rose and C. Wyplosz (1995), 'Exchange Market Mayhem: The Antecedents and Aftermaths of Speculative Attacks', *Economic Policy*, **21**: 249–312.

Eijffinger, S.C.W. (2005), 'On a Reformed Stability and Growth Pact', *Intereconomics*, **40**(3): 141–7.

Eijffinger, S. and J. De Haan, (2000), *European Monetary and Fiscal Policy*, Oxford: Oxford University Press.

Engelmann, D., H.J. Knopf, K. Roscher and T. Risse (1997) 'Identity Politics in the European Union: The Case of Economic and Monetary Union', in P. Minkkinen and H. Potomaki (eds), *The Politics of Economic and Monetary Union*, Dordrecht: Kluwer Academic Publishers.

Frieden, J. (1991), 'Invested Interests: The Politics of National Economic Policies in a World of Global Finance', *International Organization*, **45**.

Frieden, J. (1994), 'The Impact of Goods and Capital Market Integration on European Monetary Politics', Preliminary version, August.

Frieden, J., D. Gros and E. Jones (1998), *The New Political Economy of EMU*, Oxford: Rowman & Littlefield.

Gill, S. (1997), 'An EMU or an Ostrich: EMU and Neo-liberal Economic Integration Limits and Alternatives', in P. Minkkinen and H. Potomaki (eds), *The Politics of Economic and Monetary Union*, London: Kluwer.

Heipertz, M. and A. Verdun (2004), 'The Dog that Would Never Bite? What We Can Learn from the Origins of the Stability Pact', *Journal of European Public Policy*, **11**(5), October: 765–80.

Heipertz, M. and A. Verdun (2005), 'The Stability and Growth Pact: Theorising a Case in European Integration', Paper prepared for delivery at the Ninth Biennial International European Union Studies Association Conference, Austin, TX, 31 March – 2 April.

Howarth, D. (2002), 'The French State in the Euro-zone: Modernization and legitimising dirigisme', in K. Dyson (ed.), *European States and the Euro*, London: Oxford University Press.

Leblang, D.A. (2002), 'The Political Economy of Speculative Attacks in the Developing World', *International Studies Quarterly*, **46**(1), March: 69–93.

Leblond, P. (2005), 'The Political Stability and Growth Pact Is Dead. Long Live the Economic Stability and Growth Pact', Paper presented at the Political and Economic Consequences of European Monetary Integration Conference, University of Victoria, BC, 18–19 August.

McKay, D. (1999), 'The Political Sustainability of European Monetary Union', *British Journal of Political Science*, **29**: 481.

McKay, D. (2002), 'The Political Economy of Fiscal Policy under Monetary Union', in K. Dyson (ed.), *European States and the Euro*, London: Oxford University Press.

McNamara, K.R. (1994), 'Economic and Monetary Union: Do Domestic Politics Really Matter?', Paper presented at the American Political Science Association Annual Meeting.

McNamara, K. (1998), *The Currency of Ideas: Monetary Politics in the European Union*, Ithaca, NY: Cornell University Press.

Marsden, D. (1992), 'Incomes Policy for Europe? Or Will Pay Bargaining Destroy the Single European Market?', *British Journal of Industrial Relations*, **30**: 587–604.

Martin, L.L. (1994), 'International and Domestic Institutions in the EMU Process', in B.J. Eichengreen and J.A. Frieden (eds), *The Political Economy of European Monetary Unification*, Boulder, CO: Westview Press, pp. 87–106.

Marzinotto, B. (2005), 'Has EMU Made Germany Worse Off? Public Finances, Wage Bargaining and ECB Credibility from a German Perspective', Paper presented at the University of Victoria, BC, 18–19 August.

Moravcsik, A. (1993a), 'Preferences and Power in the EC: A Liberal Intergovernmentalist Approach', *Journal of Common Market Studies*, **31**(4): 474.

Moravcsik, A. (1993b), 'Integrating International and Domestic Theories of International Bargaining', in P.B. Evans, H.K. Jacobson and R.D. Putnam (eds), *Double-Edged Diplomacy: International Bargaining and Domestic Policy*, Berkeley: University of California Press.

Moravcsik, A. (1998), *The Choice for Europe: Social Purpose and State Power from Messina to Maastricht*, Ithaca, NY: Cornell University Press.

Pochet, P. (1998), 'The Social Consequences of EMU: An Overview of National Debates', in P. Pochet and B. Vanhercke (eds), *Social Challenges of Economic and Monetary Union*, Brussels: European Interuniversity Press.

Rhodes, M. (1997), 'Globalisation, Labour Markets and Welfare States: A Future of "Competitive Corporatism"?', *EUI Working Papers*, 97/36.

Rhodes, M. (2002), 'Why EMU Is, or May Be, Good for European Welfare States', in K. Dyson (ed.), *European States and the Euro*, London: Oxford University Press.

Risse, T. (1998), 'To Euro or not to Euro? The EMU and Identity Politics in the European Union', *Arena Working Papers*, WP 98/1.

Sandholtz, W. (1993), 'Choosing Union: Monetary Politics and Maastricht', *International Organization*, **47**(1): 1–39.

Streeck, W. (1994), 'Pay Restraints without Incomes Policies', in R. Dore, R. Boyer and Z. Mars (eds), *The Return to Incomes Policies*, London: Pinter.

Talani, L.S. (2000a), *Betting for and against EMU: Who Wins and Who Loses in Italy and in the UK from the Process of European Monetary Integration*, London: Ashgate.

Talani, L.S. (2000b), 'Who Wins and Who Loses in the City of London from the Establishment of EMU', in C. Crouch (ed.), *After the Euro: Shaping Institutions for Governance in the Wake of European Monetary Union*, London: Oxford University Press.

Talani, L.S. (2003), 'Interests and Expectations: A Critical Political Economy Approach to the Credibility of the Exchange Rates. The Cases of Italy and the UK in the EMS and EMU', in A. Cafruny and M. Ryner (eds), *A Ruined Fortress? Neoliberal Hegemony and Transformation in Europe*, New York: Rowman & Littlefield, pp. 123–47.

Talani, L.S. (2004), *European Political Economy: Political Science Perspectives*, London: Ashgate.

Talani, L.S. (2005), 'The European Central Bank: Between Growth and Stability', *Comparative European Politics*, **3**: 204–31.

Talani, L.S. (2007), 'The Future of EMU', in I. Stivachtis (ed.), *The State of European Integration*, Aldershot: Ashgate.

Talani, L.S. and G. Fazio (mimeo), 'Interests or Expectations: A Political Economy Model of Exchange Rate Commitments'.

Tsoukalis, L. (1997), *The New European Economy Revisited*, Oxford: Oxford University Press.

Verdun, A. and T. Christensen (2000), 'Policies, Institutions and the Euro: Dilemmas of Legitimacy', in C. Crouch (ed.), *After the Euro: Shaping Institutions for Governance in the Wake of European Monetary Union*, London: Oxford University Press.

Weale, A. (1996), 'Democratic Legitimacy and the Constitution of Europe', in R. Bellamy, V. Bufacchi and D. Castiglione (eds), *Democracy and Constitutional Culture in the Union of Europe*, London: Lothian Press.

Wren-Lewis, S. (2003), 'Fiscal Policy, Inflation and Stabilisation in EMU', working paper, University of Exeter.

Wyplosz, C. (2002), 'Fiscal Policy: Rules or Institutions?', Paper prepared for the Group of Economic Analysis of the European Commission, April.

Wyplosz, C. (2005), 'Fiscal Policy: Institutions versus Rules', *National Institute Economic Review*, **191**: 64–78.

Young, R. (1999), 'The Politics of the Single Currency: Learning the Lessons of Maastricht', *Journal of Common Market Studies*, **37**(2): 295–316.

4. Bringing domestic pressures back into the budget: Germany's Stability Pact and the new incentive structure in EMU

Benedicta Marzinotto

INTRODUCTION[1]

It is generally recognized that the proposal and approval in 1997 of the Stability and Growth Pact (SGP), an institutional device aimed at guaranteeing fiscal discipline even after Economic and Monetary Union (EMU) had started its operation, were clear-cut German inputs into the EMU design process (Dyson and Featherstone, 1999; Stark, 2001). In this light, it is certainly surprising that Germany has been the first large country to breach the 3 per cent deficit target imposed by the pact and be subject to the ensuing excessive deficit procedure in November 2002 (European Commission, 2002b).[2] Yet the political leverage of the German representation in the ECOFIN Council was such that EU institutions decided to suspend the procedure in November 2003. The period that followed was characterized by the hectic effort to address the obvious shortcomings of the SGP, and of its implementation and enforcement (Pisani-Ferry, 2002), so as to avoid financial markets reacting with a vote of mistrust against the pact, which in fact never happened (see Chapter 3). The result of this long reflection was the approval of the Stability Pact reform in March 2005. The new version of the pact asserts that national ownership of fiscal policy is to be respected and that any evaluation of EMU countries' stance with regard to the pact needs to take account of country-specific circumstances (Council of the European Union, 2005). Through this reform, two objectives have been achieved. On the one hand, the visibility of the special treatment received by Germany has faded.[3] On the other, the rules of the pact have been made so fluid that its credibility cannot be in question, whatever its future course.

This chapter adopts a domestic politics perspective to explain the collapse of the SGP in a country that has a long history of fiscal discipline mostly pursued with the tacit support of social actors. Different hypotheses have been put forward in the literature to account for Germany's undisciplined behaviour. Some observers still insist on the revolutionary impact of the 1991 re-unification on public finances. Deviation from the 3 per cent deficit target would be thus indicative of the difficulty in funding welfare programmes especially in East Germany at a time when unemployment in this part of the country remains comparatively high. For others, instead, the presence of a fiscal rule imposed from above is in itself responsible for fiscal misbehaviour in periods of slow growth. The argument is that the SGP has forced fiscal authorities into a pro-cyclical action, thus depriving economic policy of any stabilization function. A relatively stringent fiscal policy in recession is believed to further compromise growth conditions, leading to even greater fiscal imbalances in the following years. Against these explanations, this chapter suggests, firstly, that the timing of fiscal deterioration is not well explained by the re-unification shock. Fiscal discipline relaxed quite remarkably after 1999, and the same happened in most Euro-zone countries. This suggests that the coming into being of EMU probably softened the incentive structure in favour of fiscal discipline, as will be explained below. Secondly, this research addresses the issue of pro-cyclicality and argues that it is inappropriate to state that the SGP has twisted fiscal authorities' arms into pro-cyclical action. Empirical evidence shows that German fiscal policy has been fairly pro-cyclical since the early 1990s and before. In this respect, it can hardly be said that the Stability Pact, whether strictly applied or not, is a self-defeating device.

Why then is fiscal misbehaviour more evident under EMU than in the preceding period? The argument developed here is that German social actors have resorted to fiscal authorities more than in the past to obtain compensations in exchange for wage moderation. Strong domestic pressures would thus be at the root of fiscal misbehaviour. In reality, welfare programmes and tax systems have been used in the political exchange between government and social partners since the 1970s. Nevertheless, in the 1990s, the impossibility of obtaining compensations from an accommodating monetary policy left only fiscal policy to take care of side payments in most Euro-zone countries. With specific reference to Germany, the novelty of EMU was that devolution of monetary sovereignty to the new European Central Bank (ECB) disrupted the existing efficient coordination between wage and monetary policy that was the backbone of the German political economy in the Bundesbank era. Not only did wage setters accept wage moderation because they were pressurized by rising competition from abroad, but also the uncertainty about the ECB's behaviour in response to possibly excessive wage settlements in Germany further pushed towards (pre-emptive) wage restraint. European monetary unification has led in

Germany to significant wage compression relatively to the past and to parallel developments in the rest of the EU. This is in contrast to the view of some relevant literature according to which the incentives for wage moderation are weakened by EMU membership (Hall and Franzese, 1998; Iversen and Soskice, 1998).

Given such wage compression, it would have been unthinkable for labour unions to accept any form of welfare retrenchment. The failure of the Agenda 2010 programme is to be interpreted against this background. At the same time, wage setters have been pushing for lower income and labour taxes. Employers also adopted this position. As employees and employers equally share the burden of non-wage labour costs, cuts to labour taxes are welcomed by both parties. Moreover, the resulting rise in the consumption wage was a favourable prospect not only for wage earners, but also for firms at a time when production was suffering from feeble demand conditions. The preservation of the status quo on the expenditure side of the budget and pleas for lower fiscal pressure on the revenue side of the budget contributed to Germany's deviation from the pact's deficit target. The demise of the Stability Pact is thus the result of pressures from domestic sectoral interests after EMU had fundamentally altered the incentive structure in which national interest groups operate.

Needless to say, pressures are stronger where growth conditions are most disappointing.[4] This analysis confirms previous domestic actor approaches to the study of the Stability Pact, which have indicated that such a fiscal rule is hardly sustainable domestically, and especially so in periods of slow growth (McKay, 1999, 2002).[5]

1 GERMANY'S FISCAL PERFORMANCE

Figure 4.1 illustrates the evolution of fiscal aggregates in Germany. The deficit fell to below 3 per cent of GDP in 2001 and remained below this threshold until 2004. When controlling for the impact of cyclical fluctuations on public finance aggregates, the starting point of Germany's fiscal deterioration is the same. The cyclically adjusted deficit likewise deteriorated in 2001 and remained below target until 2004, even if figures for 2003 and 2004 are better than actual ones, thereby demonstrating the negative impact of the business cycle on actual deficit levels. Certainly, German discretionary fiscal policy had already started loosening in 1999. This is manifest in the evolution of the cyclically adjusted primary surplus, the aggregate that best approximates to discretionary fiscal action. Accumulated over the period 1991–99 at a time when the financial impact of re-unification should have been most visible,[6] the primary surplus is progressively eroded under EMU

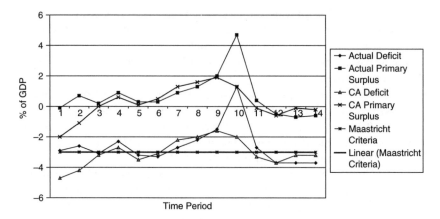

Source: European Commission, Statistical Annex, Autumn 2005

*Figure 4.1   Germany: evolution of actual and cyclically adjusted deficit
and primary surplus, 1991–2004*

(Figure 4.1). Numerous economists support the view that German public
finances remain burdened with the cost of welfare programmes, especially in
East Germany, where the unemployment rate has been systematically higher
than in West Germany since re-unification. The latest available figure shows
that the difference in unemployment is still marked. As of June 2006, unemployment in Eastern Germany is still at 16.8 per cent against a more modest
8.9 per cent in the Western part of the country (www.bundesbank.de).
Nevertheless, similar unemployment levels in the 1990s did not lead to the
same degree of deficit deterioration manifest in the period from 1999 to 2004.
Hence the timing of fiscal deterioration in Germany is not well explained by
the unification shock. Moreover, the evidence clearly indicates that the relaxation commenced in 1999, the same year in which the Euro was introduced;
this points to the fact that there might well be a relationship between the loss
of monetary sovereignty and the abandonment of fiscal discipline. Fatas and
Mihov find that the incentive for fiscal discipline is weakened in EMU in
most Euro-area member states (Fatas and Mihov, 2003).

2   THE STABILITY PACT: A SELF-DEFEATING DEVICE?

Some of the observers of EMU's fiscal framework blame the Stability Pact
for forcing EU governments to run prudent fiscal action in bad times,
thereby protracting downturns. The pact's pro-cyclical bias would be

aggravated by the fact that no positive incentive is available for countries to pursue disciplined budget policies in good times, with the result that the room for fiscal manoeuvre remains limited once the cycle turns unfavourable (Buti and Sapir, 1998; Buti *et al.*, 1998, 2005; von Hagen, 2003). In turn, the new fiscal regime is said to deprive national discretionary fiscal policies of any stabilizing function (Fatas and Mihov, 2003; Fatas *et al.*, 2003). In a similar fashion, a considerable number of analyses of the so-called German malaise would recognize the SGP as partly responsible for the country's protracted slow growth insofar as this enforced budget consolidation in face of an economic slowdown (Hein and Truger, 2005), especially in 2002 and 2003, when the slump was more severe than ever. A similar view has been expressed by the German Confederation of Trade Unions (*Deutscher Gewerkschaftsbund*, DGB), an umbrella organization that includes all the main labour unions, representing more than 7 million people. Since the inception of EMU and the coming into operation of the Stability Pact regime, the DGB has publicly criticized the pro-cyclical bias in the pact, blaming the government for agreeing to cut public expenditures just at a time when government spending was most needed to counteract recessionary tendencies. Moreover, the confederation reiterated the same criticism as that expressed by relevant economic research, that the SGP would force pro-cyclicality in downturns without offering special provisions for when national economies are booming (DGB, 2005).

While this view has been much echoed in the literature and in some influential public circles, the empirical evidence in its support remains weak. In reality, German fiscal authorities were never prompt when it came to smoothing out the cycle through fiscal policies. Germany's discretionary fiscal action had shown a tendency towards pro-cyclicality since the 1970s (see also Beetsma and Debrun, 2004: 111), so that the coming into effect of the Stability Pact does not seem to have exacerbated this predisposition,[7] nor did the shock of re-unification in the early 1990s.[8] For the sake of the present exercise, a fiscal policy stance is said to be pro-cyclical when the fluctuations in the cyclically adjusted budget balance move inversely with the output gap (for a definition, see OECD, 2003). Figure 4.2 shows how this occurred for most of the 1990s, namely in 1991–93, 1995–97, 1999–2000 and 2002–03. In other words, the implementation of the SGP in 1997 did not coincide with a structural break in the conduct of German budget policy.

Most interestingly, the relationship between the sign of discretionary fiscal policy and the growth environment is relatively symmetrical in that it is equally true that deficits rise during upturns and that they decrease in downturns, without macro-differences emerging if one compares the period before 1997 with the period after. Hence, if it is true that, under the

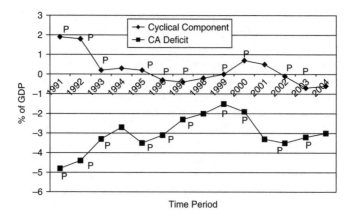

Source: European Commission, AMECO Database, July 2005

*Figure 4.2   Germany: cyclical component and cyclically adjusted deficit,
1991–2004 (based on potential GDP)*

Stability Pact regime, fiscal policy was pro-cyclical, there is no evidence indicating that responsibility for this rests with the pact. Nor is it the case that the Maastricht convergence process, with its potentially restrictive bias, induced pro-cyclicality, as, in that case, we should not have seen pro-cyclical fiscal action in good times. Instead, Germany's pro-cyclical behaviour has arguably to do with the institutional framework in which fiscal decisions are taken, and most notably with the country's federalist structure that maximizes collective action problems just when a coordinated action would be required (Braun et al., 2002).

3   WAGE RESTRAINT AND THE DEMISE OF WAGE–MONETARY POLICY COORDINATION

The period from 1999 to 2005 was characterized in Germany by significant wage compression. A diffuse argument is that strong competitive pressures in the new Single European Market (SEM) together with the realistic threat of relocation to Central and Eastern European countries (CEECs) in the wake of enlargement probably exercised a downward pressure on wages. A survey conducted by the German Association of Chambers of Industry and Commerce (DIHK) shows that, in 2003, 24 per cent of all companies surveyed were willing to relocate production activities outside of Germany, a 3 per cent rise from 1999. On the other side, there is extensive anecdotal evidence suggesting that employees have become sensitive to multinational firms' threat of moving production sites to CEECs, where labour costs remain comparatively modest. The issue ranks high in importance in German public debate (EIRO, 2006). This is by itself not surprising in a country where, historically, wage earners have 'conspired' with employers to preserve a competitive edge that would guarantee export-led growth (Katzenstein, 1987). The fact that 90 per cent of German trade is intra-European explains why it may be so important to condition the real exchange rate by means of wage policies, once nominal exchange rates vis-à-vis the principal trade partners have ceased to exist.[9] Reinforcing this historical recollection of the myth of export-led growth is the fact that German nominal bargained wages had been systematically lower than the European average since the 1970s (Table 4.1). Over the period from 1970 to 1990, average nominal compensations per employee grew by 4.9 per cent against an average in Western Europe of 8.25 per cent. Figures for nominal unit labour costs (ULC) convey a similar picture, with German ULC up by 3.1 per cent over the same period against an average rise in the rest of Europe of 6.1 per cent, thereby suggesting that West European ULC are much more decoupled from productivity gains than German ULC (Table 4.1).

Interestingly enough, the 1990s saw an equalization of nominal wage growth between Germany and the rest of the EU, with the gap between German and EU average wage rises reducing considerably, which was

Table 4.1   Germany and EU-12: wage developments 1999–2005 (annual percentage change)

	Nominal wages		Real wages		Nominal ULC		Real ULC	
	Germany	EU-12	Germany	EU-12	Germany	EU-12	Germany	EU-12
Av 71–90	**4.9**	**8.25**	**1.85**	**1.35**	**3.1**	**6.1**	**−0.35**	**−0.7**
Av. 91–98	**2.6**	**2.8**	**0.6**	**0.3**	**1.2**	**1.4**	**−0.5**	**−0.9**
1999	1.2	2.2	0.9	1	0.3	1	−0.2	−0.1
2000	2.1	2.7	0.6	0.4	1	1.3	1.2	−0.1
2001	1.7	2.8	0	0.5	1.3	2.5	0	0.1
2002	1.5	2.7	0.3	0.5	0.8	2.2	−0.7	−0.2
2003	1.6	2.5	0.5	0.6	0.7	2	−0.4	0
2004	0.1	2.1	−1.5	0.2	−1.1	0.7	−1.8	−1.2
2005	0.5	2.1	−0.8	0.2	0.4	1.3	−0.2	−0.4
Av. 99–05	**1.2**	**2.4**	**0**	**0.5**	**0.5**	**1.6**	**−0.3**	**−0.3**

Note: wages = wages per head; ULC = unit labour costs

Source: European Commission, Statistical Annex, European Economy, Spring 2005

limited to 0.2 per cent in the case of both nominal compensations per head and nominal ULC. Nevertheless, in the period 1999–2005, under the new EMU regime, German wage growth diverged again from the EU average, with a negative differential of 1.2 per cent in the case of nominal wages and of 1.1 per cent in the case of ULC (Table 4.1). The data convey an interesting message. EMU exercised an additional downwards pressure on wage growth, with the result that nominal compensations rose more slowly than in the 1990s even if, at the time, the effort to resist international competition was equally present following the completion of the European Single Market in 1992. In order to explain the relative contribution of the new EMU regime to wage moderation, the present analysis goes back to the argument about the coordination of monetary and wage policy that provided the reason for Germany's successful macroeconomic performance from the 1970s to the 1990s.

3.1 Efficient Wage–Monetary Coordination before EMU

It is generally acknowledged that the success of the German economy until the early 1990s was supported by an effective system of coordination between wage bargainers and fiscal and monetary authorities (Giersch *et al.*, 1995). The most prominent example of these 'institutional complementarities' (Hall and Soskice, 2001) was the implicit coordination between German wage setters and the independent Bundesbank. The construction of the argument rests on two pillars. First, the economics literature acknowledges that central bank independence leads to good macroeconomic performance. Independent central banks are less likely to engage in monetary expansion; by virtue of this, they are more inflation-averse than dependent central banks. Second, they are so credible in their assurances about the future course of monetary policy that wage and price contractors do not expect faster inflation and thus fail to incorporate such an expectation into their wage and price demands (Cukierman *et al.*, 1992). Wage setters also knew that excessive wage settlements could force the Bundesbank into an undesirable restrictive response; hence, they opted for wage moderation to prevent a monetary restriction. An interest rate rise is expected to dampen demand, and investment in particular, with inevitably negative implications for labour market conditions (Equation a) (Ebbinghaus and Schmidt, 1999; Soskice, 1990). Moreover, the interest rate hike is likely to induce currency appreciation, and therewith it jeopardizes export growth, and thus employment (Equation b). This second mechanism entails significant distributional implications insofar as unions concentrated in externally exposed sectors would have a stronger incentive for restraint than those in insulated sectors (Franzese and Hall, 2000; Soskice,

1990; Streeck, 1994). These mechanisms are behind the fact that Germany could enjoy relatively slow wage growth at negligible employment costs for at least three decades.[10]

$$\Delta W \to \uparrow \Delta P \to \uparrow \Delta i \to \downarrow \Delta I/C \to \downarrow \Delta Y \to \uparrow \Delta u \qquad \text{(a)}$$

$$\Delta W \to \uparrow \Delta P \to \uparrow \Delta i \to \uparrow \Delta \varepsilon \to \downarrow \Delta Y \to \uparrow \Delta u \qquad \text{(b)}$$

3.2 The New Incentive Structure under EMU

Interestingly enough, the coming into operation of EMU and the disruption of the signalling game between German wage setters and the monetary authority (i.e. the ECB) did not lead to less wage restraint, as anticipated by some relevant literature (Hall and Franzese, 1998; Iversen and Soskice, 1998), but rather to more restraint. In a nutshell, the argument works as follows. The uncertainty about the ECB's reaction coupled with the impression that their wage behaviour has the potential to affect average price conditions in the Euro-zone twisted German unions' arms into a sort of pre-emptive wage moderation.

When transposing the traditional deterrent argument into the new EMU context, the starting point in the analysis concerns the behaviour of the ECB. If the new central bank had targeted German inflation in the same way in which the Bundesbank had done over the previous three decades, then German wage setters would have continued behaving as they did, resisting excessive wage settlements to avoid a restrictive reaction function by the ECB. Nevertheless, the ECB seems to have made an effort, in the rhetoric at least, to target price conditions across the Euro-zone rather than in Germany only.[11] In practice, it might well be that both French and German price developments have been observed with special consideration, but the fact that this remains implicit and that price levels in Germany differed to a relatively significant extent from those in France – by an average of 0.8 per cent in 2001–06, according to the latest available estimate (European Commission, 2005) – is sufficient to conclude that, by and large, from 1999 to 2004, the ECB targeted inflation in the Euro-area as a whole.

Against the loss of the monetary reference partner, the expectation is that German wage setters will lose the incentive for wage restraint. The empirical evidence on wage growth presented above does not support this hypothesis.

Similarly, it is probably rushed to state that stronger international competition, especially from Central and Eastern European countries, conspired in favour of wage moderation. A country such as Austria was confronted with similar competitive pressures, not least owing to its geographic proximity to

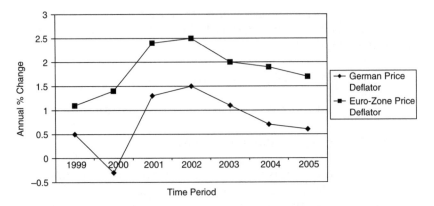

Source: European Commission, Statistical Annex of European Economy, Spring 2005

Figure 4.3   *Price deflator (GDP): Germany and the Euro-zone,*
              1999–2005

Central and Eastern Europe. Nevertheless, here, wage growth was not as slow as in Germany.

Instead, the reasons behind Germany's below-average wage growth rest with the size of its economy. The German economy represents one-third of EU GDP. This is sufficient to make of Germany a price-leader in the Euro-zone. Figure 4.3 confirms that German inflation sets the pattern for the EU as a whole. In turn, labour unions are aware of their country's leading influence. The position papers of the DGB are pervaded with references to the possible impact of Germany's nominal wage growth on general price conditions:

> An even more dynamic expansion of the economy could be achieved if the European Central Bank (ECB) would realistically consider growth an objective in the same vein as price stability. By the way, these two objectives are not alternatives. With nominal wages growing by 4 per cent on average, the distribution of output per head is not jeopardized. Real wages would thus grow together with productivity and wages per head increase by a rate that is compatible with price stability. This means that an expansionary monetary policy would not entail an inflationary potential.
>
> (DGB, 2001b: 13, author's own translation)

While awareness is there, the confederation remains dubious about the precise transmission mechanism. As a matter of fact, wage bargainers can only account for their marginal contribution to price changes in the EU,[12] but are unable to perfectly predict how this would affect the resulting EU inflation level. In other words, they are uncertain whether their bargained wage rises will push the average EU inflation level above 2 per cent, the price stability target adopted by the ECB. This distinction is of great analytical and theoretical importance. It implies that German wage setters are unable to fully internalize the ECB's reaction function given the explicit inflation target set by the ECB. At the end of the day, the prevailing feeling is uncertainty, which disrupts the process of expectation formation visualized in Equations a and b (Marzinotto, 2005b). Such a finding is not new to the economics literature. Economic models similarly show that an ambiguous monetary reaction function tends to reduce wage inflation (Grüner *et al.*, 2005).

4   THE QUEST FOR FISCAL COMPENSATIONS

German labour unions have adopted a clear-cut position in the face of the SGP. Through the DGB, labour representatives have repeatedly accused the pact of forcing the government into a restrictive stance in a period of slow growth, at a time when the role of the government would have been instead that of pushing aggregate demand upwards through deficit spending, if necessary (DGB, 2001a, 2001b, 2002b, 2004, 2005). Behind this position is the organization's strong attachment to traditional Keynesian principles (see Marzinotto, 2005a). On the other side of the spectrum, the Confederation of German Industry (BDI) reiterates its preference for fiscal discipline. Seen as a means to control inflation, financial stability is perceived as the most appropriate environment in which production activities can prosper (BDI, 2001a, 2001b, 2002a, 2002b, 2002c, 2003a, 2003b, 2005). In the game between anti- and pro-discipline interest groups, the former have prevailed given the novel incentive structure that has come into being with EMU. The reasons for this are as follows.

European economic integration and monetary unification have left German wage earners in a fairly uncomfortable situation. Competitive pressures together with the threat of relocation may have forced them into some wage restraint. But, and more originally, the uncertainty about their marginal contribution to average price conditions in the Euro-zone and about the ensuing response by the ECB have further compressed wage demands, as explained above. Whilst insistently demanding expansionary monetary conditions (DGB, 2001a, 2003), wage setters are also aware that the ECB is unlikely to respond to them directly or, if it does, only with a lag. Fiscal policy remains the only tool through which they can hope to recoup part of their diminished purchasing power.

This is not necessarily a new mechanism. Welfare programmes and tax systems have been used in the political exchange between government and social partners since the 1970s in Germany (Carlin, 1996) as well as in most other West European countries (Crouch and Pizzorno, 1978). The only difference with the past is that, whilst earlier governments could promise additional transfers, now side payments can only take the form of promises to retreat from welfare retrenchment (Streeck, 2003). This is not only because governments act under stricter financial constraints, but also because welfare states have grown to their limits. The unions' battle is fought for the preservation of the welfare status quo once they have accepted significant wage compression. This explains German unions' strong opposition to Chancellor Schröder's recent welfare reform proposal known as Agenda 2010, which has been paralysed since its launch in 2003 (*Economist*, 2005).

At the same time, the DGB has been pushing for lower income taxes (DGB, 2003). The Schröder government demonstrated itself quite attentive to these requests and implemented successive tax alleviation plans, with the result that taxes on income and wealth decreased from 12.5 per cent of GDP in 2000 to 10.2 per cent of GDP in 2004, just at a time when real compensations remained fairly modest.[13] Cuts to labour taxes were also welcome insofar as they would raise their consumption wage. This latter strategy found the approval of employers as well, considering that they shared with wage earners the burden of non-wage labour costs. Alesina *et al.* (1999) confirm that higher labour taxation reduces business investment activities.

In the political economy literature, the coordination between wage and fiscal policies is often understood in the light of the internalization of externalities. The approach is a game-theoretical one where wage bargainers are negotiators who account for current or expected fiscal policy changes when forming their wage preferences given a desired output. By way of example, in the wake of unification, once the Kohl government had clearly indicated its intention to raise social security contributions as a means to finance the transfer of West German labour market institutions to the East, German bargainers incorporated higher labour taxes into their wage demands, resulting in some significant forward shifting of taxes on wages (Tullio *et al.*, 1996).

The argument developed here foresees an opposite dynamics where wage setters accept wage moderation in exchange for lower fiscal pressure.[14] The norm is that, when income and/or labour taxes decrease, consumption wages increase automatically through a rise in disposable income, provided that labour demand does not decline too much in the face of rising wages and that the profit share is relatively small to start with. Where this is not taking place, the indication is that wage setters are accepting *preventive* wage moderation, offered to government in exchange for its current or just announced tax policy. The possibility of such a political exchange in Germany is explored by looking at the evolution of income and labour taxes as a proportion of GDP, on the one hand, and at the trend of the wage

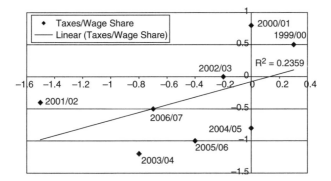

Source: European Commission, Statistical Annex, Spring 2006

Figure 4.4 *Correlation between changes in taxes and in the wage share (as a percentage of GDP), Germany 1999–2007*

share, on the other hand. With income taxes and social security contributions falling (increasing) as a percentage of GDP, the expectation is that the wage share rises (decreases) proportionally – assuming relatively constant mark-ups in conditions of close-to-perfect competition. Empirical evidence shows that from 2001 to 2007 (the EU Commission's projections are used for 2006 and 2007) decreasing income and labour taxes have been associated, quite paradoxically, with a declining wage share (Figure 4.4). The fact that lower fiscal pressure on labour has not come with a rise in the share of output wage earners have taken possession of suggests that there has been voluntary and somehow preventive wage moderation such that the typical relationship between variations in labour taxation and in the wage share has changed sign. Wages have been compressed below the level that would have been 'natural' in the case of an automatic adjustment of the wage share to tax changes. This allows us to state that wage moderation is a term of exchange in the game with a government that has implemented a labour-friendly tax policy.

Table 4.2 summarizes the evolution of wage moderation over the period 1999–2007. Bargained wage compression is measured as the difference between changes to fiscal pressure and to the wage share. A positive sign indicates that wages have risen above the level that would be 'natural' given a certain tax policy. In other words, it is indicative of discretionary wage increases that can be a sign, for example, of unions' strong bargaining (political) power. A negative sign is symptomatic of wage restraint below the 'natural' level and thus indicates discretionary wage compression, arguably used as a term of exchange in negotiations with the federal government. There is no sign of such a political exchange in the first years

*Table 4.2   Preventive wage compression, Germany 1999–2007
             (as a percentage of GDP)*

	1999– 2000	2000– 01	2001– 02	2002– 03	2003– 04	2004– 05	2005– 06	2006– 07
Wage dynamics	+0.2	+0.8	−1.9	−0.2	−2	−0.8	−1.4	−1.2

of EMU from 1999 to 2001, as wages were on the upside. Instead, German wage setters conceded to government, especially in 2001 and 2003 when (preventive) wage compression was in the realm of almost 2 per cent of GDP. This piece of evidence fits well with the facts. It was suggested above that the incentive to look for this type of political exchange is stronger in recession, and in fact the severe downturn that occurred in the third quarter of 2001 created a strong incentive for German bargainers to look for a compromise. Furthermore, the fact that preventive wage moderation remained considerable in 2006 and 2007 anticipates that significant fiscal restrictions were not expected until 2007. This is in line with the commitment that the German government has recently taken vis-à-vis the EU. In its latest Stability Programme approved in February 2006, the federal government committed itself to reducing the deficit level to below 3 per cent of GDP, starting with 2008. Moreover, the government indirectly acknowledged that the previous tax alleviation measures were excessive. And, in fact, the update of the German Stability Pact insists on the need to restore fiscal discipline by operating in particular on the revenue side of the budget, where the leeway remains significant, as the 2005 tax ratio was at a historically low 21.9 per cent of GDP (Federal Ministry of Finance, 2006).[15]

CONCLUSIONS

This chapter has looked at the fate of the SGP in Germany and argued that the new incentive structure brought in by EMU has enhanced domestic groups' pressures on the budget, with the result that discretionary fiscal policy has relaxed, leading to a significant deviation of the German deficit from the 3 per cent target. Not only has European economic integration put a constraint on wage growth in a country that has a long history of cooperation between macroeconomic authorities and social actors to preserve export competitiveness, but also the devolution of monetary sovereignty to the ECB has altered the efficient coordination game between German wage setters and monetary policy. Uncertain about their marginal contribution to average price conditions in the Euro-zone, they have opted for even further wage moderation. The result is 'excessively' slow wage growth that has left the German inflation rate well below the EU average. Germany's negative inflation differential with the rest of the Euro-zone has rendered monetary conditions stricter here than in the rest of the Euro-area, considering that the ECB has been making an effort to target average price conditions in EMU. Moreover, the disruption of the coordination game between wage setters and the monetary authority means that the former no longer have the option of obtaining a more relaxed monetary stance. Excessive wage restraint and restrictive monetary conditions leave fiscal policy as the only game in town. There is quantitative as well as anecdotal evidence showing that German wage bargainers have engaged in a political exchange with the fiscal authorities, where they guarantee wage restraint in exchange for lower fiscal pressure and for the preservation of the status quo in the case of welfare benefits. The failure of the Schröder government's Agenda 2010 is to be interpreted against this background. The German government deviated from the pact's target neither because it still suffers from the structural shock of re-unification nor because of extremely disappointing growth conditions, whether or not induced by the presence of an asymmetric fiscal rule such as the Stability Pact, but because fiscal policy has been used to compensate social actors for their sacrifices elsewhere. (For a similar interpretation see Chapter 3.)

This analysis allows us to draw come conclusions about the political economy of the Stability Pact and the future course of fiscal policy in Germany. A fiscal rule such as the SGP is the more unsustainable, the more disappointing the growth environment. Obviously, modest GDP growth has an immediate negative effect on actual deficits insofar as it maximizes social spending and minimizes revenues from taxation. It is here argued that modest growth worsens discretionary fiscal policy as well, insofar as it enhances pressures from social actors on the fiscal authorities. By affecting actual fiscal policy (economic argument) as well as discretionary fiscal policy (political economy argument), slow growth comes with a *multiplied* negative impact on fiscal aggregates.[16] Nevertheless, the recent pact's reform, with its appreciation of a more flexible approach to fiscal discipline, means that future deviations from the official 3 per cent target may not necessarily sanction the death of the SGP.

NOTES

1. I am grateful to Florin Bilbie, Stefan Collignon, Dermot Hodson, Mark Hallerberg and Manolo Palazuelos-Martinez for extremely useful comments. The usual disclaimer

applies. A previous version of this chapter was presented at the conference 'Between Stability and Growth: The Consequences of the Reform of the European Stability and Growth Pact', London School of Economics and Political Science, London, 9–10 September 2005.

2. The very first country to breach the pact's deficit target was Portugal, against which the EU Commission initiated the procedure in September 2002 (European Commission, 2002a).

3. Hancké and Soskice insist on the fact that the ECOFIN adopted a more lenient stance toward Germany because its fiscal profligacy was not such that average inflation in the Euro-zone was at risk. This meant that fiscal misbehaviour in Germany should not force the ECB to react with a restrictive response, thereby punishing all member states independently of their fiscal behaviour (Hancké and Soskice, 2003).

4. This argument is not the typical economic one, for which modest GDP growth has a negative impact on budget deficits simply because it pushes social spending upwards and reduces revenues from (progressive) taxation. It is rather a political economy argument according to which modest or negative growth has a *multiplied* negative effect on public accounts as it induces domestic groups to ask for greater compensations than they would otherwise. The impact is felt on discretionary rather than on actual fiscal policy.

5. These analyses go hand in hand with the evaluation of a few economists, who argue that the SGP is not deemed to survive (von Hagen, 2003).

6. There is no consensus amongst economists over the financial impact of unification. Bibow, for example, estimates that only one-third of the deterioration that the German public deficit experienced in the 1990s derived from the re-unification shock (Bibow, 2001). Tujula and Wolswijk reach even more extreme conclusions. In an extensive econometric study that identifies the determinants of fiscal imbalances, they find no significant effect for a German unification dummy (Tujula and Wolswijk, 2004).

7. The OECD finds a similar result for the Euro-zone as a whole (OECD, 2003).

8. Bibow confirms that German fiscal policy was pro-cyclical during the 1990s and that this modus operandi was partly responsible for the drastic deterioration of German public finances insofar as the adoption of a restrictive stance in a downturn further dampened growth (Bibow, 2001).

9. And, in fact, Germany could count on a depreciating real effective exchange rate from 1999 to 2005, which was an important boost to competitiveness and export growth (see Talani's contribution, Chapter 3 in this volume).

10. An additional and related argument developed in the literature is that German unions could actually deliver wage moderation thanks to a highly centralized system of collective bargaining. Wage moderation is possible only where wages are negotiated at firm or at national level (Calmfors and Driffil, 1988). Greater product elasticity of demand makes workers more sensitive to the firm's fate, in the first case. At the national level, instead, wage moderation prevails, as wage earners are aware that a money wage rise will lead to a proportional increase in the price level (Soskice, 1990).

11. In spite of the fact that the large German economy does indeed exercise a leading influence in the Euro-zone. This is by itself uncontroversial. Figure 4.3 shows indeed that changes in the Euro-zone price deflator reflect *tout court* changes in the German price deflator. The correlation of EU shocks with Germany seems to concern both the supply and the demand side of the economy. Eichengreen quotes high supply shock correlations with Germany in the early 1990s (Eichengreen, 1994, cited in Iversen and Soskice, 1998). Moreover, Artis demonstrates that, in the period 1970–99, real demand shocks in EU-15 correlate with Germany's by 81 per cent (Artis, 2003).

12. See note 11.

13. Even if pro-cyclicality in fiscal policy has always been there, it is not to be ruled out that the numerous tax alleviation measures introduced from 1999 to 2005 have enhanced this tendency. A study by the OECD confirms that tax cuts exacerbate pro-cyclical tendencies (OECD, 2003).

14. Hancké and Soskice (2003) have developed a similar hypothesis, albeit from a purely theoretical and scenario-based perspective. This is an empirical test of their hypothesis.
15. The Merkel government has already approved measures to raise the standard rate of VAT and insurance tax. The Programme reads: 'the increase in the rates of VAT and insurance tax is a very important element of the consolidation strategy as it makes a considerable contribution towards stabilizing the revenue side of the budget on a durable basis and allows the contribution to unemployment insurance, and thus the non-wage labour costs – which slow down economic activity – to be lowered' (Federal Ministry of Finance, 2006: 12).
16. This conclusion shares common traits with arguments developed elsewhere, according to which the slow-growth environment of the 1990s undermined Germany's corporatist patterns and consensual policy-making style so that striking a compromise has become increasingly difficult (Streeck, 2003).

BIBLIOGRAPHY

Alesina, A., S. Ardagna, R. Perotti and F. Schiantarelli (1999), 'Fiscal Policy, Profits and Investment', Working paper 7207, National Bureau of Economic Research, Cambridge, MA.

Artis, M.J. (2003), *Analysis of European and UK Business Cycles and Shocks*, London: HM Treasury.

BDI (2000a), *Höher Wachstumspfad fuer 2000 erreichbar – Schlüsselrolle für Wirtschafts- und Tarifpolitik*, 19 January, Berlin: BDI.

BDI (2000b), *BDI zum Gutachten des Sachverständigenrats: Arbeitsmarkt muss flexibler werden*, 15 November, Berlin: BDI.

BDI (2001a), *BDI zum Herbsgutachten: Finanzpolitische Spielraüme ausschöpfen, 23 October, Berlin: BDI.*

BDI (2001b), *BDI-Präsident Rogowski: Zinsentscheidung der EZB stabilitäts- und kojunkturegerecht- Schröder muss wirtschaftlichpolitish flankieren*, 8 November, Berlin: BDI.

BDI (2002a), *BDI-Präsident Rogowski: 'Hände weg vom Stabilitätspakt'*, 8 May, Berlin: BDI.

BDI (2002b), *BDI-Präsident Rogowski zum Herbsgutachten: Stabilitätspakt nicht nur in Schönwetterzeiten einhalten*, 22 October, Berlin: BDI.

BDI (2002c), *Rogowski zur Haushaltsdebatte: Wachstum und Arbeitsplätze nur durch Reform in den Sozialen Sicherungsssytem*, 4 December, Berlin: BDI.

BDI (2003a), *BDI-Präsident Rogowski zum Gutachten des Sachverständigenrates: Eindringliche Mahnung zur Konsolidierung zur rechten Zeit*, 12 November, Berlin: BDI.

BDI (2003b), *Rogowski: Dieser Haushalt ist den Euro-Stabilitätsstreit nicht wert*, 27 November, Berlin: BDI.

BDI (2004), *BDI-Präsident Rogowski: 'Trotz kräftiger Exportimpulse kommt Konjunktur nicht richtig in Schwung'*, 21 July, Berlin: BDI.

BDI (2005), *Stabilitäts- und Wachstumpakt: Reform mit grossen Risiken*, 21 March, Berlin: BDI.

Beetsma, R.M.W.J. and X. Debrun (2004), 'Reconciling Stability and Growth: Smart Pacts and Structural Reforms', *IMF Staff Papers*, **51**(3): 431–56.

Bibow, J. (2001), 'The Economic Consequences of German Unification: The Impact of Misguided Macroeconomic Policies', Levy Economics Institute of Bard College, New York.

Bibow, J. (2005), 'Germany in Crisis: The Unification Challenge, Macroeconomic Policy Shocks and Traditions, and EMU', *International Review of Applied Economics*, **19**(1), January.

Braun, D., A.-B. Bullinger and S. Wälti (2002), 'The Influence of Federalism on Fiscal Policy Making', *European Journal of Political Research*, **41**: 115–45.

Buti, M. and A. Sapir (1998), *Economic Policy in EMU: A Study by the European Commission Services*, Oxford: Clarendon Press.

Buti, M., D. Franco and H. Ongena (1998), 'Fiscal Discipline and Flexibility in EMU: The Implementation of the Stability and Growth Pact', *Oxford Review of Economic Policy*, **14**(3): 81–97.

Buti, M., S. Eijffinger and D. Franco (2005), 'The Stability Pact Pains: A Forward-Looking Assessment of the Reform Debate', Discussion paper, Tilburg University, August.

Calmfors, L. and J. Driffil (1988), 'Centralization of Wage Bargaining', *Economic Policy*, April, 13–61.

Carlin, W. (1996), 'West German Growth and Institutions 1945–1990', in N. Crafts and G. Toniolo, *Post-War European Growth*, Cambridge: Cambridge University Press.

Council of the European Union (2005), 'Presidency Conclusions', 7619/05, Luxembourg: Council of the European Union.

Crouch, C. and A. Pizzorno (1978), *The Resurgence of Class Conflict in Western Societies since 1968*, London: Holmes and Meier.

Cukierman, A., M.A. Kiguel and N. Liviatan (1992), 'How Much to Commit to an Exchange Rate Rule: Balancing Credibility and Flexibility', Policy Research Working Paper No 931, The World Bank.

DGB (2000), *Zum Jahresgutachten 2000/2001 des Sachverständigenrates*, 20 December, Berlin: DGB.

DGB (2001a), *Bundeshaushalt 2002: Mehr Mittel für öffentliche Investitionen und Arbeitsmarktpolitik erforderlich*, 11 September, Berlin: DGB.

DGB (2001b), *Offensive Strategies für mehr Wachstum und Beschäftigung*, 18 October, Berlin: DGB.

DGB (2002a), *Die Steuerpolitik der rot-grünen Bundesregierung*, 31 May, Berlin: DGB.

DGB (2002b), *Bundeshaushalt 2003: Chancen fuer Beschäftigung und soziale Sicherheit nutzen*, 13 September, Berlin: DGB.

DGB (2003), Offensive für Beschäftigung und Wirtschaftswachstum, 11 March, Berlin: DGB.

DGB (2004), *Finanzpolitik muss für Wachstum sorgen*, 26 April, Berlin: DGB.

DGB (2005), *Stellungnahme des Deutschen Gewerkschaftsbundes zu dem Antrag der Koalitionsfraktionen Stabilitäts- und Wachstumpolitik fortsezten – den Europäischen Stabilitäts- und Wachstumspakt stärken*, 21 January, Berlin: DGB.

Dyson, K. and K. Featherstone (1999), *The Road to Maastricht: Negotiating Economic and Monetary Union*, Oxford: Oxford University Press.

Ebbinghaus, M. and J.U. Schmidt (1999), *Prüfungsmethoden und Aufgabenarten*, Bielefeld: Bertelsmann Verlag.

Economist (2005), 'Germany's Surprising Economy' and 'Ready to Motor?', 20 August: 9, 62–4.

EIRO (2006), 'Relocation of Production and Industrial Relations', http://www.eiro.eurofound.eu.int/2005/11/study/tn0511101s.html.

European Commission, AMECO Database.

European Commission (2002a), 'Commission Adopts Report on Government Finances in Portugal as a First Step of the Excessive Deficit Procedure', IP/02/1360.

European Commission (2002b), 'Commission Adopts Report on Government Finances in Germany as a First Step of the Excessive Deficit Procedure', IP/02/1705.

European Commission (2005), *Statistical Annex of European Economy*, Spring, Brussels: European Commission.

Fatas, A. and I. Mihov (2003), 'Fiscal Policy and EMU: Challenges of the Early Years', in M. Buti and A. Sapir (eds), *EMU and Economic Policy in Europe*, Cheltenham, UK and Northampton, MA, USA: Edward Elgar.

Fatas, A., A. Hughes-Hallett, A. Sibert, R. Strauch and J. von Hagen (2003), *Stability and Growth in Europe: Towards a Better Pact*, London: CEPR.

Federal Ministry of Finance (2006), German Stability Programme, February 2006 Update, Berlin.

Franzese, R.J. and P.A. Hall (2000), 'Institutional Dimensions of Coordinating Wage Bargaining and Monetary Policy', in T. Iversen, J. Pontusson and D. Soskice, *Unions, Employers, and Central Banks: Macroeconomic Coordination and Institutional Change in Social Market Economies*, Cambridge: Cambridge University Press, pp. 173–204.

Giersch, H., K.-H. Paqui and H. Schmieding (1995), *The Fading Miracle: Four Decades of Market Economy in Germany*, Cambridge: Cambridge University Press.

Grüner, H.P., B. Hayo and C. Hefeker (2005); 'Unions, Wage-Setting and Uncertainty', ECB Working Paper Series 490, June.

Hagen, J. von (2003), 'Fiscal Discipline and Growth in Euroland: Experiences with the Stability and Growth Pact', ZEI Working Paper B06.

Hall, P.A. and R.J. Franzese Jnr (1998), 'Mixed Signals: Central Bank Independence, Coordinated Wage Bargaining, and European Monetary Union', *International Organization*, **52**(3): 505–35.

Hall, P.A. and D. Soskice (2001), *Varieties of Capitalism: The Institutional Foundations of Comparative Advantage*, Oxford: Oxford University Press.

Hancké, B. and D. Soskice (2003), 'Wage Setting and Inflation Targets, in EMU', *Oxford Review of Economic Policy*, **19**(1): 149–60.

Hein, E. and A. Truger (2005), 'Macroeconomic Policies, Wage Developments, and Germany's Stagnation', Working paper 1/2005, Macroeconomic Policy Institute.

Iversen, T. and D. Soskice (1998), 'Multiple Wage Bargaining Systems in the Single European Currency Area', *Oxford Review of Economic Policy*, **14**(3).

Katzenstein, P.J. (1987), *Policy and Politics in West Germany: the Growth of a Semi-Sovereign State*, Philadelphia, PA: Temple University Press.

Marzinotto, B. (2005a), 'Germany and Italy: Stumbling Giant and Prodigal Son? Social Pacts and the Political Economy of Fiscal Consolidation 1991–1998', Ph.D. thesis, unpublished.

Marzinotto, B. (2005b), 'At the Forefront or at the Back of Europe? Public Finances, Wage Bargaining and ECB Credibility from a German Perspective', mimeo.

McKay, D. (1999), 'The Political Sustainability of European Monetary Union' *British Journal of Political Science*, **29**: 519–41.

McKay, D. (2002), 'The Political Economy of Fiscal Policy under Monetary Union', in K. Dyson (ed.), *European States and the Euro*, Oxford: Oxford University Press.

OECD (2003), 'Fiscal Stance over the Cycle: The Role of Debt, Institutions, and Budget Constraints', *OECD Economic Outlook*, December, Paris: OECD.

Pisani-Ferry, J. (2002), 'Fiscal Discipline and Policy Coordination in the Euro-zone: Assessment and Proposals', mimeo.

Soskice, D. (1990), 'Wage Determination: The Changing Role of Institutions in Advanced Industrialised Countries', *Oxford Review of Economic Policy*, **6**(4).

Stark, J. (2001), 'Genesis of a Pact', in A. Brunila, M. Buti and D. Franco (eds), *The Stability and Growth Pact: The Architecture of Fiscal Policy in EMU*, London: Palgrave, pp. 77–105.

Streeck, W. (1994), 'Vincoli benefici: sui limiti economici dell'attore razionale', *Stato e Mercato*, **41**.

Streeck, W. (2003), 'From State Weakness as Strength to State Weakness as Weakness: Welfare Corporatism and the Private Use of the Public Interest', *Max Planck Working Papers*, **03**(2).

Tujula, M. and G. Wolswijk (2004), 'What Determines Fiscal Imbalances? An Empirical Investigation in Determinants of Changes in OECD Budget Balances', ECB Working Paper 422.

Tullio, G., A. Steinherr and H. Buscher (1996), 'German Wage and Price Inflation before and after Unification', in P. De Grauwe, S. De Micossi and G. De Tullio (eds), *Inflation and Wage Behaviour in Europe*, Oxford: Oxford University Press, pp. 3–29.

WSI Tarifarchiv (2005), www.dgb.de.

5. Notes on the reformed SGP: creating and implementing effective macroeconomic frameworks

Robert Woods[1]

1 INTRODUCTION

This chapter sets out some general principles for an effective macroeconomic framework and looks at the Stability and Growth Pact (SGP)[2] in this context. It goes on to consider how the recent reforms[3] are likely to affect the functioning of the SGP. The final section considers some of the future challenges in the implementation of the reformed SGP.

Effective macroeconomic policy frameworks help to achieve high and stable levels of economic growth and employment. Section 2 considers some general principles for effective policy frameworks characterized in terms of credibility, flexibility and legitimacy. Experience has pointed countries to frameworks with 'constrained discretion' with: clear long-term goals; a pre-commitment to sound institutional arrangements; and maximum transparency.

Section 3 discusses how the SGP performed against the three criteria of credibility, flexibility and legitimacy in the past and the extent to which the recent reforms have improved operation of the SGP. In particular, it highlights how key areas of the reforms are aimed at:

- improving credibility, for example by the increased focus on debt levels and long-term fiscal sustainability;
- increasing flexibility by giving greater attention to cyclical factors and the quality of public spending, including public investment; and
- enhancing legitimacy from a more robust economic rationale and greater scope for judgement in the application of the SGP.

Finally, Section 4 discusses some future challenges in implementing the pact including: the development of complementary national fiscal frameworks and increasing ownership; taking structural reforms into account;

the challenge of EU enlargement; discretionary fiscal stabilization in the context of a monetary union; and data, surveillance and transparency.

2   EFFECTIVE MACROECONOMIC FRAMEWORKS

A strong macroeconomic framework supports the achievement of high and stable levels of economic growth and employment by ensuring low and stable inflation and sound public finances. Large fluctuations in output, employment and inflation add to uncertainty for firms, consumers and the public sector and can reduce the economy's long-term growth potential. Stability allows businesses, individuals and the government to plan more effectively for the long term, improving the quality and quantity of investment in physical and human capital and helping to raise productivity. From having among the most unstable macroeconomic conditions, the UK has been the most stable of all the G7 economies since 1997 (Figure 5.1).

Effective macroeconomic frameworks can be characterized in terms of having:

- credibility – so that policy makers have public trust;
- flexibility – allowing a prompt and timely response to economic developments; and
- legitimacy – meaning there is widespread support for the framework.

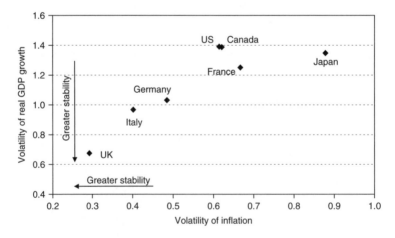

Source: OECD, national indices

Figure 5.1   Volatility of real GDP growth and inflation in the G7, 1997–2004 average

A robust macroeconomic framework must be both comprehensive and coherent, encompassing both monetary and fiscal policy. In establishing macroeconomic frameworks, policy makers have recognized the need for a credible framework that solves the 'time-inconsistency'[4] problem. With complete discretion, policy makers have found it hard to resist short-term pressures or to shape long-term expectations. In the fiscal context this has been reflected in problems of deficit bias and pro-cyclical fiscal policies. Policy makers have also learnt from frameworks that were based on overly mechanistic rules. While such frameworks forced governments to commit to long-term policy goals, rigid rules that do not allow any flexibility to respond to economic shocks can lead to substantial adjustment costs. Alternatively, inflexible rules may end up being ignored, especially as they tend to lose legitimacy, and thus they fail to make the intended long-term credibility gains.

The 'constrained discretion' approach combines the discretion necessary for effective short- to medium-term economic policy with a credible institutional framework and constraints on policy makers to deliver clearly defined long-term policy objectives. Constrained discretion can be operationalized by putting in place:

- clear and well-defined long-term policy objectives;
- pre-commitment to sound institutional arrangements which could allow credible and flexible policy responses in the face of shocks; and
- maximum transparency.

Box 5.1 describes the approach taken in the UK.

BOX 5.1   THE UK FISCAL FRAMEWORK

In 1997, the new government embarked on a radical overhaul of the frameworks which guide monetary and fiscal policy, against a legacy of a poor track record in macroeconomic policy making. The design of the UK fiscal framework reflects the three reinforcing principles set out above. These principles are not only features of the fiscal policy framework but are evident in the monetary policy framework and public spending framework, strengthening the UK's overall macroeconomic framework through a principled approach.

Clear and well defined long-term policy objectives
The government has set two objectives for fiscal policy:

- over the medium term, to ensure sound public finances and that spending and taxation impact fairly within and between generations; and
- over the short term, to support monetary policy and, in particular, to allow the automatic stabilizers to help smooth the path of the economy.

These objectives are implemented through two fiscal rules, against which the performance of fiscal policy can be judged. The fiscal rules are:

- the golden rule – over the economic cycle, the government will borrow only to invest and not to fund current spending; and
- the sustainable investment rule – public sector net debt as a proportion of GDP will be held over the economic cycle at a stable and prudent level. Other things being equal, net debt will be maintained below 40 per cent of GDP over the economic cycle.

Pre-commitment to sound institutional arrangements
The Code for Fiscal Stability, which was given legal backing in the 1998 Finance Act, underpins the fiscal framework and demonstrates the government's commitment to improve the conduct of fiscal policy, ensuring that fiscal policy is conducted in an open and transparent manner.

Maximum transparency
The principle of transparency is a central feature of the Code for Fiscal Stability, and the government has taken a number of steps designed to increase transparency. These include:

- having the key assumptions used in the public finances independently audited by the National Audit Office to assess whether they are reasonable and cautious; and
- regular publication of data on the public finances in the Budget and Pre-Budget Report combined with more detailed publications such as the End of Year Fiscal Report, and the Long-Term Public Finance Report (available on http://www.hm-treasury.gov.uk).

A **credible framework** is one in which the policy maker's commitment to long-term stability commands trust from the public, business and markets so that they do not expect policy makers to sacrifice their long-term goals in response to short-term pressures.[5] Credibility can be enhanced by setting clear policy objectives that are consistent with achieving stability. Underlying these objectives, well-defined policy rules and procedures need to be established against which performance can be judged. In terms of fiscal policy, governments have a range of options to build credibility. They could, for example, establish explicit fiscal rules, legal requirements that commit governments to set long-term objectives and account for their performance, and public expenditure management procedures to ensure that spending plans are consistent with the fiscal objectives of the government as a whole.

Greater transparency means it is easier to hold policy makers to account for their performance. The public are able to examine the arguments and issues that lie behind policy decisions and are given a thorough explanation of those decisions. It also helps governments to respond to shocks through discretionary policy actions without damaging long-term credibility, as they can clearly explain why they are undertaking such actions and how the expected outcome is consistent with long-term goals and policy frameworks.

Clear objectives and rules by themselves are insufficient to ensure credibility, however. Governments must also demonstrate their commitment to achieving their objectives in the face of short-term pressures. This commitment can be demonstrated by a track record of consistently delivering on their objectives over time. However, building up a track record takes time, and the process of building up credibility can be usefully accelerated through the establishment of sound institutional arrangements, including clear lines of accountability and greater transparency and openness.

A robust framework will also provide sufficient **flexibility** to allow policy makers to respond to shocks. This flexibility must, however, be delivered while maintaining the credibility of the government's commitment to its long-term objectives. Where there is a credible commitment to long-term stability, policy makers will be able to exercise discretion in response to shocks without affecting long-term expectations. Without a commitment to long-term goals, credibility could suffer in the face of short-term discretionary action that agents could perceive as opportunistic. Flexibility can enhance policy credibility given that policy rules have been undermined in the past by their rigidity under changing circumstances.

Macroeconomic frameworks must demonstrate **legitimacy** in the sense that they command widespread support. This can be achieved through building a consensus about the appropriate goals and about the institutional arrangements through which they are delivered. Legitimacy allows policy makers to take difficult decisions in the public interest without losing public support. Transparency and accountability are key to ensuring legitimacy.

These three principles are interrelated. Policy makers that respond flexibly and decisively to economic developments and national circumstances will be able to build a track record for delivering long-term stability. Insufficient flexibility could lead to large fluctuations in output and unemployment, which can quickly undermine legitimacy as well as credibility.

Policy coordination is also important, especially where responsibility for monetary and fiscal policies rests with different institutions. The monetary and fiscal authorities need to understand each other's policy objectives and reaction functions. If they do not, there may be welfare losses, for instance if their initial guesses are some way from the true outcome. This highlights the need for transparency, clear objectives and responsibilities, and the appropriate mechanisms to ensure effective policy coordination takes place. Box 5.2 discusses the UK's arrangements.

BOX 5.2   FISCAL AND MONETARY POLICY COORDINATION IN THE UK

The UK's macroeconomic framework includes procedures to ensure that fiscal and monetary policy is properly coordinated. This is facilitated by:

- The government setting the objectives for both monetary and fiscal policy. Indeed, both arms of policy have the same fundamental objective of helping to achieve economic stability. Monetary policy does this by aiming to deliver price stability, while fiscal policy aims to deliver sound public finances.
- Clear objectives and operating rules with transparent procedures so that both sets of policy makers fully understand what the other is trying to achieve and how they would react to news including their policy decisions.
- The presence at Monetary Policy Committee (MPC) meetings of a non-voting representative from HM Treasury who is able, in particular, to provide information on fiscal policy. This includes presentations on the Budget and the Pre-Budget Report.

Enhanced transparency built into the Bank of England Act 1998 and the Code for Fiscal Stability requires the MPC and the Treasury to put greater emphasis on communicating the policy stance not only to expert commentators but also to the general public. Greater clarity in macroeconomic policy enhances public debate and scrutiny of monetary and fiscal policies and has helped to establish credibility and legitimacy.

In addition, fiscal policy is constrained by the inflation target because the Treasury must take into account the likely response of the MPC to different fiscal policy settings. Thus when deciding on the fiscal stance, the Treasury is effectively setting the policy mix. The clarity of objectives for both monetary and fiscal policy, based on a symmetric inflation target and clear fiscal rules, has therefore enhanced the coordination of monetary and fiscal policy. (See O'Donnell and Bhundia, 2001a and b.)

3 REFORMING THE STABILITY AND GROWTH PACT

This section appraises the Stability and Growth Pact (SGP) in terms of the three principles – credibility, flexibility and legitimacy – outlined above. It assesses why reforms were needed and considers the recent reforms against these same principles. The agreement on the revision of the rules of the pact was launched by the European Commission with its September 2004 communication.[6] Discussions concluded on 22 March 2005 when the EU heads of state and government endorsed the Report of the ECOFIN Council entitled 'Improving the Implementation of the Stability and Growth Pact'.[7] The report lays out the guiding principles and specific changes to be made to the pact, as well as stating the spirit in which it is to be implemented. The two numerical anchors from the Maastricht Treaty continue to hold their place at the centre of the pact: the 3 per cent deficit-to-GDP ratio and the 60 per cent gross debt-to-GDP ratio.[8] Before discussing the difficulties encountered in implementing the pact in the past it is worth briefly reviewing what the SGP was intended for.

3.1 What is the SGP for?

Protecting other member states from the cost of unsustainable policies in one particular member state is at the heart of the justification for the pact. If the costs of unsustainable policies fall entirely within the country that carries them out, they need not be the concern of area-wide rules. In a monetary union, however, there may be adverse spill-over effects on other countries. A country within a monetary union that became unable to finance its expenditure would face three options. It could:

1. default on its debts;
2. receive direct transfers from other members of the monetary union or another international organization to finance its expenditure; or
3. put pressure on the central bank to relax monetary policy.

All three options would be harmful, both for the country involved and for other member countries.

Even if a country were not about to default, there could be some other undesirable effects of high levels of debt. The extensive evidence on fiscal developments and long-term interest rates has been summarized in two recent literature surveys.[9] While the conclusions reached by different authors are mixed, and there is considerable difficulty in disentangling the different drivers of interest rates (there is, for example, evidence that European long-term interest rates are influenced by international rates, particularly those in the USA[10]), the emerging conclusion is that some fiscal aggregates can affect long-term interest rates. The strongest results come from debt or high and prolonged or permanent changes in expected fiscal deficits (which would in turn increase debt). In addition, there is also some evidence that the effect of increased debt on long-term interest rates is non-linear, and greatest for those countries which already have high debt levels.[11]

All this should provide countries with an incentive not to incur excessive debts themselves. But there is also the issue of the extent to which one country's fiscal policy has a spill-over effect on the interest rates of other countries, especially in the context of Economic and Monetary Union (EMU). There has recently been some discussion as to why there has been so little differentiation among the government bonds of the Euro area countries. Schumacher (2005) outlines four possible explanations: 'greater fiscal soundness after EMU, a perceived implicit bail-out guarantee for member countries, a subsidy for lower rated bond yields through the ECB's repo business,[12] and the "hunger for yield" among investors in the current low yield environment'. Schumacher rejects the first three explanations: on the first, the pressure to consolidate has waned since the start of EMU; on the second, he regards the possibility of a bail-out as unconvincing; and the third factor appears to have only a limited impact. This leaves the last explanation, and as a consequence he concludes: 'In time, we expect that financial markets will discriminate more between the bonds of EMU member states, especially if the fiscal situation in any country were to deteriorate further.'

If financial markets were to discriminate more between Euro area members this would leave open the question as to whether an SGP were needed at all. This has not been the position of the UK government, however. In the current circumstances where the European Central Bank (ECB) and member states' attitudes have not been tested in a crisis situation[13] there is clearly a precautionary case for avoiding reaching a position where a country might default. Secondly – and arguably this has been a problem with the SGP (see section 4.1) – without the SGP, many EU countries would not have a fiscal framework at all. Thirdly, as noted, there has been very little differentiation by financial markets so far[14] and even if this were to happen, as for example Schumacher expects, the change is likely to be abrupt and potentially very disruptive. The markets' response would not necessarily discriminate properly between individual countries in EMU either, implying that member states could be affected adversely by the actions of others.

3.2   Credibility and the SGP

The historical problems of fiscal policy in the EU member states are well known. During the 1980s and early 1990s high and persistent budget deficits fed an ever-growing stock of public debt. Against this backdrop, the objectives and rules in the Maastricht Treaty and the SGP played an important role in enhancing the credibility of EU governments' commitment to fiscal discipline in the run-up to EMU. Figure 5.2 shows that the average deficits and debts in the Euro area were both steadily reduced over the second half of the 1990s.

While the deficit for the Euro area as a whole has remained below 3 per cent of GDP since the late 1990s, debt remains above the reference value. Debt-to-GDP ratios fell slightly in the run-up to EMU, but the average level for the Euro area countries is now around 70 per cent of GDP and it is expected to rise in the coming years. Moreover, some countries still have debt levels over 100 per cent of GDP. Progress on debt consolidation appears to have stalled, suggesting there may be insufficient incentives in the SGP to reduce debt levels.

A forward-looking focus on maintaining prudent debt levels should help ensure that EU member states address the long-term challenges to public finances, such as those posed by population ageing. Indeed, issues concerning long-run sustainability were increasingly being recognized amongst EU member states before the recent SGP reforms. For example, Stability and Convergence Programmes were required to include information on

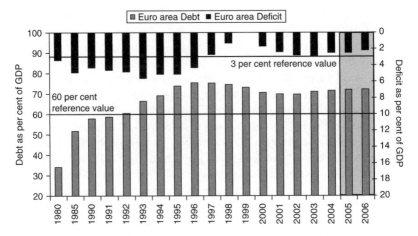

Note: 2005 and 2006 are forecasts

Source: European Commission Spring Forecasts 2005

Figure 5.2 Euro area debt and deficits

longer-term sustainability under the Code of Conduct. However, joint work at the EU level[15] suggests that, if current policies remain unchanged, some EU countries face substantial increases in age-related spending in the coming decades (Figure 5.3). As shown in HM Treasury (2004a), the UK appears relatively well placed to face the challenges of an ageing population.

Reforms affecting credibility

While the SGP's corrective arm already had the 60 per cent debt ratio as one of the reference values that could be used to trigger an excessive deficit procedure (EDP) if debt was not 'sufficiently diminishing and approaching the reference value at a satisfactory pace', the debt trigger has never been used to launch an EDP. The reformed SGP takes note of the need to increase the focus on both debt and long-term sustainability and reaffirms a commitment to reducing debt below 60 per cent of GDP. The Council will, from now on, formulate recommendations for countries above the debt level in the opinions of the Stability and Convergence Programmes. The recommendations will be set out in qualitative terms and take account of macroeconomic conditions, debt dynamics and debt management strategies.[16] In addition in the preventive arm, the Medium-Term Objective (MTO) will take into account the initial level of debt in the country and it will be set to ensure that debt moves under the reference value in a suitable time-frame.

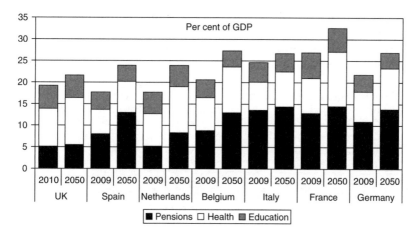

Note: For UK, pension spending equivalent to state pension spending as defined in HM Treasury (2004a). For other countries, as defined in 2004 Updates of Stability Programmes. Comparisons of projections need to be treated with caution as some include the cost of long-term care within health projections

Source: European Commission Services working documents on member states' Stability and Convergence Programmes 2005

Figure 5.3 Age-related spending in selected EU countries

Success in this aspect of the pact is closely related to the extent to which national policy makers demonstrate their commitment to fiscal prudence and the principle of legitimacy looked at later (see section 3.4). Enhancing credibility also requires further progress on developing comprehensive and reliable assessments of long-term sustainability and the commitment to policy reforms to underpin it.

Other aspects of the reforms have increased the automaticity of the rules, for example in the corrective arm: countries in excessive deficit are required to achieve a minimum fiscal effort of 0.5 per cent of GDP as a benchmark (in cyclically adjusted terms net of one-off and temporary measures); and the Commission's report under Article 104(3) is automatic if there is a deficit above 3 per cent of GDP. And, in the preventive arm, the Euro area and ERM II countries will have to pursue an annual adjustment towards meeting their medium-term budgetary objective in cyclically adjusted terms, net of one-offs and other temporary measures, of 0.5 per cent of GDP as a benchmark. While this greater automaticity introduces a transparent predictability to the operation of the pact, it will be important to apply the additional economic judgement the new pact allows to avoid the application of automatic fiscal adjustments being overly mechanistic and thereby impinging on the greater flexibility afforded by the reforms (see section 3.3).

Also within the preventive arm, the ECOFIN (2005) Report encourages greater fiscal consolidation in 'good times':

> Member States should commit at a European level to actively consolidate public finances in good times ... Member States that have not yet reached their medium-term objective should take steps to achieve it over the cycle. Their adjustment effort should be higher in good times; it could be more limited in bad times ... Good times should be identified as period where output exceeds its potential level.

If effective, this would also enhance credibility. A greater focus on debt levels should also increase the incentives on member states to do more in good times.

3.3   Flexibility

Experience has also shown that credible macroeconomic frameworks must have sufficient flexibility. This section considers two aspects of flexibility: the flexibility to take account of the economic cycle without jeopardizing the credibility of governments' long-term goals for sound public finances; and the flexibility to undertake public investment.

Taking account of the economic cycle

In the short term, provided that rules are adhered to and sustainability is not in doubt, fiscal policy should be flexible enough to be able to support monetary policy in smoothing economic fluctuations and stabilizing output. A first step is to allow the automatic stabilizers to operate in full – this should mean the budget position moves counter-cyclically, including running smaller deficits/larger surpluses when output is above trend (in the 'good times'). Leaving the automatic stabilizers to operate can also be justified in efficiency terms because of tax-smoothing considerations.[17] In the UK, the fiscal rules are set over the economic cycle (see Box 5.1), which allows the automatic stabilizers to operate in full. The rules also allow for discretionary changes in the fiscal stance to restrain or stimulate demand where appropriate, with the safeguard that any discretionary fiscal stimulus in a downturn would need to have been matched by at least as large a restraining measure in the upturn.

In a single currency area, with monetary policy no longer able to react to country-specific shocks, or where common shocks have a differential impact across member states due to different structures, there could be a greater need for discretionary fiscal policy at a national level. Section 4.4 briefly considers some of the issues.[18]

Without an adequate focus on the cycle there is a risk that economies will not tighten fiscal policy sufficiently when the economy is growing strongly. Moreover, the 3 per cent Treaty deficit limit is defined in terms of the actual deficit, not the cyclically adjusted deficit. This could lead to pressure to override the automatic stabilizers in a downturn to meet the 3 per cent limit. This underlay the desire to address the issue of encouraging fiscal consolidation in 'good times' in the reforms noted above. It could be argued that the SGP permits as much short-run stabilization as a country wants, so long as the country has achieved a high enough surplus in normal times to permit it.[19] However, structural surpluses (or balanced budgets) in countries with low and sustainable debt positions could be undesirable for at least two reasons. If the current generation bears more than its fair share of the burden of maintaining a sound fiscal position it could harm inter-generational equity. Alternatively, it could result in a squeeze in public investment which might harm future generations by damaging a country's infrastructure or the capacity of the public sector to deliver public services.[20] The problem of public investment is discussed further below.

It is worth considering the extent to which fiscal policy has helped to support monetary policy. So far under the SGP the automatic stabilizers have been able to operate at least partially in Euro area countries. However, Figure 5.4, which shows the changes in the cyclically adjusted deficit, suggests that on average fiscal policies in the Euro area have not been strongly counter-cyclical in recent years and there is a suggestion that policy was somewhat pro-cyclical over the period 2000–02. Figure 5.5 illustrates that the change in the monetary policy stance, measured as the change in real interest rates, has also been rather limited in the Euro area (at least by comparison with the UK over the same period). Figure 5.5 also suggests that fiscal and monetary policies have not been particularly closely coordinated in the Euro area on these measures.[21]

While the recognition of cyclical factors in the implementation of the SGP had evolved prior to the recent reforms,[22] it was perhaps understandable at the outset that, dealing with so many countries, the pact would be interpreted in rather mechanistic terms rather than by guiding principles that could afford some constrained discretion. A particular concern has been that the SGP did not have a mechanism to promote stronger fiscal policies in the above-trend phase of the cycle.

Flexibility to invest

For countries with sound public finances and economic stability, the fiscal framework should allow governments to implement structural reforms and improve the quality of public finances. In particular, there should be room

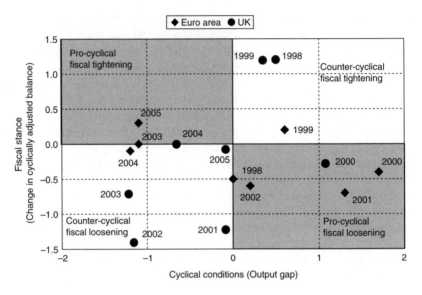

Note: 2005 is a forecast

Source: European Commission Spring 2005 Forecasts and HM Treasury

*Figure 5.4   UK and Euro area fiscal stance and cyclical conditions,
1998–2005*

for policies that help deliver structural reforms and promote public investment which have long-term benefits but require significant upfront costs.

The UK fiscal and spending frameworks distinguish between capital and current expenditure.[23] One reason for making this distinction was the historical bias against public investment in the UK, especially in periods of fiscal consolidation. Unlike current spending, public investment adds to the public capital stock and it provides an ongoing flow of benefits to society. Borrowing for investment can therefore help to match the flow of benefits with the costs of providing the asset,[24] and it is consistent with the principle of inter-generational equity. Ideally, as in the UK framework, investment should be net of depreciation so as to match the costs and benefits of investment over time.

Public investment also contributes to the provision of high-quality public services and it can help to underpin a flexible, high-productivity economy. There is an analogy here with areas of *current* expenditure that promote the accumulation of non-physical capital, such as education spending, and other costs related to making successful structural reforms. For example, reforms to the tax system may entail a significant upfront

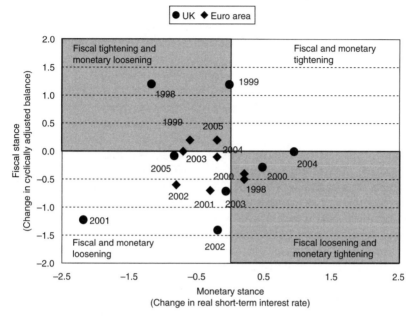

Note: UK fiscal data in financial years

Source: European Commission Spring Forecasts 2005 and ONS

Figure 5.5   *Euro area and UK policy mix – change in cyclically adjusted balance*

cost, while delivering a stream of future benefits as a result of stronger trend growth. Fiscal or expenditure rules that do not recognize this might discourage such reforms. The difficulty is that, while the costs of such reforms are often clear, the benefits are often not well defined and are difficult to calculate with any precision (whereas investment expenditure is defined according to internationally agreed conventions). For this reason in the UK, a cautious approach is taken where the potential impact of structural reforms on trend growth is not included in the assumptions for the fiscal projections until the effects are clearly seen in the data.

While inter-generational fairness depends on the flow of costs and social (often non-financial) benefits, the sustainability of the public finances depends on the net financial benefits of public investment. Plans for capital expenditure, therefore, need to be fully consistent with ensuring long-term sustainability and maintaining low and stable debt levels.[25]

The original SGP framework recognized the importance of public investment to an extent. Article 104(3) of the EC Treaty states that the assessment of whether a country's deficit is excessive should take into account 'whether the government deficit exceeds government investment expenditure'. Indeed, initial proposals for a fiscal stability pact explicitly called for 'priority in government spending for public investment'.[26] However, in practice the SGP could have benefited from greater recognition of the importance of measures that have longer-term benefits, even if they entail upfront costs in the short run. In addition to the 3 per cent deficit reference value, the Medium-Term Objective of close to balance or in surplus for the deficit was largely set in uniformity for all member states, with little variation to take account of debt levels or levels of public investment.

Overall, there is some evidence that public investment has suffered. For example, Blanchard and Giavazzi (2003) noted that, in the run-up to EMU between 1993 and 1997, public investment fell by 0.8 per cent of GDP, a period marked by a pronounced fiscal consolidation. Balassone and Franco (2000) found the adjustment to investment was particularly marked in high-debt countries, Italy, Belgium and (at that time) Ireland. In some cases, some reduction in public investment may have been appropriate. However, the UK experience suggests that, while cutting back public investment can be sustained for a long time, ultimately it is not sustainable if the government remains responsible for the provision of public infrastructure and public services. This suggests a fiscal consolidation focused solely on reducing deficit and debt indicators which involved cutting net investment may give a misleading impression of the longer-term sustainability of the public finances. (In addition, running down the capital stock and then building it back up is likely to be more expensive than maintaining a capital stock at the appropriate level.)

Reforms affecting flexibility
Flexibility in the new SGP has been enhanced in both the preventive and corrective arms.[27] For example, there has been an increased recognition of the importance of taking account of the economic cycle through a change in the definition of 'severe economic downturn' in the corrective arm. Previously, a severe economic downturn was defined as 'an annual fall of real GDP of at least 2 per cent'. Not only was this too restrictive, but it had little economic rationale. The ECOFIN (2005) Report's definition now refers to periods of: 'an excess over the reference value which results from a negative growth rate or from the accumulated loss of output during a protracted period of very low growth relative to potential growth'. The reference to the accumulated loss of output and potential growth also allows for the heterogeneities between member states' underlying growth rates (discussed further in section 4.3).[28]

Building on this, reforms have also introduced greater flexibility by extending the time-frame for taking effective action to correct an excessive deficit, and to repeat the steps of the procedure if there are unexpected adverse economic events when effective action has been taken. These changes have been important in the excessive deficit procedures agreed for Portugal and Italy (Box 5.3).

BOX 5.3   EXCESSIVE DEFICIT PROCEDURE FOR ITALY AND PORTUGAL

The Commission launched an excessive deficit procedure on Italy on 7 June 2005 by adopting a report under Article 104(3) of the EU Treaty. It found that the Italian general government budget deficit had been above 3 per cent of GDP, albeit slightly at 3.2 per cent, in 2003 and 2004 and was expected to be above 4 per cent of GDP in 2005 and 2006 unless there was a policy change. In July, the Council issued the following Recommendation to Italy:

- To correct the excessive deficit by the end of 2007. This gives Italy one additional year beyond that normally required under the SGP. Under the new regulations in the case of special circumstances, the initial deadline for correcting an excessive deficit could be set one year later, i.e. the second year after its identification and thus normally the third year after its occurrence. In particular, the Council text stated that with 'the current cyclical weakness in Italy together with the size of the required adjustment to bring the deficit below the 3% of GDP reference value by 2006 . . . special circumstances exist and an extension of the deadline for the correction of the excessive deficit to 2007 is warranted'.
- A deadline of four months at the most for effective action to be taken by Italy to correct the excessive deficit. However, this was extended by a further two months when the new regulations were applied at the end of July.

Portugal's Stability Programme projects a correction of its excessive deficit by 2008. Its fiscal deficit is expected to be above 6 per cent of GDP in 2005, significantly above the SGP reference value. Similar to Italy, Portugal was given an additional year to correct its excessive deficit. Even though the circumstances were different (for instance, Italy was in recession in the first quarter of the year, and Portugal recorded low but positive growth) the wording in the recitals to the Recommendations for special circumstances was identical for both Portugal and Italy. The Council established a deadline of 19 March 2005 for the Portuguese government to take effective action regarding the measures envisaged to achieve the deficit target.

In the context of the reforms to the SGP these EDPs mainly illustrate the increased flexibility the pact now allows for correcting an EDP and how the process takes account of the cycle.

In terms of accounting for investment, in the preventative arm of the pact, the Medium-Term Objective has now been modified to take investment needs into account, providing debt is sufficiently low. The ECOFIN Report states:

> The Council therefore proposes developing medium-term objectives that, by taking account of the characteristics of the economy of each Member State, pursue a triple aim. They should firstly provide a safety margin with respect to the 3% deficit limit. They should also ensure rapid progress towards sustainability. Taking this into account, they should allow room for budgetary manoeuvre, in particular taking into account the needs for public investment.

Based on this commitment, countries can deviate from the medium-term goal of close to balance or in surplus of the previous pact subject to: low-debt and high-potential-growth countries having a deficit target of between 1 per cent and surplus; and high-debt and low-potential-growth countries having a target of balance or in surplus.[29] However, while the new Medium-Term Objectives build in greater flexibility in this way as noted, there is a requirement for Euro area and ERM II countries to pursue an annual adjustment towards meeting their medium-term budgetary objective in cyclically adjusted terms, net of one-offs and other temporary measures, of 0.5 per cent of GDP as a benchmark. As noted above, it will be important to apply the additional economic judgement the new pact allows to avoid this dimension becoming overly mechanistic in its implementation.

There is also now explicit recognition of the importance of structural reforms (which is looked at further in section 4.2).

Flexibility to allow for investment, structural reforms and the cycle are also included in the list of 'other relevant factors' (applicable to the definition and adjustment path towards the Medium-Term Objective in the preventive arm, and to assessing the existence and correction of an excessive deficit in the corrective arm).[30] While the provision for 'other relevant factors' already existed in the Treaty, in practice it had not played a significant role in the past as it was not clear what it referred to. The ECOFIN (2005) Report states that when preparing the assessment of whether an excessive deficit exists the Commission must consider any other factor which may have contributed to an excess over the deficit limit, provided the excess is close and temporary.

3.4 Legitimacy and the SGP

Legitimacy means that the policy framework engenders lasting public and parliamentary support. Accountability and transparency can help promote legitimacy. But legitimacy can also be measured by whether the policy framework gives policy makers the democratic mandate to take action on behalf of the public.

The multilateral surveillance provided for under the SGP could enhance legitimacy. For example, the annual publication of Stability and Convergence Programmes has increased the transparency of member states' fiscal positions. Assessment of these programmes by the European Commission[31] and the ECOFIN Council provides for an element of peer review. Transparency was also promoted by the Council publishing its opinions on individual member states' Stability and Convergence Programmes, as well as any decisions that an excessive deficit existed in a member state.

The SGP faced a number of challenges that suggested further steps could be undertaken to enhance the legitimacy of the framework. Particular criticisms included:

- rules were not based on a clear economic rationale;[32]
- relatedly, the targets were applied mechanistically; and
- there was a perceived lack of transparency and consistency.

The lack of a clear economic justification may have contributed to difficulties in distinguishing between a breach of the rules by a state with fundamentally sound policies and one without. The SGP as originally implemented left little scope to differentiate between countries on the basis of their individual economic circumstances beyond deficit levels.

Some serious statistical difficulties have been highlighted, compromising both the credibility and the legitimacy of the SGP. The existence of an excessive deficit in Portugal for 2001 was only identified by ECOFIN in November 2002 following the release of substantially revised statistics. In 2004 and 2005 the fiscal deficit data for Greece were revised by very large magnitudes right back to 1997, with deficits of over 5 and 6 per cent recorded in 2003 and 2004 respectively. The use of one-off measures to reduce the reported deficit in several countries has also been a concern.

There are fewer formal parliamentary mechanisms for ensuring accountability at an EU level than at national level, although the Treaty does require that the president of the Commission and the Council report to the European Parliament on the results of multilateral surveillance and the Parliament can call the president of the Council to appear. And there has also been some role for national parliaments.[33]

In considering whether the SGP has the necessary high degree of legitimacy, it is important to examine the division of responsibilities. With fiscal policy decisions remaining firmly within the national competence, legitimacy is achieved through the usual democratic mandate, i.e. decisions made by elected politicians (Hodson and Maher, 2000). Although the European Commission has the right of initiative on, for example, recommending that a member state has an excessive deficit, the Council has the ultimate right of decision and can choose whether to accept or reject Commission recommendations. The Council represents member states and therefore, together with the fact that the Council makes the final decisions, the system ensures legitimacy. As Hodson and Maher state: 'the case of the EDP shows that even when economic policy is defined in terms of regulations (the most rigorous form of legal rule within the EU legal order) it remains fundamentally intergovernmental'.

Reforms affecting legitimacy

The importance of legitimacy is reflected in the emphasis on the role of national fiscal rules and national governance arrangements, and the need to strengthen national ownership in the ECOFIN (2005) Report. (Some of these issues are taken up in section 4.1.) The recent reforms have made advances in improving the economic rationale and increasing the scope for judgement in the application of the rules the better to reflect the realities of operating fiscal rules in an enlarged EU. The measures to promote flexibility should allow the SGP to reflect national differences better in an economically sensible way and they should help to build legitimacy and ownership, for example in the greater differentiation in the Medium-Term Objective noted above. In addition, to help ensure that sufficient economic judgement is used in assessing whether there is an excessive deficit, a set of 'other relevant factors'[34] will be considered, as mentioned above.

There have also been moves to improve the reliability of statistics. In June 2005, ECOFIN endorsed work on a package of measures to improve the integrity of the European Statistical System. In particular, the Council welcomed the European Statistics Code of Practice, which will help spread best practice among national statistical institutes through a peer review process. It has also indicated its support for ongoing work that might give Eurostat the right to review countries' methodology in the event that there is considerable evidence of serious risks to their data. Finally, the Council called for an acceleration in work to rebalance the priorities in the

European Statistical System. This will help ensure that resources are withdrawn from areas that have ceased to be a priority, and refocused on producing high-quality, timely statistics. Work on these areas is ongoing. In the light of earlier problems, greater attention is now also being paid to stock-flow dynamics. A greater focus on debt levels should also help in this respect.

Table 5.1, reproduced from Buti (2006), summarizes all the main changes.

Table 5.1 Main changes to the Stability and Growth Pact following the Council agreement of 20 March 2005

	Original	Revised
1. Changes in the preventive arm		
Medium-Term Objective (MTO)	All member states (MS) have a medium-term budgetary objective (MTO) of 'close to balance or in surplus'.	• Country-specific differentiation of MTOs according to stock of public debt and potential growth. • MTOs for Euro area and ERM II are set between −1% of GDP and balance or surplus (in cyclically adjusted terms and net of one-offs). • Implicit liabilities to be taken into account at a later stage, when modalities for doing so are agreed by the Council.
Adjustment path towards the MTO	No specific provisions.	• MS to take active steps to achieve the MTO. • Annual minimum adjustment for MS of the Euro zone or of ERM II of 0.5% of GDP. • The effort should be higher in 'good times'. • 'Good times' are identified as periods where output exceeds its potential level, 'taking into account tax elasticities'.
Early policy advice	Early warnings are adopted/addressed by the Council, upon recommendation of the Commission.	In addition, the Commission can issue direct 'early policy advice' to encourage MS to stick to their adjustment path, to be replaced by 'early warnings' in accordance with the Constitution once applicable.

Table 5.1 (continued)

	Original	Revised
Structural reforms	No specific provision.	Reforms will be taken into account when defining the adjustment path to the MTO and may allow a deviation from it under the following conditions: • Only major reforms (direct/indirect impact on sustainability); • safety margin to the 3% reference value is guaranteed; • the deficit returns to the MTO within the programme period; • detailed information is provided in the Stability/Convergence Programmes. Special attention to systemic pension reforms.

2. Differences in the corrective arm

	Original	Revised
Preparing a report under Article 104(3)	No obligation for the Commission to prepare a report if a deficit exceeds 3%.	• The Commission will always prepare a report in case there is a deficit above 3%. • The report will examine whether the exceptions in Article 104(2) apply. • It will take into account whether the deficit exceeds government investment expenditure and all 'other relevant factors'.
Severe economic downturn	'Severe economic downturn' if there is an annual fall of real GDP of at least 2% for the preparation of report under Art. 104(3) by the Commission, and in decisions under 104(6) by the Council, if observations by the member state concerned show that the downturn is	An economic downturn may be considered 'severe' in case of a negative growth rate or accumulated loss of output during a protracted period of very low growth relative to potential growth.

Table 5.1   (continued)

	Original	Revised
	exceptional in light of evidence of the abruptness of the downturn and the accumulated loss of output with respect to past trends. The member states commit not to invoke the severe economic downturn when growth is above -0.75%.	

'Other relevant factors' *(ORF)*	No specific definition of 'ORF' and their role in the excessive deficit procedure.	• The Commission report under Art. 104(3) will take into account:
		  • Developments in the medium-term economic position (potential growth, cyclical conditions, implementation of policies);
		  • Developments in the medium-term budgetary position (public investment, quality of public finances, as well as fiscal consolidation in 'good times', debt sustainability);
		  • Any other factors, which in the opinion of the MS, are relevant in order to assess the excess over the reference value.
		• 'ORF' will be considered in the steps from Article 104(4) to (6) only if the excess over the reference value is temporary and the deficit remains close to the reference value. Any deficit above 3% that is neither close to the reference value nor temporary will be considered excessive.
		• If the Council has decided that an excessive deficit exists, the ORF will also be considered in the subsequent procedural steps of Article 104

Table 5.1 (continued)

	Original	Revised
		(except in Article 104(2), i.e. abrogation, and when deciding to repeat steps in the EDP).
Systemic pension reforms	No specific provision.	• These are treated like an 'ORF', but under strict conditions also with a role in abrogation. • Consideration to the net cost of the reform will be given regressively for the initial five years after an MS has introduced the reform (or five years after 2004).
Increasing the focus on debt and sustainability	No specific provision.	• The debt criterion and in particular the concept of a debt ratio 'suficiently diminishing and approaching the reference value at a satisfactory pace' will be applied in qualitative terms. • The Council will formulate recommendations on the debt dynamics in its opinions on the Stability and Convergence Programmes.
Extending deadlines for taking effective action and measures		Deadlines are extended: • for a decision under 104(6) – from 3 to 4 months after notification; • for taking effective action following 104(7) – from 4 to 6 months; • for moving to 104(9) – from 1 to 2 months; • for taking action following a notice under 104(9) – from 2 to 4 months.
Minimum fiscal effort	No specific provision.	Countries in excessive deficit are required to achieve a minimum fiscal effort of at least 0.5% of GDP as a benchmark.
Initial deadline for correcting the excessive deficit	The excessive deficit has to be corrected in the year following its identification,	The rule remains; possible extension by one year based on 'ORF' and on the condition that minimum fiscal efforts have been taken.

Table 5.1 (continued)

	Original	Revised
	unless there are 'special circumstances'.	
Repetition of steps in the EDP	Not foreseen.	Deadlines for correcting the ED can be extended if: • effective action has been taken by the MS concerned in compliance with the initial recommendation or notice, and • unexpected adverse economic events with major unfavourable budgetary effects occur during the correction phase.

Source: Commission services

4 FUTURE CHALLENGES IN IMPLEMENTATION

4.1 Developing National Frameworks and Increasing National Ownership

The reforms have taken some important steps forward in recognizing both the theoretical and the operational shortcomings of the pact. An important challenge in terms of legitimacy will be to ensure greater national ownership of the fiscal rules in the pact and embedding this within national fiscal frameworks.

The modifications to the SGP should help improve ownership by national policy makers by taking greater account of the economic and fiscal heterogeneity across member states, so that the application and enforcement of the rules and provisions are enhanced. In addition, the Council Report itself highlights the importance of improving governance and strengthening national ownership of the fiscal framework.

One aspect of this is that it has been argued that the SGP is an incomplete fiscal framework in some ways, reflecting the degree to which member states are comfortable with placing supra-national constraints on their fiscal policies.[35] This remains an issue and suggests a need to supplement the SGP with complementary national fiscal frameworks. It remains to be seen, for example, how effective the measures to consolidate fiscal positions in 'good times' prove to be, especially if the implementation of the SGP were not to succeed in raising the focus on debt levels by much.

4.2   Taking Account of Structural Reforms

Structural reforms[36] are needed to maintain prosperity for European citizens in the face of profound economic and social changes that have already begun to take place, including the ageing of populations and the substantial, ongoing changes in the international division of labour. These changes are bound to have deep-seated effects not only on public finances, but more generally on the economy and the society. Structural reforms, aimed at strengthening economic growth and the sustainability of public finances, are needed in many countries in order to preserve high standards of living.

The populations in most developed countries and some developing countries are ageing. This trend is not new but it is expected to continue and even accelerate over the coming decades. Underlying this general development are three distinct population trends:

- The post-war baby-boom generation is gradually reaching retirement age. As a result the number of people above working age will rise. However, everything else being equal, this increase will only have a temporary impact on the age structure, as subsequent cohorts are smaller again.
- There is a general ageing of the population, with life expectancy expected to continue to rise over the coming decades. Continued increases in longevity will have a permanent demographic effect.
- The fertility rate is expected to remain below the natural replacement rate, leading to expected absolute reductions in the population of working age in some countries.[37]

While it is useful to quantify the required policy action in terms of fiscal adjustment, this can be misleading as a policy prescription. A fiscal tightening now to deal with future ageing only makes sense as long as ageing is a one-off process. This is only the case for the cohort effect from the baby-boom generation. A fiscal tightening alone is not sufficient if life expectancy were to continue to increase over the coming decades and beyond.[38] Nor will it help resolve issues related to a declining working population due to low fertility rates. Moreover, there are certain structural reforms which might improve both long-term growth and the sustainability of public finances, which might have a negative effect on the budget in the short run. This might happen for a variety of reasons: conventions in national accounting, as is the case for certain pension reforms; the fact that reforms might take time to produce beneficial effects on growth and/or the budgetary situation; and the fact that temporary increases in expenditure might be necessary to make structural reforms viable from a political point of view.

In some countries the fiscal challenges might arise from the pension system, in other countries from the health or long-term care system. Addressing the source of the projected imbalance will often be a more appropriate policy response than using a fiscal tightening.

The appropriate response to the challenges and opportunities offered by the process of globalization is greater innovation and productivity-enhancing investment in human and physical capital.[39] Structural reforms in labour, product and capital markets will be needed to foster this process. Regulation must be streamlined and made more efficient and effective so as to reduce the burden on enterprises. Also the quality of public expenditure has to improve to raise the value for money in the provision of public services.

The original SGP did not emphasize the importance of country-specific structural reforms, which might improve the long-term sustainability of the public finances. Instead it focused on the deficit criterion, with a rather short-term focus. Under the reformed SGP, structural reforms and pension reforms are given special consideration in the preventive and corrective arms of the pact. The ECOFIN Report lays out the following:

- If the Medium-Term Objective has been met, a temporary deviation can be permitted provided the 3 per cent of GDP reference value is guaranteed and the objective is achieved within the projection period in the Stability and Convergence Programme.
- If the Medium-Term Objective is yet to be achieved, structural reforms will be taken into account when defining the adjustment path towards the Medium-Term Objective.
- An excess close to the reference value which reflects the implementation of pension reforms introducing a multi-pillar system that includes a mandatory, fully funded pillar should be carefully considered, including when deciding whether an excessive deficit has been corrected.

Within this framework, specific structural reforms will be taken into account which can be shown to have (through detailed cost–benefit analysis): 'direct long-term cost saving effects, including by raising potential growth'.[40]

This raises the challenge of identifying what qualifies as a structural reform, how the evidence base is to be compiled, and how the uncertainty over the costs and particularly the longer-term benefits should be considered.

It is clear that a mechanical, one-size-fits-all taxonomy would be inappropriate given the heterogeneities discussed. This is reinforced by analysis carried out by the European Commission (EC)[41] which suggests that on average the change in the structural balance is not significantly different following the implementation of reforms compared with years without reforms; and that reforms are not less frequent in years when there is budgetary consolidation. However, these broad conclusions vary significantly depending on the specific characteristics of the reforms. Therefore, when assessing structural reforms under the pact the EC proposes that: 'a mechanistic, one-size fits all approach where all reforms, or all reforms belonging to some broad categories, are considered the same way should be avoided. This means careful judgement is needed on a case-by-case basis and considering the relevant features of the specific reforms at stake.'[42] Achieving a successful balance of promoting sufficient fiscal consolidation while leaving room for appropriate structural reforms with uncertain benefits will be a challenge.

4.3   Managing a More Diverse EU

Enlargement brought ten countries into the EU with very different economic characteristics from the existing members. As Figure 5.6 illustrates, most of them have low levels of public gross debt, around 40 per cent of GDP on average, versus an EU-15 average above 60 per cent of GDP. Many of the new member states are running budget deficits exceeding the 3 per cent Treaty threshold in 2004, however. The new member states are also very dynamic economies, growing at 5 per cent in 2004[43] (when EU-15 growth was 2.3 per cent). To the extent that exchange rates are fixed, the faster long-term growth also implies that they are likely to have higher (sustainable) inflation rates owing to the Balassa–Samuelson effect.[44] Finally, ongoing structural reform and the likelihood that their initial capital stocks are low suggest that the new member states are likely to need to maintain relatively high levels of public investment. These stylized facts have significant implications for the application of the SGP to the new member states.[45]

A **credible framework** should deliver long-term fiscal sustainability. A country's sustainable level of debt can be assessed in terms of the government's solvency constraint that the current value of debt must be equivalent to the net present value of future primary surpluses.[46] This has a number of implications for the new member states:

- Higher equilibrium inflation rates due to Balassa–Samuelson effects imply lower real interest rates, and mean that (other things being equal) the new member states can sustain a higher debt level.

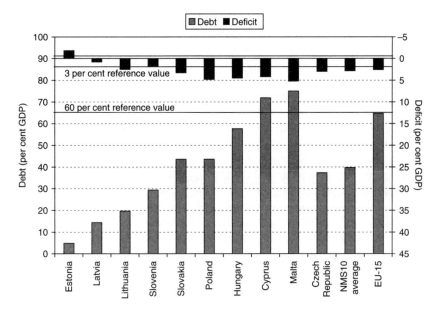

Source: HM Treasury

Figure 5.6   Debt and deficits in the new member states, 2004

- Higher growth rates also mean that a higher initial debt level can be sustained.
- Temporarily higher spending now can be accommodated if it is offset by lower spending and/or higher taxes in the future.

Since strong growth and low real interest rates reduce the effective burden of any existing debt, the new member states can sustain somewhat higher levels of debt. In addition, they have a strong starting position owing to their relatively low initial debt levels. Some of these countries should be allowed to run larger deficits now if long-run projections suggest that they are sustainable on reasonable assumptions (e.g. if the country wanted to make large investments in public infrastructure now in order to generate higher growth in the future).

A number of the new member states have taken steps to counteract the effects of an ageing population, for instance by reforming their pay-as-you-go pension systems or establishing funded schemes. These often involve short-term transitional costs. The reformed SGP has taken a step forward by taking these transitional costs into account, which will assist reforming countries such as Hungary and Poland.

As noted, a robust framework should also provide **short-term flexibility** to allow policy makers to respond to shocks, providing the government's commitment to its long-term objectives is credible. Since, as noted above, the new member states seem well placed in terms of fiscal sustainability, the SGP should give them additional flexibility. However, the new member states are very open economies and are heavily influenced by international portfolio investors' attitudes to risk.[47] This may make them more vulnerable to economic shocks. While this means that they may need to have recourse to greater flexibility in the event of negative shocks, it also suggests that they may need to be relatively cautious in considering what longer-term debt levels are safe for them to assume.[48]

It is important for the SGP to give the new member states maximum capacity to implement structural reforms that require significant public investment in the short run. They need to invest in order to improve their infrastructure – both to fulfil promises to implement the acquis that they made during accession negotiations and in order to create good conditions for self-sustaining growth.

Figure 5.7 demonstrates that gross public investment is higher on average in the new EU member states than in the EU-15 (only Latvia was below the EU-15 average). However, on a net basis the difference is likely to be even more marked as the new member states have a smaller public capital stock.

Finally, macroeconomic frameworks must have widespread and lasting support to gain **legitimacy**. As noted, there is a close connection between legitimacy and credibility and flexibility. If the SGP were to take account

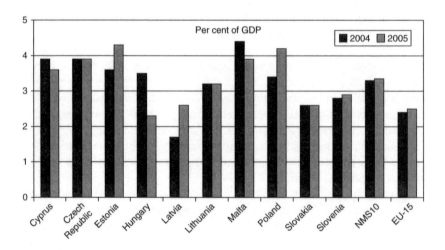

Source: European Commission Spring 2005 Forecasts

Figure 5.7   Public investment in the new EU member states

of how well the new member states stand in terms of fiscal sustainability, and gave them the flexibility to increase public investment and respond to shocks, then it is likely to be perceived as more legitimate.

The way the excessive deficit procedure has been applied to the new member states provides an example of a way each country's circumstances can be taken into account, rather than imposing mechanistic targets. It was recognized that 'special circumstances' apply to five of the six new member states with excessive deficits.[49] They were therefore given more than a year to correct their excessive deficits. The special circumstances included the fact that these countries' deficits were considerably above the 3 per cent Treaty threshold, making it unrealistic to expect them to eliminate their deficits in a year, but also the fact that they were undertaking substantial structural reforms.

In all five cases, the Council made a recommendation that they reduce their deficits over the medium term, in line with projections in the countries' own convergence programmes. Accordingly, Malta was given until 2006 to correct its excessive deficit, Poland and Slovakia until 2007, and the Czech Republic and Hungary until 2008. The fact that these deadlines were drawn from each country's own convergence programme should encourage national ownership and therefore enhance legitimacy.

All these points apply to the EU-15 members as well. Besides marked differences in initial debt levels, the countries also differ substantially in terms of likely longer-term projected growth rates, owing to both differential rates of productivity growth and wide differences in likely rates of employment growth.[50]

4.4 Macroeconomic Stability and Fiscal Stabilization in EMU

In a monetary union there is no scope for monetary policy or exchange rates to move in response to asymmetric shocks or different responses to common shocks. Labour, product and capital markets will ultimately promote adjustment, but even if they are relatively flexible, which they are not in some EU countries, the process of adjustment will take time. In the context of a small, calibrated macroeconomic model, HM Treasury (2003a, 2003b) illustrated the potential scope for discretionary fiscal policy in these circumstances. In the benchmark model output is 20 per cent more volatile in EMU and inflation is over 36 per cent more volatile (Table 5.2). In these circumstances, using a discretionary fiscal policy could substantially reduce output and inflation volatility.

Other studies, such as Kirsanova *et al.* (2004), also suggest there may be significant gains from operating simple fiscal stabilization rules in EMU.

Table 5.2 Long-run volatility comparison inside EMU versus outside EMU

	Ratio of volatility	
	Inflation	Output
Benchmark model	1.36	1.20
Augmented fiscal policy (in EMU only)[1]	1.11	0.92

Note: [1] Assumes a discretionary fiscal policy rule responding to both inflation and the output gap inside EMU only

Source: HM Treasury (2003b: 94). A ratio greater than 1 indicates greater volatility inside EMU

There is a long way between illustrative model simulations and effective policy action, however. As reviewed in HM Treasury (2003a), the history of discretionary fiscal policy is not very auspicious, with particular problems associated with lagged responses and the deficit bias problem manifested in a tendency to do more in downturns than upturns. In view of this, HM Treasury (2003a)[51] proposed a symmetric fiscal stabilization rule triggered by large deviations in output from trend (similar to the Swedish Commission's proposal, 2002) or by large deviations in inflation. The paper considered other institutional changes that might need to go alongside such a rule[52] and which fiscal instruments might prove the most effective.

Given the early experience with EMU, the potential scope for fiscal stabilization measures is significant even if relatively wide deviations of output or inflation are tolerated, i.e. even if the authorities were to pursue 'coarse tuning' rather than 'fine tuning'. Figure 5.8 shows a number of cases where the estimated output gap has been more than 1.5 percentage points or inflation has deviated from a (country-specific[53]) target by more than 1 percentage point.

The SGP, even as reformed, has not been designed to handle a discretionary fiscal policy. However, following the reforms to the SGP a possible way through can be seen. In particular, one can see how greater flexibility might be allowed if a country could show that satisfactory counter-cyclical measures had been made in 'good times' which ensured long-term sustainability and that they had a rigorous national framework to ensure discretionary interventions were symmetric. However, it would be useful to clarify the procedures further, before any country actually embarked on such a course.

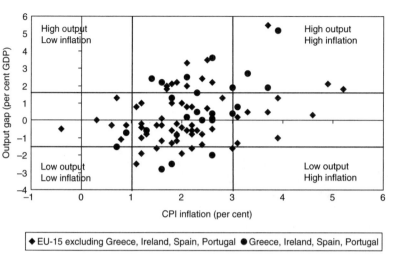

Source: European Commission Spring Forecasts 2005

Figure 5.8 *Output gap and inflation in the EU-15 countries, 2000–05,
adjusted for Balassa–Samuelson effects*

4.5 Data, Surveillance and Transparency

There are three interrelated challenges to improve the data, surveillance
and transparency underlying the SGP processes. As discussed above, at the
EU level, measures are being taken to improve the quality of data following the emergence of serious problems. In the UK there has also been
ongoing work to develop the data on the public finances:

- First, a project is underway to produce consolidated public sector
  accounts using Generally Agreed Accounting Principles. The first
  Whole of Government Accounts on this basis are planned to cover
  the financial year 2006–07 and they will be published once the
  methodological issues raised by the development work have been
  addressed. These data will strengthen some of the data sources for
  the national accounts, such as on depreciation and physical assets,
  and provide new areas of consolidated data in other areas, such as on
  provisions and contingent liabilities.
- Second, the Atkinson review, which considered the issues surrounding the measurement of public sector output, reported in January
  2005. It described a number of methodological developments which
  are now being implemented by the Office for National Statistics. This

work is important in the context of having a better-informed discussion of issues such as the quality of the public finances.

There is scope for member states to think further about strengthening the role of independent surveillance within their national fiscal frameworks.[54] This is unlikely to take the form of delegating the functions of fiscal policy as has sometimes been suggested in the literature[55] – this would go too far in compromising governments' responsibility and accountability for fiscal policy. In the UK, the National Audit Office[56] has a role in auditing the key assumptions underlying the public finance projections, including, for example, trend growth, equity prices, oil prices and unemployment. In 2005 the Chancellor announced[57] that he would invite the National Audit Office to audit the point at which the previous economic cycle ended.[58] A wide range of independent forecasts of the economy and the public finances are also collected by the Treasury and published every month and referred to in the Budget and Pre-Budget documents.[59] The European Commission (2005: 103) highlights the range of different national institutional arrangements across the EU. There may be greater scope for member states to learn from each other in this area, and also with respect to improving fiscal transparency.

CONCLUSION

The chapter has reviewed the workings of the SGP and key features of the recent reforms. As noted by the European Commission (2005), the reforms took place against the background of deteriorating fiscal situations and the changed circumstances of the enlarged EU. Within this context the reforms can be characterized as making greater allowance for the heterogeneity of member states and allowing for more economic judgement. Key areas of the reforms are aimed to:

- enhance credibility with more focus on debt and long-term sustainability, more automaticity in the application of the procedures, and greater focus on fiscal consolidation in 'good times';
- increase flexibility through the definition of a severe downturn, the time-frame for correcting an excessive deficit, the application of other relevant factors, and the allowance for investment and structural reforms;
- improve legitimacy through a clearer economic rationale which leaves more scope for judgement to allow for country-specific circumstances.

As noted, with regard to the greater automaticity of fiscal adjustments, it will be important to apply the additional economic judgement the new pact allows to avoid them becoming overly mechanistic and thereby impinging on the greater flexibility afforded by the reforms.

The challenge now is to implement the new SGP effectively. The chapter highlights five significant challenges including:

- the development of complementary national fiscal frameworks and increasing national ownership;
- promoting structural reforms to prepare the EU economy better for the challenges of an ageing population and globalization;
- managing a more diverse EU, especially in the context of the recent enlargement;
- consideration of the scope for using fiscal policy more actively in an EMU context; and
- improving data, surveillance and transparency.

NOTES

1. The views expressed in this chapter are those of the author and do not necessarily represent the views of HM Treasury. The author is grateful for the support of Preya Sharma in helping with the chapter.
2. For the purpose of the chapter the 'SGP' is taken to comprise the Treaty, the regulations and the Code of Conduct. See Appendix 5.1 for further information.
3. The reforms discussed in this chapter refer to the ECOFIN report, endorsed on 22 March 2005 by the EU heads of state and government entitled 'Improving the Implementation of the Stability and Growth Pact'.
4. The problem that policy makers find it hard to commit to long-term goals if short-term pressures point in another direction.
5. Blinder (1999) argued that credibility means people believe policy makers will do what they say.
6. Available at http://europa.eu.int/comm/economy_finance/publications/sgp/2004/comm 581_en.pdf.
7. Available at http://register.consilium.eu.int/pdf/en/05/st07/st07423.en05.pdf.
8. Appendix 5.1 provides a brief summary of how the SGP operates and illustrates the distinction between the preventive and corrective parts of the SGP which is used in the text (essentially the corrective arm relates to the excessive deficit procedure, and the preventive arm covers the multilateral surveillance of stability and convergence programmes).
9. The first is Brook (2003); and the second is European Commission (2004).
10. Brook (2003) cites a number of studies showing that US interest rates have in the past had a greater impact on European rates than vice versa. On the other hand, Chinn and Frankel (2003) find evidence that since EMU there are now two-way effects.
11. O'Donovan, Orr and Rae (1996) and Conway and Orr (2002) both find this result.
12. As suggested by Buiter and Sibert (2005), for example.
13. The ECB's formal independence and the no-bail-out rule are, of course, enshrined in the Maastricht Treaty.
14. Based on the 2004 data, Schumacher estimates that spreads would widen by about 15 bps if the government debt of a country rose from 50 per cent to 100 per cent of GDP.

15. See the Economic Policy Committee's Report (October, 2003).
16. However, EC (2005) notes: 'The SGP remains silent on how to apply the Excessive Deficit Procedure in the case of violation of the public debt criterion of the Treaty.'
17. Barro (1979).
18. HM Treasury (2003a) and Woods (2004a) consider these issues in more detail.
19. Partly for this reason, the Swedish Government Commission on Stabilisation Policy recommended that the Swedish government ran surpluses of over 2 per cent of GDP in normal times. See Government of Sweden (2002).
20. Easterly (1999) claims that the Maastricht deficit rules harmed many public investment projects.
21. A positive correlation between the monetary and fiscal stance might be expected if there were a close coordination.
22. The 2001 Code of Conduct placed greater emphasis on the implementation of fiscal consolidation in higher-debt countries, particularly when the economy is above trend, and to combine that with greater flexibility by allowing the automatic stabilizers to operate fully over the economic cycle.
23. See Toigo and Woods (2005) for a discussion of the interaction between public investment and fiscal policy.
24. Blanchard and Giavazzi (2003) summarize this: 'Investment implies future returns: its costs should thus be distributed over time as those returns accrue.'
25. See Toigo and Woods (2005) for a further discussion of this issue.
26. Waigel (1995: 3).
27. See Appendix 5.1 for brief details of how the pact operates.
28. In countries with high trend growth rates, a sustained period of negative growth would indicate a much wider output gap opening up than for countries with low trend growth rates. Moreover, with projected long-term reductions in the population of working age, trend growth in some EU countries could fall to rather low levels, making periods of negative growth more likely.
29. For Euro area and ERM II countries.
30. Article 2(3) of Council Regulation (EC) No. 1056/05.
31. Supported by ongoing work undertaken at the EU level on fiscal issues, such as the programme of work on long-run fiscal sustainability and the work on estimating trend output.
32. Buiter and Grafe (2003) stated that the SGP's rules were not credible because they 'are arbitrary and rigid in design'. Mélitz (2002) argues that: 'The means of enforcing the ceiling are too weak, and this is true in no small extent because of the limp justification for the ceiling.' Pisani-Ferry (2002) commented: 'It is a fact of life that a law that has lost justification is not considered legitimate any more and cannot be credibly enforced for long.'
33. For example, in the UK, the Treasury Select Committee and the EU Committee of the House of Lords have both considered recent developments in the SGP. The UK government also has a legal obligation under section 5 of the EC (Amendment) Act 1993 to submit its annual update of the UK Convergence Programme before both Houses of Parliament. The government has also adopted the practice of submitting the Council opinions on its programme and on the programmes of all other member states for scrutiny by Parliament.
34. Article 2(3) of Council Regulation (EC) No. 1056/05.
35. Mortensen (2004: 25) describes: 'a latent and lasting conflict between two equally valid features of the construction of the Union: (1) The need to ensure a high degree of consistency, notably in the medium and long run, between monetary and budgetary policy; and (2) The principle of 'subsidiarity' which can be taken as the theological argument assigning the full competence in the field of fiscal affairs and social policy to the national (or regional) governments'.
36. Including in line with the Lisbon Strategy.
37. This is true even taking into account that women now have children at a later stage in their lives.

38. Demographers have often assumed that increases in longevity would decline over time and converge to zero but increases in longevity have been systematically underestimated.
39. HM Treasury (2004b) described the policy challenges in terms of: entrenching macroeconomic stability; promoting enterprise; harnessing science and innovation; opening up the acquisition of skills for all; combining greater flexibility with fairness in balancing work and family commitments and supporting sections of society who face barriers to work; and tackling global environmental issues.
40. ECOFIN (2005) Report.
41. European Commission (2005).
42. European Commission (2005: 7).
43. Unweighted average.
44. If an economy grows rapidly because of strong productivity growth in the tradable sector, but wage growth is uniform across the economy, then unit labour costs will rise in the non-tradable sector where productivity growth is slower. This will translate into a higher equilibrium inflation rate than in the country's trading partners unless the nominal exchange rate appreciates.
45. See Buiter and Grafe (2002, 2004) for a fuller discussion.
46. Alternatively in considering fiscal sustainability, for any given debt ratio, to maintain the debt ratio the required primary balance to GDP ratio (PSPB/Y) is given by: PSPB/Y = $(r-g).(d/Y)$, where r is the real interest rate, g is the real growth rate and d is the debt level. It is clear from this that, for a given debt level, a larger surplus on the primary balance is required: the higher r, the lower g and the lower Y (which will include the effect of real growth and inflation).
47. European Commission (2005) also notes that the stock of contingent liabilities is relatively high, creating a risk of sudden upward changes in debt levels.
48. Woods (2004b) discusses some of the issues in setting debt rules.
49. The five were the Czech Republic, Hungary, Malta, Poland and Slovakia. It was decided that there were no special circumstances in the case of Cyprus, as its authorities felt confident they could eliminate their excessive deficit in a year.
50. Differences in projected growth of the working age population alone are marked for otherwise comparable countries. For example, in the decade starting 2031 Italian working population growth is projected to average -1.75 per cent a year as against 0 per cent in the UK.
51. For further discussion see Woods (2004a).
52. Such as a fiscal open letter system; see HM Treasury (2003a and b), Chapter 6.
53. The adjustment for Balassa–Samuelson effects around an assumed 2 per cent inflation target mainly affects Greece, Ireland, Spain and Portugal. See Woods (2004a) for details.
54. HM Treasury (2004a: 33) argued that: 'as part of a robust institutional framework, where the Council retains responsibility and accountability for enforcing fiscal discipline while exceptionally sanctioning fiscal stabilisation, there would also be a case at the EU level for strengthening the role of independent monitoring, surveillance and transparency'.
55. Ball (1996); Calmfors (2003); Gruen (2000); Seidman (2001); Wren-Lewis (2002); Wyplosz (2005).
56. The National Audit Office reports directly to Parliament and is independent of the government.
57. Statement to the Treasury Select Committee, 19 July 2005.
58. This has a particular significance in the UK framework given that the golden rule is measured 'over the cycle', as the end of the previous cycle marks the start of the next cycle. The audit was completed by the National Audit Office alongside the 2005 Pre-Budget Report.
59. For example, 41 separate forecasts are included in the July 2005 edition; see http://www. hm-treasury.gov.uk/forecasts.

BIBLIOGRAPHY

Balassone, F. and D. Franco (2000), 'Assessing Fiscal Sustainability: A Review of Methods with a View to EMU', *Fiscal Sustainability*, Rome: Banca d'Italia.

Ball, L. (1996), 'Disinflation and the NAIRU', Working paper W5520, National Bureau of Economic Research, Cambridge, MA. Available at SSRN: http://ssrn.com/abstract=3221.

Barro, R. (1979), 'On the Determination of Public Debt', *Journal of Political Economy*, **87**(5): 940–91.

Berglöf, E., B. Eichengreen, G. Roland, G. Tabellini and C. Wyplosz (2003), 'Built to Last: A Political Architecture for Europe', CEPR, *Monitoring European Integration*, **12**.

Blanchard, O. and F. Giavazzi (2003), *Improving the SGP through a Proper Accounting of Public Investment*, http://econ-www.mit.edu/faculty/download_pdf.php?id=787.

Blinder, A.S. (1999), 'Central Bank Credibility: Why Do We Care? How Do We Build It?', Working paper 7161, National Bureau of Economic Research, Cambridge, MA.

Brook, A.-M. (2003), *Recent and Prospective Trends in Real Long-Term Interest Rates: Fiscal Policy and Other Drivers*, Working paper 367, OECD Economic Department.

Buiter, W. and C. Grafe (2002), 'Patching Up the Pact: Some Suggestions for Enhancing Fiscal Sustainability and Macroeconomic Stability in an Enlarged European Union', CEPR Discussion paper 3496.

Buiter, W. and C. Grafe (2003), 'EMU or Ostrich', in HM Treasury, *Submissions on EMU from Leading Academics*, London: HMSO.

Buiter, W. and C. Grafe (2004), 'Patching Up the Pact: Some Suggestions for Enhancing Fiscal Sustainability and Macroeconomic Stability in an Enlarged European Union', *Economics of Transition*, **12**(1): 67–102.

Buiter, W.H. and A. Sibert (2005), 'How the Eurosystem's Treatment of Collateral in its Open Market Operations Weakens Fiscal Discipline in the Eurozone (and What To Do about It)', CEPR Discussion paper 5387.

Buti, M. (2006), 'Will the New Stability and Growth Pact Succeed? An Economic and Political Perspective', European Economy European Commission Directorate-General for Economic and Financial Affairs Economic Papers, Number 241, January.

Buti, M., C. Eijffinger and D. Franco (2003), 'Revisiting the Stability and Growth Pact: Grand Design or Internal Adjustment?', CEPR Discussion paper, http://www.cepr.org/pubs/dps/DP3692.asp.

Calmfors, L. (2003), *Nominal Wage Flexibility and Fiscal Policy: How Much Can They Reduce Macroeconomic Variability in the EMU?*, London: HM Treasury.

Chinn, M. and J. Frankel (2003), 'The Euro Area and World Interest Rates', Paper presented at CEPR/ESI conference The Euro Area as an Economic Entity, Eltville, September.

Conway, P. and A. Orr (2002), 'The GRIM: A Global Interest Rate Model', Westpac Institutional Bank Occasional Paper, September.

Easterly, W. (1999), 'When Is Fiscal Adjustment an Illusion?', *Economic Policy*, **14**(28), April: 55–86.

European Commission (2004), The Benefits of Fiscal Discipline, Part III of *Public Finances in EMU 2004*, Brussels: European Commission.

European Commission (2005), *Public Finances in EMU 2005*, Brussels: European Commission.

Government of Sweden, Government Commission on Stabilisation for Full Employment in Event of Swedish Membership in the Monetary Union (2002), 'Stabilisation Policy in the Monetary Union'. An English translation of the summary chapter is available at http://www.finans.regeringen.se.

Gruen, N. (2000), 'Greater Independence for Financial Insititutions', 21st Annual Meeting of Senior Budget Officials, Paris, 29–30 May.

HM Treasury (2003a), *Fiscal Stabilisation and EMU: A Discussion Paper*, London: HMSO.

HM Treasury (2003b), *Modelling Shocks and Adjustment Mechanisms in EMU: EMU Study by Dr. Peter Westaway*, London: HMSO.

HM Treasury (2004a), *Long-Term Public Finance Report: An Analysis of Fiscal Sustainability*, London: HMSO.

HM Treasury (2004b), *Long-Term Global Economic Challenges and Opportunities for the UK*, London: HMSO.

Hodson, D. and I. Maher. (2000), 'EMU: Balancing Credibility and Legitimacy in the Policy Mix', London School of Economics working paper, 12/00.

Kell, M. (2001), 'An Assessment of Fiscal Rules in the United Kingdom', IMF working paper WP/01/91, July.

Kirsanova, T., M. Satchi and D. Vines (2004), 'Monetary Union: Fiscal Stabilisation in the Face of Asymmetric Shocks', mimeo, January.

Kopits, G. and S. Symansky (1998), 'Fiscal Policy Rules', IMF Occasional Paper, 162, International Monetary Fund, Washington, DC.

Mélitz, J. (2002), 'Revisiting The Evidence about the Costs and Benefits of EMU', in HM Treasury, *Submissions on EMU from Leading Academics*, London: HMSO.

Mortensen, L. (2004), 'Economic Policy Coordination in EMU: What Role for the SGP?', CEPS working document, 202, June.

O'Donnell, G. and A. Bhundia (2001a), 'UK Policy Coordination: The Importance of Institutional Design', *Fiscal Studies*, **23**(1), 105–33.

O'Donnell, G. and A. Bhundia (2001b), 'Policy Frameworks in the UK and EMU', EMU paper, HM Treasury.

O'Donovan, B., A. Orr and D. Rae (1996), 'A World Interest Rate Model', Financial Research Paper No. 7, National Bank of New Zealand.

Pisani-Ferry, J. (2002) 'Fiscal Discipline and Policy Coordination in the Eurozone: Assessment and Proposals', in *Budgetary Policy in E(M)U: Design and Challenges*, The Hague: Ministerie van Financien.

Schumacher, D. (2005), 'Financial Markets and Fiscal Discipline', *Goldman Sachs Euroland Weekly Analyst*, 22 July.

Seidman, L. (2001), 'Reviving Fiscal Policy', *Challenge*, **44**(3): 17–42.

Toigo, P. and R. Woods (2005), 'Public Investment in the UK', Paper presented at the 7th Banca d'Italia Public Finance Workshop.

Waigel, T. (1995), 'Stability Pact for Europe', Communication to the ECOFIN Council, November. Available at http://www.ecu-activities.be/1996_2/ecofin.htm.

Woods, R. (2004a), 'Fiscal Stabilisation and EMU', CESifo Working Paper No. 1338.

Woods, R. (2004b), 'The Role of Public Debt in the UK Fiscal Rules', Paper presented at the 6th Banca d'Italia Public Finance Workshop.

Wren-Lewis, S. (2000), 'The Limits to Discretionary Fiscal Stabilisation Policy', *Oxford Review Economic Policy*, **16**: 92–105.

Wren-Lewis, S. (2002), 'Fiscal Policy, Inflation and Stabilisation in EMU', Paper for Workshop on the Interactions between Fiscal and Monetary Policies in EMU, Brussels, 8 March.

Wyplosz, C. (2005), 'Fiscal Policy: Institutions versus Rules', *National Institute Economic Review*, **191**(1): 64–78.

APPENDIX 5.1

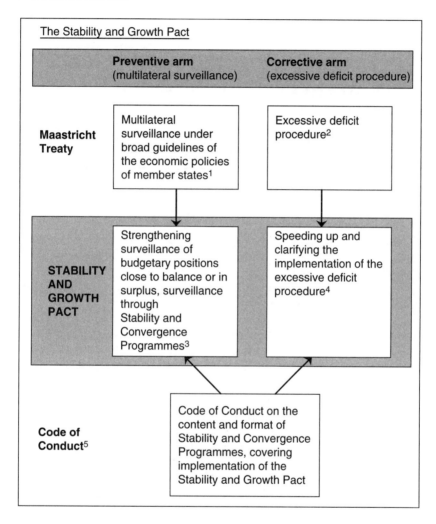

Notes:
[1] Article 99 (ex 103), February 1992.
[2] Article 104 (ex 104c), February 1992.
[3] Regulation 1466/97, June 1997.
[4] Regulation 1467/97, June 1997.
[5] EFC Opinion endorsed by ECOFIN, revised June 2001.

Figure A.5.1   The Stability and Growth Pact

6. The revision of the Stability and Growth Pact: the Medium-Term Objective

Michael J. Artis and Luca Onorante[1]

INTRODUCTION: THE MTO

The Medium-Term Objective, or MTO, is the concept around which the preventive arm of the Stability and Growth Pact operates. The 'preventive arm', in turn, is (at least in theory) the core of the SGP, in the sense that it should guide fiscal policies in normal times.

In practice, insufficient consolidation in good times, as mandated by the preventive arm of the SGP, implies that the corrective arm has been the one used more often. Many countries hit the 3 per cent deficit during the recent economic stagnation. The improvement in balances experienced until 1999 was largely due to the favourable economic upswing in the second phase of the EMU (1998–2001), and the structural surpluses turned out to be insufficient to allow the automatic stabilizers to work fully through the recession which started in 2001. This conclusion is confirmed by von Hagen (2002), who argues that after entry to the Union most countries, and especially the big ones, abandoned the process of fiscal consolidation. As a result, some countries adopted a restrictive pro-cyclical fiscal stance in order to respect the 3 per cent threshold during the recent economic slowdown, possibly increasing its amplitude.

The current emergency phase seems to be at least partially finishing, putting the preventive arm in a central role again. According to the European Commission's autumn 2006 economic forecasts, the general government deficit of the Euro area is projected to decline from 2.4 per cent of GDP in 2005 to 2.0 per cent in 2006 and 1.5 per cent in 2007. Among the Euro area countries subject to excessive deficit procedures, deficits would be brought – and remain – below 3 per cent of GDP in Germany, France and Greece, and would remain close to (or above) 3 per cent in Italy and Portugal.

In parallel, increasing criticism led to the revision of both the preventive and the corrective arm of the pact, with the declared aim of increasing the economic rationale of the rules. It has, among other things, led to the substitution of the common MTO of 'close to balance or in surplus' with country-specific MTOs related to the debt ratios and the trend growth of each country.

This chapter compares the new MTOs with the previous criterion of 'close to balance or in surplus' and shows that there is a solid economic rationale for these revised MTOs. It also argues that it is crucial to apply in a better way the preventive arm of the pact, to avoid insufficient consolidation in good times leading once again to the massive application of the corrective arm of the pact.

The chapter is organized as follows. After an introductory section a set of structural VARs, one for each Euro-zone country, is introduced and estimated. The VARs are identified via long-run restrictions that are relatively uncontroversial and compatible with most theoretical models of fiscal policy; they also take into account the effect of monetary policy in order to avoid misspecification. The estimated models are then used to estimate new MTOs.

1 ECONOMIC AND HISTORICAL BACKGROUND OF THE PACT

The fiscal rules laid down in the Treaty of Maastricht and the Stability and Growth Pact (SGP) are the result of a perception that qualification for participation in the monetary union would remove the incentive to conduct disciplined fiscal policies.

According to Bini-Smaghi *et al.* (1994), the binding thresholds on deficit and debt were adopted on the ground that market discipline alone would not have a sufficient disciplinary effect on the public finances of the countries in the Euro area. The approach adopted in the Maastricht criteria and reiterated in the Stability and Growth Pact associated binding nominal thresholds with a procedure for assessing excessive deficits which provided for margins of discretion, thus mediating between the two extreme views advocating on the one side strict binding rules and on the other simple reliance on market-imposed discipline.

The threshold values were chosen somewhat arbitrarily. The debt ceiling of 60 per cent was simply more or less the Community average, and was not intended as a limit of acceptability for the debt, but simply as a threshold after which changes in debt become relevant and a close look at the deficit is necessary. The deficit ceiling of 3 per cent of GDP, although broadly compatible with the 60 per cent deficit ratio and a nominal growth of 5 per cent, was criticized as being potentially too strict and inflexible. However, the excessive deficit procedure was supposed to provide the necessary margins for discretion. All the alternative proposals were rejected on practical grounds; the so-called 'golden rule' required a strict and harmonized differentiation between current and capital expenditure which was not available at the time; a proposal for assessing the budgetary position over a number of years was rejected on the ground that it would be heavily based on intentions for the future rather than on measurable facts. In the end, the limits were set on nominal annual figures.

Although it is only a few years since the start of EMU, the SGP has undergone an extensive process of revision. This may appear surprising, as the Maastricht criteria, very similar to those in the SGP, were never subject to discussion. Two elements may help to explain this difference.

First, the structure of incentives has changed. While the possibility of being excluded from participation in the EMU proved to be a powerful incentive to support fiscal restraint, the stick of the sanctions provided by the excessive deficit procedure of the SGP is relatively weak and uncertain.

Second, the experience of the first few years of EMU has highlighted that the SGP rules were not correctly implemented in the conduct of fiscal policies. The correct or incomplete implementation can be attributed to several factors, some of which are summarized by Buti and Giudice (2002). First, the requirement of budgets close to balance or in surplus in the medium run is confronted with a lack of consensus on how an output gap, and therefore a structural balance, should be measured. As a result, the only binding (nominal) rule in the SGP makes it intrinsically asymmetric in that it sanctions excessive deficits but does not provide incentives for fiscal consolidation in good times. Second, in the presence of current expenses that are difficult to cut, the balanced budget requirement may result in an insufficient level of investment. More generally, Buiter and Grafe (2003) remark that the enforcement of uniform nominal deficit and debt rules may cause problems for EU members whose initial conditions or medium-term growth and inflation rates are different from the EU average. This problem is particularly relevant for the new member states, whose catch-up process may imply a need for higher public investment in infrastructures.

Finally, respect for the 3 per cent deficit threshold of the Treaty does not explicitly address nor automatically ensure sustainable public finances,[2] and may in theory still expose the ECB to the 'unpleasant monetaristic arithmetic' of Sargent and Wallace (1981).

2 THE MEDIUM-TERM OBJECTIVE AND ITS REFORM

The Council Regulation No. 1466/97 of 7 July 1997 on the strengthening of the surveillance of budgetary positions and the surveillance and coordination of economic policies established a common 'medium term objective of budgetary positions of close to balance or in surplus, to which all Member States are committed', and a related obligation 'to take the corrective budgetary action they deem necessary to meet the objectives of their stability and convergence programmes, whenever they have information indicating actual or expected significant divergence from the medium-term budgetary objective'.

The economic rationale of the MTO would be that 'adherence to the medium-term objective of budgetary positions close to balance or in surplus will allow Member States to deal with normal cyclical fluctuations while keeping the government deficit within the 3% of GDP reference value'. In other words, the MTO would allow fiscal policies to stabilize the economic cycle and avoid the application of the corrective arm.[3]

The surveillance of the adherence of fiscal policies to the MTOs proceeds as follows. Every year, each member state submits to the Council and the Commission its Stability Programme, in which the Medium-Term Objective for the budgetary position of close to balance or in surplus and the adjustment path towards this objective for the general government deficit are specified. The Council then monitors the budgetary position against the benchmark of the MTO of the Stability Programme. Article 6.2 of the regulation specified that:

> In the event that the Council identifies significant divergence of the budgetary position from the medium-term budgetary objective, or the adjustment path towards it, it shall, with a view to giving early warning in order to prevent the occurrence of an excessive deficit, address, in accordance with Article 103 (4), a recommendation to the Member State concerned to take the necessary adjustment measures.[4]

The European Council of 22–23 March 2005 agreed on a reform of the Stability and Growth Pact. Regulation 1055/2005 of 27 June 2005 amended Regulation 1466/97 on the strengthening of budgetary surveillance and coordination of economic policies and redefined the MTO according to the following criteria:

- The new medium-term budgetary objective should be differentiated for individual member states, to take into account the diversity of economic and budgetary positions and developments as well as of fiscal risk to the sustainability of public finances, and prospective demographic changes.
- The country-specific medium-term budgetary objectives, expressed in cyclically adjusted terms,[5] net of one-off and temporary measures, would lie between −1 per cent of GDP and balance or surplus.

Therefore, MTOs may (and normally will) diverge from close to balance for individual member states.[6]

The scope of the MTO is enlarged and now comprises three parts:

- to deal with normal cyclical fluctuations while keeping the government deficit below the 3 per cent of GDP reference value, as before;
- to ensure rapid progress towards fiscal sustainability; and
- taking this into account, to allow room for budgetary manoeuvre, in particular for public investment.

The third point is extremely difficult to quantify; the second improves the rationale of the MTO by putting the emphasis on the sustainability of public finances.

In order to reach their medium-term budgetary objective, member states of the Euro-zone or of ERM2 should pursue a minimum annual adjustment in cyclically adjusted terms, net of one-offs and other temporary measures, which is quantified as 0.5 per cent of GDP as a benchmark.[7]

Finally, some extra elements of flexibility apply under the new pact. When defining the adjustment path towards the MTO, major structural reforms which have direct long-term cost saving effects, including by raising potential growth, will be taken into account. A safety margin with respect to the 3 per cent reference value must, however, be maintained at all times.

3   METHODOLOGICAL ASPECTS

3.1   The Empirical Literature on Fiscal Policy

The investigation requires, as a first step, the identification of the interaction between fiscal policy and macroeconomic developments.

Structural regressions have been widely used to disentangle the components of fiscal policy. Van den Noord (2000) groups the structural methods into three categories. A first approach runs regressions of fiscal variables on different sets of explanatory variables. For instance, Galí and Perotti (2003) estimate fiscal rules for the discretionary budget deficit, using data on EMU countries on a sample period very similar to the one of this chapter. This approach gives reliable results only if the set of explanatory variables is sufficiently wide, but may suffer from misspecification if the correct lags are not included. A second approach uses macroeconometric models, whose equations are calibrated. Macro models have the advantage of allowing the identification of different kinds of shocks, but suffer from the problems just described, because the equations need first to be estimated in order to calibrate the elasticities in the model. The third approach is used by OECD, and consists of a mix of different methodologies. The elasticities of the cyclical components of taxes and expenditure are computed relative to a measure of the output gap independently estimated.

A different approach tries to overcome the difficulties of correctly specifying a model by using vector autoregression models (VARs), which require only minimal identifying assumptions and normally fit the data well.

VAR models are widely used in empirical studies of monetary policy, but their use in the analysis of fiscal policy is fairly recent. The lack of high-frequency fiscal data or of long annual data series is partially responsible for this lack of interest. However, a number of important contributions have shown that the approach can give useful results. Blanchard and Perotti (1999) use a Structural Vector Autoregression Model (SVAR) with taxes, government spending and GDP, all expressed in real terms, to investigate the dynamic effects of shocks in government spending and taxes in the US. A similar approach, with a different specification of the model, can be found in Fatás and Mihov (1999). De Arcangelis and Lamartina (2001) use different identifying restrictions to explore the existence of different fiscal policy regimes. Perotti (2002) studies the effects of fiscal policy on GDP, prices and interest rates in five OECD countries. Favero and Monacelli (2003) and others have shown that fiscal and monetary policy cannot be estimated separately, because the interaction effects would bias the estimates.

Following Blanchard and Quah (1989), other authors use long-run restrictions, which are relatively easy to reconcile with economic theory. This is the case of Bayoumi and Eichengreen (1992), who apply the long-run restriction to divide between supply and demand shocks, and more recently of Dalsgaard and de Serres (2000), who estimate a SVAR for 11 EMU countries.[8] Garcia and Verdelhan (2001) use a specification scheme à la Clarida–Galí, including both short- and long-run restrictions. They apply it to synthetic Euro area data, including yearly GDP, inflation, real short-term interest rate and budget balance, and manage to identify four types of shocks: supply, demand, monetary and fiscal. They also estimate cyclically adjusted budget balances and a synthetic indicator of policy mix.

Since our emphasis is on the statistical fit of the model to the data, the unrestricted VAR methodology is particularly suitable for the present study. We do not even need to identify a fiscal shock; therefore the usual criticisms about identification do not apply here. Instead, we use the estimated model as the basis of stochastic simulation, taking advantage of the fact that, 'given the size and simplicity of most VAR models, these models are particularly well-suited to an investigation of the various types of

uncertainty that influence forecasts, and their use in decision making'
(Garratt *et al.*, 2006).[9]

3.2 The Model

The structure of the reduced-form model used for estimation is the following one:

$$Y = \sum_{L=1}^{p} C(L) Y \sum_{L=1}^{q} D(L) X + e$$

where C(L) and D(L) are polynomials in the lag operator and the matrices
are defined as follows:

$$Y = \begin{bmatrix} \gamma \\ d \\ \pi \end{bmatrix}; X = \begin{bmatrix} r \\ oil \\ b \end{bmatrix}; e = \begin{bmatrix} e_{\gamma} \\ e_{d} \\ e_{\pi} \end{bmatrix}$$

The model expresses the deficit/GDP ratio d_t, the growth rate γ_t and the
inflation rate π_t as a linear function of their own lagged values and of
the debt/GDP ratio b_t, the interest rate on debt r_t (or, in a robustness check,
the long-run interest rate) and the oil price index oil_t. The reduced form
residuals e are assumed to be identically and independently distributed with
mean zero and variance–covariance matrix $= E(ee')$.

Our structural model contains three structural shocks: an aggregate
supply shock ε_t^s, an aggregate demand (non-fiscal) shock ε_t^D, and a fiscal
shock ε_t^F. In order to identify these shocks we can rewrite the reduced-form
model in moving average (MA) form. Omitting the exogenous component
we have:

$$Y = \sum_{L=0}^{\infty} A(L) e$$

where $A(L) = [I - C_1 - \ldots - C_p]^{-1}$ and $A(0) = I$ are known.

Structural form residuals ε_t are assumed to have a normalized covariance
matrix: $E(\varepsilon\varepsilon') = I$. They are linked to the reduced form residuals e by the
linear transformation S:

$$\varepsilon_t = \begin{bmatrix} \varepsilon_t^S \\ \varepsilon_t^F \\ \varepsilon_t^D \end{bmatrix} = S^{-1} e_t \quad \forall t$$

Taking into account that $SS^{-1} = I$, the moving average form can be rewrit-
ten as:

$$Y = \sum_{L=0}^{\infty} A(L)SS^{-1}e = \sum_{L=0}^{\infty} B(L)\varepsilon$$

where

$$B(L) = A(L)S \quad \forall L$$

$$B(1) \equiv \sum_{L=1}^{\infty} B(L) = \sum_{L=0}^{\infty} A(L)S \equiv A(1)S$$

Three identifying restrictions are required to identify the structural innovations from the reduced-form VAR. Following a solidly established tradition, we identify the supply shocks ε_t^s, as the only shocks to have a permanent long-run effect on growth. This is equivalent to restricting to zero the (1,2) and (1,3) elements of matrix $B(1)$. Moreover, the aggregate (temporary) demand shock ε_t^D, is assumed to have no long-run impact on the deficit/GDP ratio. This is equivalent to restricting to zero the (2,3) element of matrix $B(1)$. The fiscal shock ε_t^F is left free. After imposing these restrictions, the long-run matrix $B(1)$ looks like:

$$B(1) = \begin{bmatrix} b_{11} & 0 & 0 \\ b_{21} & b_{22} & 0 \\ b_{31} & b_{32} & b_{33} \end{bmatrix}$$

After imposing these restrictions, the signs of some of the elements of the S matrix need to be normalized.[10] We choose a normalization such that the structural disturbances correspond to what are normally considered positive shocks.

3.3 The Variables

Our dataset contains 26 annual observations of six variables for each of the EMU countries, with the exception of Luxembourg, over the years 1980–2005. The beginning of the sample in 1980 is chosen in order to concentrate on monetary regimes that stabilize inflation around a target value and to avoid modelling the impact of the two oil shocks.

The endogenous variables are: the rate of inflation (GDP-deflator based) π_t, the real GDP growth rate γ_t, and the deficit/GDP ratio d_t. A negative value of d_t indicates a deficit, a positive value a surplus. The exogenous variables include the interest rate on debt (the implicit interest rate, calculated as general government interest as a percentage of the gross public debt of the preceding year) r_t, the oil price index expressed in national currency oil_t, and the debt/GDP ratio b_t. The use of annual data when working with a dataset containing fiscal variables is in line with the literature and due to the absence of non-interpolated data at higher frequencies. The interest rate on debt is introduced to take into account the relationship between financial and monetary developments and the interaction between fiscal variables, inflation and real GDP. A robustness check uses long-term bond yields, leading to similar results. Oil prices are used to capture the world economic cycle and exchange rate movements. The lagged value of government debt is introduced on the basis of the arguments contained in Favero and Monacelli (2003) and OECD (2003), according to which sustainability problems associated with indebtedness seem to be an important determinant of whether the fiscal stance is pro-cyclical.

3.4 The EMU Effect

A problem arising in this simulation exercise is that the beginning of EMU towards the end of the sample could have led to a structural break in the conduct of economic policies. More specifically, it has been argued that the EMU could have provoked a structural break in governments' behaviour. The adoption of a common currency eliminates exchange rate risk and the associated interest rate premia among the participating countries. Furthermore, additional deficit can be financed more easily because the cost of the additional borrowing in terms of higher interest rates is partly spread across the entire currency area. Both factors may in principle lead to an increase in the deficit bias of fiscal policies. Fiscal developments since 1999 seem to suggest that after the beginning of EMU fiscal consolidation indeed stopped and even reversed in some countries. This hypothesis is tested by adding a dummy from 1999 to the end of the available data[11] and testing for its relevance. The results, reported in Table 6.1, show that this dummy is often not significant; when it is, the sign is not always the one expected.

The few available data after 1998 do not allow for a test for structural breaks. However, we have compared the out-of-sample forecasts of the models estimated until 1998 with the observed variables until 2005. The forecasting ability of the model estimated until 1998 turns out to be quite good. One can thus conclude that the structural break is not statistically relevant and that pre-EMU estimated VARs are a good approximation of the economic structure in the whole sample. Following this conclusion, the model is re-estimated using the whole 1981–2005 sample.

Finally, a structural change certainly induced by the EMU is that the monetary authority, now targeting Union-wide aggregates, will appear as not very or not at all reactive to the national policy makers. While this phe-

Table 6.1   Convergence and EMU dummies in the model

		Betas		T-stats	
		D 94–98	D 99–04	D 94–98	D 99–04
Belgium	Y=	−0.05	−0.01	−0.53	−0.29
	S=	0.05	0.02	1.15	0.86
	P=	−0.02	0.01	−0.27	−0.19
Germany	Y=	−0.06	−0.01	−0.26	−0.47
	S=	0.16	0.04	2.71	1.97
	P=	0.06	0.01	1.14	1.96
Greece	Y=	−0.08	−0.01	−0.68	−0.04
	S=	0.25	0.02	2.41	0.66
	P=	0.02	−0.01	0.10	−0.05
Spain	Y=	0.11	0.02	1.33	1.60
	S=	0.12	0.05	1.98	3.07
	P=	−0.04	0.00	−0.39	0.16
France	Y=	0.10	0.01	1.76	0.22
	S=	0.03	−0.01	1.01	−0.15
	P=	0.04	0.01	0.64	0.27
Ireland	Y=	0.19	0.00	1.76	0.10
	S=	−0.06	−0.04	−0.83	−1.97
	P=	−0.08	−0.03	−0.61	−0.84
Italy	Y=	0.21	0.01	3.24	1.35
	S=	−0.01	0.01	−0.16	0.15
	P=	0.20	0.02	2.10	1.22
Netherlands	Y=	0.05	0.02	1.37	0.62
	S=	0.13	0.04	2.03	1.33
	P=	0.00	−0.02	−0.13	−0.57
Austria	Y=	−0.01	−0.01	−0.32	−0.69
	S=	0.00	0.02	−0.28	1.73
	P=	0.03	0.01	0.76	0.83
Portugal	Y=	−0.02	0.00	−0.20	−0.61
	S=	−0.12	−0.01	−1.31	−1.10
	P=	−0.07	−0.01	−0.29	−0.41
Finland	Y=	0.17	0.05	0.93	1.08
	S=	0.05	0.04	0.32	1.16
	P=	−0.10	−0.02	−0.54	−0.28

nomenon does not affect our estimations much, since we do not aim to estimate an interest rate rule, the out-of-sample simulation will be run using a constant interest rate equal to the one observed in the country in 2005. This is a compromise solution in the absence of information about the future developments of the interest rate.

4   RESULTS

In this section we calculate for each country a 'safety margin with respect to the 3 per cent of GDP government deficit ratio' and a second 'safety margin ensuring rapid progress towards sustainability'. These two conditions motivate the introduction of the new country-specific Medium-Term Objectives (MTOs) of the new Stability Pact, which would be, in cyclically adjusted terms and net of one-off and temporary measures, between −1 per cent of GDP and 'in balance or surplus'.

4.1   The Safety Margin with Respect to the 3 Per Cent of GDP

This section finds numerical values for a 'safety margin with respect to the 3 per cent of GDP government deficit ratio' and a 'safety margin ensuring rapid progress towards sustainability', and compares them with the MTOs of the reformed SGP and with the results of Artis and Buti (2000). In order to perform statistical analysis, we resort to dynamic stochastic simulation (DSS). As a statistical methodology, DSS is based on two assumptions: first, that the estimated model provides an adequate description of the economic phenomenon under consideration over the simulation period; second, that the original distribution of estimated residuals is an adequate empirical measure of economic shocks, embracing a sufficiently ample spectrum of possibilities to form an adequate basis for the bootstrapping exercise.[12] For any period in the simulation, the DSS requires that the following steps are taken:

1.   A shock is randomly chosen among the residuals of the estimated model (bootstrapping).
2.   A new (simulated) data point is obtained by applying this shock to the estimated model.
3.   This new data point is added to the data.
4.   For every period over the simulation horizon, points 1 to 3 are repeated. At every step, statistics of interest are collected.

Replicating the simulation described in steps 1–4 a congruous number of times (10 000 in our case for each country), each time with a new set of shocks randomly chosen from the original distribution, it is possible to construct an ample set of alternative paths the economy might follow on the basis of the structure of the model and of the original distribution of residuals. These replications are the basis for our subsequent analysis.

The 'safety margin' is defined as the target for the cyclically adjusted deficit which prevents the nominal deficit from breaching the 3 per cent limit under normal economic fluctuations. In order to identify the safety margin, two pieces of information are necessary: the knowledge of the probability of breaching the 3 per cent reference value given an initial deficit value, and a (per force subjective) assessment of what can be considered a sufficiently prudent probability p*.

The first of the two elements, the probability of exceeding the 3 per cent threshold conditional on different levels of deficits, can be calculated on the basis of our simulations. As expected, a higher initial deficit implies higher probabilities of excessive deficits given normal economic fluctuations.

As for the prudent probability p*, since the main scope of the safety margin is to prevent the occurrence of deficits above 3 per cent, it should be fixed to a fairly low level, to make sure that the probability of future excessive deficits is not too high. Given the arbitrariness of choosing a 'prudent probability', we pick up probabilities which are consistent with the rest of the rules contained in the pact: the safety margin will then be such that the probability of trespassing the 3 per cent limit under normal economic fluctuations is *grosso modo* the same as the probability of applying the exceptional circumstances clause, under which a deficit higher that 3 per cent is allowed. Looking at the real growth figures for the Euro-zone countries in the period 1980–2004, we observe that growth has been below –2 per cent in 1.45 per cent of the cases, below −0.75 per cent in 6.91 per cent of the cases and below 0 per cent in 9.82 per cent of the cases. The first two probabilities correspond to 'prudent probabilities' of the old SGP; the third is derived from the new set of rules.

The one-year-ahead safety margin for a country is then defined as the level of the deficit/GDP ratio which keeps the probability of that country's deficit being greater than 3 per cent one year ahead below the prudent probability p*. Analogously, the two-years-ahead safety margin is defined as the level of the deficit/GDP ratio associated with a p* per cent probability of being greater than 3 per cent two years ahead.

The values corresponding to the different safety margins are reported in Table 6.2.

The resulting safety margins one year ahead calculated for the 0 per cent threshold of the 'new pact' (that is for a prudent probability of 9.82 per cent) are as high as 2.2 per cent deficit for Germany, where the shocks are relatively small, and as small as 0.3 per cent for Greece, a country whose estimated model tends to produce systematic high deficits, and 0.2 per cent for Finland, whose bootstrapped shocks include the fall of the Soviet Union at the beginning of the 1990s. The average safety margin is around 1.4 per cent. Looking at the safety margins two years ahead, they are slightly more restrictive, as one might expect, with an average of around 0.9 per cent and a maximum at 1.9 per cent (again Germany). These results are

Table 6.2   Safety margin with respect to the 3 per cent threshold

	Probability: 1.45%		Probability: 6.91%		Probability: 9.82%	
	1yr ahead	2yr ahead	1yr ahead	2yr ahead	1yr ahead	2yr ahead
Belgium	−0.4%	−0.4%	−1.2%	−1.2%	−1.4%	−1.5%
Germany	−1.6%	−1.1%	−2.1%	−1.7%	−2.2%	−1.9%
Greece	1.4%	3.1%	0.1%	0.9%	−0.3%	0.4%
Spain	−0.9%	−0.2%	−1.7%	−1.1%	−1.9%	−1.3%
France	−1.1%	−0.3%	−1.8%	−1.4%	−2.0%	−1.6%
Ireland	−0.8%	−0.5%	−1.3%	−1.1%	−1.4%	−1.3%
Italy	−0.9%	−0.2%	−1.6%	−1.1%	−1.8%	−1.4%
Netherlands	−0.2%	1.0%	−1.2%	−0.7%	−1.4%	−1.0%
Austria	−0.9%	0.0%	−1.4%	−0.9%	−1.6%	−1.2%
Portugal	0.7%	1.0%	−0.6%	−0.5%	−1.0%	−0.8%
Finland	1.6%	4.0%	0.1%	2.1%	−0.2%	1.3%

Note: Negative numbers are deficits

very similar to those obtained by Dalsgaard and de Serres (1999) with a similar methodology.

A similar exercise has already been undertaken by Artis and Buti (2000), who use output gap and elasticities of the budget balance to the cycle. The methodology used in this section is different, in that it does not use any outside information on output gap or elasticities. This difference in methodology is partially reflected in the results; in their paper (Artis and Buti, 2000), Germany, Greece, France, Italy and Austria could aim for a deficit slightly above 1 per cent of GDP, while the other countries should remain below.

4.2   Debt Sufficiently Diminishing and Approaching the 60 Per Cent Reference Value

As a second requirement, the Medium-Term Objectives would be defined in such a way that the debt would be 'sufficiently diminishing and approaching the 60 per cent reference value at a satisfactory pace'.

Debt sustainability is listed among the relevant factors that the Commission has to take into account when preparing a report under Article 104(3) of the Treaty. It has been agreed that the debt condition should be evaluated in qualitative terms, but it cannot be ruled out that the reaffirmed commitment to debt reduction may actually lead to the definition of a more specific framework of assessment. In the present chapter the definition of the debt ratio sufficiently diminishing and approaching the 60 per cent reference value at a satisfactory pace is quantified by the following general form:

$$b_t - b_{t-1} = -\lambda(b_{t-1} - b^*)$$

in which the required rate of debt reduction $b_t - b_{t-1}$ declines linearly with the deviation from debt target $b_{t-1} - b^*$ at a constant adjustment speed λ. Budget dynamics in terms of GDP ratios are expressed by:

$$b_t = def_t + \frac{b_{t-1}}{(1 + y_t)(1 + \pi_t)}$$

where def_t is deficit (including interest payments), y_t is real GDP growth and π_t is inflation. Putting together the required consolidation and the equation of debt dynamics we obtain the following expression:

$$def_i = \lambda b^* + \left(1 - \lambda - \frac{1}{(1 + y_t)(1 + \pi_t)}\right) b_{t-1}$$

which shows that for every nominal growth rate $(1+y_t)(1+\pi_t)$ the required deficit level def_t is a positive function of the debt target b^* and, for realistic values of the parameters,[13] a negative function of the previous level of debt b_{t-1}. Taking long-run values for π and y, the last equation identifies for each debt level a safety margin ensuring rapid progress towards sustainability.

In order to implement the simulation, numerical values are needed for the parameters. We choose $\lambda = 0.05$ and experiment with both $b^* = 0.4$ and $b^*=0.6$. The first value of b^* implies that a country with a high debt ratio around 100 per cent of GDP will be initially required to reduce this ratio by 3 per cent yearly, while the required debt reduction will be of 1 per cent for a debt ratio just above 60 per cent of GDP; as a consequence, the 60 per cent debt criterion would be satisfied in a finite number of years. The second value of b^* would drive the debt ratio to 60 per cent only asymptotically. The long-run value for inflation is set to $\pi = 0.02$, a value compatible with the objective of price stability of the ECB. Two values of structural growth are tried in order to provide robust evidence, the structural growth provided from the estimated model and the average real growth observed in the 2001–05 period. The results are summarized in Table 6.3.

4.3 Resulting Medium-Term Objectives

The resulting Medium-Term Objectives vary extensively from country to country. With the adoption of the more restrictive debt target at 40 per cent of GDP and the average 2000–05 growth, both of which imply a higher consolidation effort, Belgium, Germany, France and Portugal should aim at structural deficits between 0 and 1 per cent of GDP. Greece, Spain,

Table 6.3   Medium-Term Objectives such that the debt would be
*   'sufficiently diminishing and approaching the 60 per cent*
*   reference value at a satisfactory pace'*

	Debt in 2005	Thresholds based on average real growth 2001-05		Thresholds based on structural growth from model	
λ		*0.05*	*0.05*	*0.05*	*0.05*
b*		*60%*	*40%*	*60%*	*40%*
Belgium	93%	−1.7%	−0.7%	−2.4%	−1.4%
Germany	68%	−1.6%	−0.6%	−1.8%	−0.8%
Greece	108%	−4.1%	−3.1%	−4.0%	−3.0%
Spain	43%	−3.0%	−2.0%	−2.8%	−1.8%
France	67%	−2.0%	−1.0%	−2.3%	−1.3%
Ireland	28%	−3.5%	−2.5%	−3.8%	−2.8%
Italy	106%	−0.6%	0.4%	−1.4%	−0.4%
Netherlands	53%	−2.1%	−1.1%	−2.3%	−1.3%
Austria	63%	−2.1%	−1.1%	−2.1%	−1.1%
Portugal	64%	−1.5%	−0.5%	−1.6%	−0.6%
Finland	41%	−2.9%	−1.9%	−3.1%	−2.1%

Note: Negative numbers are deficits

Ireland, The Netherlands, Austria and Finland would achieve the necessary debt reduction in the presence of higher structural deficits, while Italy should target a surplus of about 0.4 per cent of GDP. The less demanding 60 per cent target would allow for structural deficits 1 per cent higher, while the adoption of the growth estimated from the models generally implies slightly less demanding targets (the exceptions are Spain and Greece).

In order to derive numbers comparable with the medium-term budgetary objective of the new SGP, which must both provide a safety margin with respect to the 3 per cent of GDP government deficit ratio and ensure rapid progress towards sustainability, the lowest numbers from both exercises must be considered. In a somewhat arbitrary choice, the one-year-ahead safety margins and the second column of Table 6.3 are considered in Table 6.4. The resulting picture is overall supportive of the new MTOs from 1 per cent deficit to close to balance or in surplus; Ireland and Spain could be allowed less demanding targets, also taking into account that their main reason for the MTO is not linked to the sustainability of debt, whilst Italy should target a structural surplus in order to reduce the debt ratio.

It should however be noted that the data used in the simulation are overall deficits, while the MTOs are defined on deficits excluding temporary

Table 6.4   Estimated Medium-Term Objectives

Country	Threshold deficit	Reason for the threshold
Belgium	−0.7%	Sustainability of debt
Germany	−0.6%	Sustainability of debt
Greece	−0.3%	Safety margin from 3%
Spain	−1.9%	Safety margin from 3%
France	−1.0%	Sustainability of debt
Ireland	−1.4%	Safety margin from 3%
Italy	0.4%	Sustainability of debt
Netherlands	−1.1%	Sustainability of debt
Austria	−1.1%	Sustainability of debt
Portugal	−0.5%	Sustainability of debt
Finland	−0.2%	Safety margin from 3%

measures and implicit liabilities. The results are therefore to be considered as indicative.

CONCLUSIONS

The present chapter compares the new country-specific MTOs with the previous criterion of 'close to balance or in surplus' and assesses them against the two criteria of providing a safety margin against the risk of breaching the 3 per cent reference value and of implying a declining debt ratio.

A set of structural VARs, one for each Euro-zone country, is estimated and used to perform a set of country-by-country dynamic stochastic simulations. The simulations are the base for assessing the possible effects of alternative fiscal policies to the paths of deficit and debt.

The analysis shows that there is a solid economic rationale for the new country-specific Medium-Term Objectives from 1 per cent deficit to close to balance or in surplus; possibly Ireland and Spain could be given less demanding targets, while Italy should target a structural surplus in order to reduce the debt ratio.

These results are derived under the assumption that the new MTOs will be taken seriously and applied thoroughly. This has not been the case in the past. If, as it seems, the new MTOs respond to a sound economic rationale, it is then important that it is enforced within the preventive arm of the pact, to avoid insufficient consolidation in good times leading again to the massive application of the corrective arm.

The results of this study should be interpreted with caution. First, the estimation of the model assumes that government behaviour estimated over the 1980–2005 period can be conveniently represented by a unique model with some dummies. Second, it is assumed that governments do not change behavioural preferences in the EMU. In reality a more lenient pact may incline governments towards a more relaxed attitude on deficits. Third, trend growth may in the future be lower than in the past so that instances with negative or even significantly negative growth may become more frequent than expected according to the estimated models.

NOTES

1. The authors would like to thank Marco Buti, Ilian Mihov and Rick van der Ploeg for their comments, and Roberto Perotti, Jürgen von Hagen, Carlo Favero, Olivier Blanchard, Jose Marín Arcas, Ludger Schuknecht, Jean-Pierre Vidal and Paolo Paesani for very useful discussions and insights. All mistakes are ours. The views expressed in this chapter do not necessarily reflect those of the European Central Bank.
2. For instance, one-off measures can be used by the national governments as substitutes for structural changes in the budget, and issues such as an ageing population are not considered at the moment.
3. The corrective arm, in principle, would apply only in special cases, to ensure fiscal discipline when the first part failed. Given the nature of 'emergency break' of the corrective arm, the emphasis was more on constraining the deficit than on ensuring an optimal fiscal policy over the cycle, and a nominal threshold of 3 per cent of GDP was chosen. Clearly, this nominal threshold would often force fiscal consolidation in difficult times.
4. Article 6.3. further specifies that 'In the event that the Council in its subsequent monitoring judges that the divergence of the budgetary position from the medium-term budgetary objective, or the adjustment path towards it, is persisting or worsening, the Council shall, in accordance with Article 103 (4), make a recommendation to the Member State concerned to take prompt corrective measures and may, as provided in that Article, make its recommendation public.'
5. The production function approach of the European Commission provides a common framework for calculating cyclically adjusted budgets. For a description of the Commission's production function approach, see Denis *et al.* (2002).
6. The adoption of new, looser medium-term targets implicitly recognizes the lack of rationale of the close-to-balance or in-surplus requirement which, if respected, would drive the debt ratios to zero or even to negative values.
7. An ambiguous provision is the one that 'The Council shall take into account whether a higher adjustment effort is made in economic good times, whereas the effort may be more limited in economic bad times.'
8. Their restrictions are that only supply shocks have a permanent effect on output, and that nominal shocks have a permanent impact on prices only.
9. For a model with variables similar to ours see Canova and Pappa (2003).
10. See Christiano *et al.* (1999) for a discussion of this issue.
11. The choice of 1999 as the first year coincides with the beginning of the third phase of the EMU. From the purely economic point of view, it presents a margin of arbitrariness, as argued in Canova and Pappa (2003), according to whom previous years (1997 and 1998) may already belong to the new regime. However, Canova and Pappa also find that the qualitative conclusions do not change by omitting these two years. An earlier break

date would probably be opportune in a monetary policy rule, but we do not model monetary policy as an endogenous variable.
12. In this context, the DSS assumes that the cyclical behaviour of the economies has not changed with the advent of EMU. This hypothesis is unlikely to hold in the long run. Artis and Buti (2000) point out that, 'as the cyclical behavior of the Euro-area economy adapts to the new EMU environment, the medium-term targets will need to be re-addressed'.
13. For small values of λ,y and π the condition to have a negative coefficient is $\lambda > y + \pi$.

BIBLIOGRAPHY

Artis, M.J. and B. Winkler (1998), 'The Stability Pact: Safeguarding the Credibility of the European Central Bank', *National Institute Economic Review*, January: 87–98.

Artis, M.J. and M. Buti (2000), 'Close to Balance or in Surplus: A Policy Maker's Guide to the Implementation of the Stability and Growth Pact', CEPR Discussion Papers 2515.

Bayoumi, T. and B. Eichengreen (1992), 'Shocking Aspects of European Monetary Integration', in F. Torres and F. Giavazzi (eds), *Adjustment and Growth in the European Monetary Union*, Cambridge: Cambridge University Press, pp. 193–229.

Beetsma, R. and X. Debrun (2007), 'The New Stability and Growth Pact: A First Assessment', *European Economic Review*, **51**(2), 453–77.

Bini-Smaghi, L., T. Padoa-Schioppa and F. Papadia (1994), 'The Transition to EMU in the Maastricht Treaty', *Essays in International Finance*, **194**, November.

Blanchard, O. and D. Quah (1989), 'The Dynamic Effects of Aggregate Demand and Aggregate Supply Shocks', *American Economic Review*, **79**(4): 655–73.

Blanchard, O. and R. Perotti (1999), 'An Empirical Characterization of the Dynamic Effects of Changes in Government Spending and Taxes on Output', Working paper 7269, National Bureau of Economic Research, Cambridge, MA.

Bruneau, C. and O. De Bandt (1999), 'Fiscal Policy in the Transition to Monetary Union: A Structural VAR Model', *Banque de France Notes d'Etudes et de Recherche*, **60**.

Buiter, W. and C. Grafe (2003), 'Reforming EMU's Fiscal Policy Rules', in M. Buti (ed.), *Monetary and Fiscal Policies in EMU: Interactions and Coordination*, Cambridge: Cambridge University Press, pp. 92–145.

Buti, M. and G. Giudice (2002), 'Maastricht's Fiscal Rules at Ten: An Assessment', *Journal of Common Market Studies*, **40**(5), December.

Buti, M., J. In 't Veld and W. Roeger (2001), 'Stabilising Output and Inflation: Policy Conflicts and Co-operation under a Stability Pact', *Journal of Common Market Studies*, **39**: 821–8.

Calmfors, L. and G. Corsetti (2003), 'How to Reform Europe's Fiscal Policy Framework', *World Economics*, **4**(1), January–March.

Canova, F. and E. Pappa (2003), 'Price Dispersions in Monetary Unions: The Role of Fiscal Shocks', CEPR Discussion Papers 3746.

Christiano, L., M. Eichenbaum and C. Evans (1999), 'Monetary Policy Shocks: What Have We Learned and to What End?', in J. Taylor and M. Woodford (eds), *Handbook of Macroeconomics*, **1A**. Amsterdam: Elsevier North-Holland.

Dalsgaard, T. and A. de Serres (1999), ' Estimating Prudent Budgetary Margins for

11 EU Countries: A Simulated SVAR Model Approach', OECD Economics Department Working Papers 216, OECD Economics Department.

Dalsgaard, T. and A. de Serres (2000), 'Estimating Prudent Budgetary Margins for EU Countries: A Simulated SVAR Model Approach', *OECD Economic Studies*, **30**(1): 115–47.

De Arcangelis, G. and S. Lamartina (2001), 'Fiscal and Policy Regimes in Some OECD Countries', in R. Beetsma, C. Favero, A. Missale, A. Muscatelli, P. Natale and P. Tirelli (eds), *Monetary Policy, Fiscal Policies and Labour Markets: Macroeconomic Policy Making in the EMU*, Cambridge: Cambridge University Press, pp. 224–55.

Denis, C., K. McMorrow and W. Röger (2002), 'Production Function Approach to Calculating Potential Growth and Output Gaps: Estimates for the EU Member States and the US', European Commission Economic Papers No. 176.

EEAG (European Economic Advisory Group) (2003), *Report on the European Economy*, Munich: CESifo.

European Commission (2002), 'Strenghtening the Co-ordination of Budgetary Policies', Communication from the Commission to Council and the European Parliament 668, November.

Fatás, A. and I. Mihov (1999), 'Government Size and Automatic Stabilizers: International and Intranational Evidence', CEPR Discussion Papers 2259.

Fatás, A. and I. Mihov (2003), 'The Case For Restricting Fiscal Policy Discretion', *Quarterly Journal of Economics*, MIT Press, **118**(4): 1419–47.

Favero, C.A. and T. Monacelli (2003), 'Monetary–Fiscal Mix and Inflation Performance: Evidence from the US', CEPR Discussion Papers 3887.

Galí, J. and R. Perotti (2003), 'Fiscal Policy and Monetary Integration in Europe', *Economic Policy*, Blackwell Publishing, **37**: 533–72.

Garcia, S. and A. Verdelhan (2001), 'Le policy-mix de la zone euro: une évaluation de l'impact des chocs monétaires et budgétaires', *Economie et Prévision*, **148**: 40.

Garratt, A., K. Lee, M.H. Pesaran and Y. Shin (2006), *Global and National Macroeconometric Modelling: A Long-Run Structural Approach*, Oxford: Oxford University Press.

Giavazzi, F. and M. Pagano (1996), 'Non-Keynesian Effects of Fiscal Policy Changes: International Evidence and the Swedish Experience', *Swedish Economic Policy Review*, **3**: 69–103.

Hagen, J. von (2002), 'More Growth for Stability: Reflections on Fiscal Policies in Euroland', ZEI papers, University of Bonn, June.

Höppner, F. (2000), 'An Empirical Analysis of the Effects of Fiscal Policy in Germany', Unpublished mimeo, University of Bonn.

Lütkepohl, H. (1993), *Introduction to Multiple Time Series Econometrics*, 2nd edn, New York: Springer-Verlag.

Mélitz, J. (2000), 'Some Cross-Country Evidence about Fiscal Policy Behaviour and Consequences for EMU', *European Economy*, **2**: 3–21.

Noord, P. van den (2000), 'The Size and Role of Automatic Fiscal Stabilisers in the 1990s and Beyond', OECD Economics Department Working Papers 230.

OECD (2003), *OECD Economic Outlook*, **74**, December.

Perotti, R. (2002), 'Estimating the Effects of Fiscal Policy in OECD Countries', Working paper series 168, European Central Bank.

Sargent, Thomas J. and Neil Wallace (1981), 'Some Unpleasant Monetaristic Arithmetic', *Federal Reserve Bank of Minneapolis Quarterly Review*, Fall: 1–17.

APPENDIX 6.1   ADF UNIT ROOT TESTS OF THE VARIABLES

Probability of unit root	GDP real growth		Deficit ratio		GDP deflator	
	Intercept	No intercept	Intercept	No intercept	Intercept	No intercept
Belgium	0.00	0.02	0.84	0.20	0.41	0.22
Germany	0.10	0.10	0.23	0.47	0.30	0.08
Greece	0.53	0.64	0.34	0.46	0.84	0.17
Spain	0.00	0.34	0.75	0.37	0.35	0.02
France	0.05	0.19	0.13	0.58	0.09	0.00
Ireland	0.20	0.30	0.58	0.04	0.19	0.03
Italy	0.03	0.06	0.89	0.40	0.01	0.00
Netherlands	0.02	0.19	0.50	0.29	0.03	0.05
Austria	0.01	0.36	0.29	0.31	0.42	0.09
Portugal	0.00	0.08	0.24	0.20	0.71	0.08
Finland	0.15	0.06	0.15	0.02	0.27	0.03

Note: HO: Unit root exists. Probability of unit root reported. Lag length in the test: Schwartz info criterion

APPENDIX 6.2   THE IDENTIFICATION OF THE MODEL

The three long-run restrictions on B(1) imply that:

$$A(1)SS^{-1}e = B(1)\varepsilon = B(1)S^{-1}e$$
$$A(1) = B(1)S^{-1}$$
$$A(1)S = B(1)$$

where $A(1)$ is totally known and the zeros of the $B(1)$ are the long-run restrictions. The restrictions apply to the transition matrix S.

Finally, the normalization of restricted residuals implies that $E(\varepsilon\varepsilon')=I$ and, since $\varepsilon = S^{-1}e$ or $S\varepsilon = e$, then $E(ee') = E(S\varepsilon\varepsilon'S')=SS'=\Sigma$.

Conclusions: the demise and reform of the SGP and the future of EMU: towards the disruption of the European integration process?

Leila Simona Talani

This book focused on the future of the monetary union in relation to the fate of its fiscal constraints as enshrined in the European Union's Stability and Growth Pact. The book has offered an interdisciplinary perspective: by its nature the fiscal governance of a single currency area includes inter-related economic and political dimensions.

Reacting to national and/or international economic developments, economists have offered a variety of prescriptions designed to enhance fiscal cooperation within the Euro-zone. From an economic point of view, the reforms of the SGP deeply modified its original philosophy, norms and practices. The reforms of the SGP were enacted in the context of deteriorating fiscal conditions; uneven economic growth; vast discrepancies in the scope and extent of structural reforms, especially in the area of labour and pensions; and the changed circumstances of the enlarged EU. They need to be assessed within this context. Because they make greater allowance for the heterogeneity of member states and permit more discretion in the application of the fiscal rule, they enhance credibility, increase flexibility, and elicit greater legitimacy through a clearer economic rationale which leaves more scope for judgement to allow for country-specific circumstances.

Hence, the member states must meet the challenge of implementing the new SGP. As Woods argues (Chapter 5), the capacity of the new SGP to be effective depends largely on the ability of the member states of the Euro-zone to develop complementary national fiscal frameworks and promote structural reforms.

Artis and Onorante (Chapter 6) concur that the member states will play the key role in deciding the fate of the SGP and, consequently, the future of EMU. They show that there is a clear economic rationale for the new differentiated country-specific Medium-Term Objectives (MTOs) from 1 per cent deficit to close to balance or surplus. However, these results are derived under the assumption that the new MTOs will be taken seriously and applied strictly by the governments. In sum, the effectiveness and success of the reformed MTOs (and, therefore, of the reformed SGP) depend on the political will of the Euro-area member states. This throws a spotlight on domestic politics.

The absence of a fiscal polity and the resultant centrality of domestic politics have led political scientists to apply a state-centric perspective to the analysis of the SGP, as reflected in the contributions of Talani and Fazio (Chapters 1 and 3) and Marzinotto (Chapter 4), while Cafruny and Ryner (Chapter 2) have broadened the scope of the analysis to the transatlantic context. It seems that many of the answers to the future of EMU may be found within the framework of a revised, 'embedded' version of intergovernmentalism. According to this theoretical framework, the decision to abide by strict monetary and exchange rate commitments is related to the existence of a strong socio-economic consensus in the domestic constituencies of the most powerful European member states, namely France and Germany. In turn, the existence of such consensus provides for the credibility of the commitments themselves.

Where does this emphasis on the nation state leave the process of European integration? What is the impact of this particular form of EMU, as defined at Maastricht and refined by the old and the new SGP, on the EU as a political project? With respect to these questions the debate is still very open. Especially since the crisis of the SGP many scholars, including Cafruny and Ryner (Chapter 2), have explored the disruptive potential of EMU on the European integration process, resulting from the lack of fiscal and political union. De Grauwe (in Talani *et al.*, 2008), for example, emphasizes the need for a political union to reduce the impact of asymmetric shocks on the public opinion's assessment of EMU. From this point of view the credibility of the member states' commitments to EMU is higher the closer EMU is to an optimal currency area (OCA). OCA theory suggests that, if the benefits of the monetary union exceed the costs, member countries form an optimal currency area and have no incentive to exit. In the language of game theory the members are in a Nash equilibrium, and the monetary union is sustainable. Thus political union and the adoption of a common fiscal policy increase the benefits of a currency union. Moreover, by increasing fiscal support to countries in a business cycle downturn, a single budgetary policy could ease the support for EMU and facilitate the legitimacy and implementation of structural reforms. These are necessary as flexibility is another essential dimension of an OCA. In the absence of political and fiscal union, De Grauwe suggests that the credibility of the member states' commitment to EMU is reduced and that the project will ultimately collapse, producing a disruptive impact on the broader European integration process.

Cafruny and Ryner in Chapter 2 concur with De Grauwe that the crisis of EMU, in the lack of political union, may have a disruptive impact on the European integration process. They trace back the origins of this crisis to two fundamental contradictions. First, the political and economic imperatives of EMU as presently constituted undermine essential features of European welfare capitalism. Second, because of its neo-liberal underpinnings EMU is incompatible with the further development of European solidarity and, hence, the establishment of a common fiscal policy and, more broadly, a polity that can provide social and political cohesion. Far from promoting greater integration, as its architects predicted, EMU serves to intensify conflict among and within member states by accelerating uneven development, dramatizing regional and international inequalities, and provoking demands in some quarters for the re-nationalization of monetary policy.

Do the demise and reform of the SGP necessarily signal a crisis of EMU? Adopting a structural definition of the credibility of the commitment to EMU as proposed in Chapter 1, it can be argued that the answer is no. Despite the crisis of the SGP and the domestic struggles over structural reforms, the leading socio-economic actors in the Euro member states continue to support the set of anti-inflationary and supply-side policies which were enshrined in EMU from the onset and which will guarantee the competitiveness of the German and French manufacturing sectors. Indeed, it was precisely because the SGP had turned into an obstacle for the implementation of those same policies that its stricter constraints were abandoned for the time being by Germany and France with the full support of their socio-economic constituencies. In the context of this analysis, the emphasis of the French and German business sectors is still on increasing competitiveness. After having relied on the competitive devaluation of the Euro, favoured by the monetary and exchange rate policy of the ECB (Talani, 2005), with the reversal of this trend, they turned to the reduction of taxes and the implementation of structural reforms (Chapter 3). In turn, the adoption of structural reform in a neo-corporatist system required the support of the trade unions, which was sought by relaxing the adherence to the SGP (Chapter 4). The broader project of EMU was not called into question by the crisis and reform of the SGP, and financial markets did not react negatively to the crisis of the European fiscal rule. Indeed, after the decision by the ECOFIN not to impose sanctions on France and Germany, financial markets did not reduce the value of the Euro, which kept on increasing vis-à-vis the Dollar, nor did they ask for higher yield to keep assets denominated in Euros.

In brief, the future of EMU is safe.

BIBLIOGRAPHY

Talani, L.S. (2005), 'The European Central Bank: Between Growth and Stability', *Comparative European Politics*, **3**: 204–31.

Talani, L.S., C. Spagnolo and S. Baroncelli (2008), *Back to Maastricht: Obstacles to Constitutional Reform within the EU Treaty (1991–2007)*, Newcastle, UK: Cambridge Scholars Publishing.

Index